EDUCATION, WORK AND WOMEN

An Enquiry into Gender Bias

M.M. REHMAN
KAMALAKANTA BISWAL

Commonwealth

Education, Work and Women

ISBN : 81-7169-251-6

Edition : 2024

Published by :
COMMONWEALTH PUBLISHERS (P) LTD.
4831/24, Govind Lane,
Ansari Road, Darya Ganj,
New Delhi - 110002
Ph. : 23272541, 23242541
e-mail : commonwealthpublishers2016@gmail.com

Distributed by :
ARJUN PUBLISHING HOUSE
4831/24, Govind Lane,
Ansari Road, Darya Ganj,
New Delhi - 110002
Ph. : 23272541, 23242541
e-mail : arjunbooks2001@gmail.com

Laser Typesetting by :
Dimple Computers
Delhi

Printed at :
Divine Digital Press
Delhi

To our Mothers

KANCHANABALA
K. NISHA

It is for man to establish the reign of liberty in the midst of the world of the given. To gain the supreme victory, it is necessary, for one thing, that by and through their natural differentiation men and women unequivocally affirm their brotherhood.

Simone de Beauvoir

FOREWORD

It is only in recent years that gender related inequalities have attracted such wide attention. From time immemorial woman has been accorded a second place in our society. Her position in the social system though apparently and ambivalently exalted at times, in practice she has always been subordinated within and outside the family sphere.

In the last two centuries, the human civilization has witnessed two important events - first, the industrial revolution which has dramatically altered the patterns of production and social relations; and second, the democratic framework of governance by state organization. Both these breakthroughs have changed human relations significantly and, in many cases, new paradigms have been developed to place men and women at equal level in various spheres of life, be it education, employment or any other area, where human beings, as men and women, interact and perform a mutually complementary role.

The present book, authored by M.M. Rehman and Kamalakanta Biswal, provides many insights into the present situation of women and immediacy of the problems which are arising out of the issues of gender relations that pervade all aspects of our life because of unequal treatment meted out to women. In the modern world, the role of woman goes much beyond the home and bringing up of children. She is now adopting autonomous career of her own and sharing equally with man the responsibility for the development of society in all its aspects.

This book, drawing data on education and employment from wide range of sources, presents a picture which outlines the contours of discrimination against women in the world in general and India in particular. This volume, I hope, will help all those who are responsible for framing and implementing policies designed for achieving equality for women and also those who want to be informed about the gender differentiation and crusade for elimination of all forms of discrimination against women.

Baldev Mahajan
Joint Director
National Institute of Educational
Planning and Administration
New Delhi
INDIA

PREFACE

Women constitute half of the human race. But their position in society is ambiguous. They have been subjected to all forms of discrimination, and in every institutional structure extending from family to state. Discriminations have led to her subordination which is defined as gender gap between man and woman. The subordination of women could be measured by the levels of their disproportionate representation in various areas of life such as education, employment, politics, health, etc.

This book attempts to measure the gender disparities that exist today in various fields. It specially focuses on representations of women in education and employment sectors at global, national, village and individual levels.

We have made our best to marshall data and information from different sources. Along with the secondary sources, we have conducted our own study to generate data on gender differentiation at grassroots level. The purpose was to measure the gender based gaps at various levels to furnish a comprehensive and, at the same time, a precise picture of differentiation.

This book consists of six chapters. Chapter One discusses gender related issues and subordination of women in the historical perspective. It also outlines the concerns of the international and national bodies for women's development. This chapter also provides a global picture of women's representation in education and employment in various regions/ countries. Chapter Two describes the position of women in the education sector at its various levels. It also shows the intra-gender disparities existing in their representation. Chapter Three examines the employment scenario and women's position therein, and provides information with regard to women's education specific employment status. Chapter Four describes perceptions of an individual woman about her situation, while Chapter Five examines situation of gender differentiation in education and employment at grassroots level. Chapter Six discusses gender issues from a theoretical perspective, provides some ideas as policy direction and identifies some future research areas.

However, here, we would like to make it clear that, in this volume, the attempt is to examine, by using secondary as well as primary data, to bring into surface the glaring phenomenon of sex differentiation at different points of time in India. We have not been much analytical in providing explanations of sex differentiation in our society ; partly, because of non-availability of comparable time series data, particularly on employment of women; and partly, because of the fact that our basic objective in this volume is to show that women have been and continue to be "discriminated" against even after nearly four and half decades of independence.

We are grateful to many people for their cooperation in writing this book. First and foremost, we would like to express our gratitude to Kanta Wadhwa who provided us her support throughout the preparation of this book. We also thank S.B. Roy who was persistently at us to complete this book. Our thanks are also due to Sudhir Dagar, to whom we are specially grateful for his unstinted support throughout the preparation of this volume. We would like to thank Nirmal Malhotra, Deepak Makol and B.D. Joshi of the NIEPA library for their cooperation. We are also indebted to P.N. Tyagi who has lent his cartographic excellence to this book. We express our gratitude to Kausar Wizarat and Rajender Kumar for their support and encouragement. We cannot forget Michael Rehman who extended his support in many little ways. We are especially grateful to Baldev Mahajan, Joint Director of NIEPA, New Delhi, who kindly consented to write the foreword to this volume. Finally, we express our gratitude to Suresh Kumar for laser typesetting and B.R. Verma of Commonwealth Publishers for bringing out this volume in the shortest possible time.

M.M. REHMAN
KAMALAKANTA BISWAL

January 26, 1993
New Delhi

CONTENTS

List of Tables

List of Figures

List of Boxes

CHAPTER ONE

PERSPECTIVES ON GENDER DIFFERENTIATION

PROLOGUE

Women's role in socio-economic, political, and cultural development has been recognised only partially in the recent past. Their activities which contribute equally as that of men to development process are yet to get full economic recognition in all its dimensions. Their activities have also been gender-stereotyped over the centuries and their roles in different fields have been characterised on the basis of their sex status and reproduction function. Gailey delineates this point very clearly in the following terms:

> Sex differences are not gender differences. Few people would say that being a female means being womanly or being a male means being manly. Sex differences are physiological features related to procreation, to biological reproduction. The sex division of labor in reproduction is well understood. Males produce sperm, females produce eggs; females bear youngs. Sex differences are found in all mammals. However, humans from their very origin have interpreted and reshaped their physical and social environment through symbolizing. Humans are self-reflective, culture-creating animals. Humans have sex differences, but like all other aspects of physcial differentiation, they are experienced symbolically. In human societies, sex differences are experienced as gender.
>
> While sex differences are physical, gender differences are socially constructed. Concepts of gender are cultural interpretations of sex differences. Gender is related to sex differences but not necessarily to physiological differences as we see them in our society. Gender depends on how society views the relationship of male to man and female to woman. Every culture has prevailing images of what men and women are "supposed" to be like (1987 : 33-34).

The cultural image of sex status of women has not originated and developed on its own. It has emerged out of economic and social needs for perpetuating the status of some groups by weakening them culturally, economically and politically for establishing the basis of an exploitative system in which one is subordinated for conveniences of another. In this process female became the first victim, and systematically and slowly, in the historical process, she has not only been deprived of her status as equal creature materially but she also has been psychologically prepared to accept her relegated status as 'naturally' as she has accepted her reproductive function.

The ancient socio-political and cultural forms are epitomised in the concept of "religion"- man's one of the most brutal instruments of subjugation of women in particular and others in general. Each religion has handed down such traditions and practices for centuries onwards that have successfully helped in perpetuating the idea of gender discrimination against women in innumerable ways and by means of dictates. In the historical process the most serious harm which has been done to woman is by depriving her of the right to property. This single most obstacle has helped to subjugate her in a manner that man wished. Her identity has remained linked to man's assumptions about her sex defined concepts : a daughter, sister, wife, mother and a grandmother. She has been perpetuating the human race since the dawn of human being's appearance on this earth. But she did not own its heritage, and its physical outcomes. Her existence has remained equal to a prisoner of procreation of human beings and its perpetuation (see Engels, 1977).

She has not only been deprived of her right to natural and human created resources but also been deprived of her name. She, despite her possessing equal potentials as that of man, has been systematically thwarted to realize and achieve them. She has been, for ages, subjected to all forms of discrimination on the ground of her sex status. For her, options for development have been very limited and circumscribed by man who has promulgated laws to direct, control and regulate her actions within certain prescribed boundaries. Stepping out of those boundaries was severely restricted, and invited man's reprisal.

Man's imaginations about woman are not only contradictory, they are also groundless. She has been, on one side, depicted as a frightening creature while, on the other, a venerated madonna and purely as sex objects (Hunter College, 1983). These contradictory images are not without purpose.

> The social distancing established by the notion of women as 'other' provides an excuse for the actual devaluation of women, for the treatment of women as less than human, for exploitation and abuse, and for the denial of their rights to self-determination. The same ideological devices are used against various ethnic and social groups and social

> classes exploited by the elites of a stratified and unequal social order. What is distinctive about this treatment of women is that it is so widespread, so ancient, and so pervasive. This makes the challenge to change it extra- ordinarily formidable (Hunter College, 1983 : 37).

Every society, everywhere, has discriminated against women, with a few exceptions. The result of this discrimination is reflected in every country's intense effort to correct the mistakes made against women for centuries and barriers created to wrest them to realise their potentials. At both the international and national levels, many efforts have been made to eradicate all forms of discrimination against women and opening and providing opportunities to realise their potentials in equal terms with men.

In this chapter we have made an attempt to discuss and outline, though briefly, the situation of women in socio-economic and cultural contexts against historical backdrop. We have also made an effort to examine various endeavours made by international bodies and the national government to ameliorate women's conditions. Apart from these, a brief but precise account has also been furnished here with regard to women's position in education and employment at global level.

Here, we shall provide a brief review of the strategies so far adopted by various international bodies to enhance and develop the status of women and their participation in various areas such as education, employment and training and credit facilities, and share of resources.

INTERNATIONAL LEVEL

One of the landmark endeavours of the United Nations Organisation was the declaration of 1976-1985 as the Decade for Women. The Decade for Women proclaimed in Mexico that the problem of status of women was a global issue. The conference also observed that in order to enhance the status of women the entire human race had to participate. "It has been established, accordingly, that this is not a problem that has to be or can be resolved by women alone, but rather as a part of the entire complex of economic, political and social problems of the world and of each country respectively with active participation of men and women as agents and beneficiaries of development. In the Declaration of Mexico on the 'Equality of Women' and their contribution to Development and Peace is also expressed the recognition that women of the entire world, whatever differences exist between them, share the painful experience of receiving or having received unequal treatment, and that as their awareness of this phenomenon increases they will become natural allies in the struggle against any form of oppression" (Tomsic, 1982 : 5-6).

In the same year of the Declaration of the Decade for Women the International Labour Organisation also adopted a Declaration on Equality of Opportunity and Treatment for Women Workers and it adopted a Plan of Action "to eliminate all forms of discrimination against women in all sectors of social and economic activity and at all levels of skill and responsibility".

In the first half of the UN Decade for Women, considerable efforts had been made by UN and its various specialised agencies to ensure social development for creating conditions in which women would find enough space to realise their potentials as that of men. It also implied that in the development process women and men would not be objects. They would be the subjects.

The World Conference of the UN Decade for Women adopted a Programme of Action in Copenhagen in 1980. The Programme of Action formulated a more realistic aproach to women's role and position :

> Development is here interpreted to mean total development including development in the political, economic, social, cultural and other dimensions of human life, as also the development of economic and other material resources and also the physical, moral, intellectual and cultural growth of the human person. The improvement of the status of women required action at the national and local levels and within the family. It also requires a change in the attitudes and roles of both men and women. Women's development should not only be viewed as an issue in social development but should be seen as an essential component in every dimension of development. To improve the status of women and their role in the process of development, such development should be an integral part of the global project for the establishment of a NIEO based on equity, sovereign equality, interdependence, common interest and cooperation among all States (UN, 1980 : para 4).

The Copenhagen Conference also emphasized that to provide equal opportunity to women their employment in various sectors of the economy should be ensured. The measures on which it emphasised, were :

> To ensure that women and men receive equal remuneration for work of equal value..., to improve the working conditions and occupational mobility of women workers, to ensure equal rights and opportunities for gainful employment of rural women both in agricultural and non-agricultural jobs under proper working conditions, to promote occupational mobility for women by encouraging the provision of maternity

protection, childcare facilities, technical training and health protection... (UN, 1980 : para 109).

Apart from the UN system, the Non-Aligned Movement also showed its concern for women's development. In a conference, held in Baghdad in 1979, the Non-Aligned Movement considered various aspects of women's development vis-a-vis development of economy. "It was requested from all coordinating countries for the cooperation of Non-Aligned countries and from all important meetings of the Non-Aligned countries to include in their activities also the dimension of the role of women in development" (Tomsic, 1983).

In 1985 came the ILO resolution which envisaged "constructive measures to foster economic development in such a way that the situation of women will improve within a framework of general policies for achieving economic recovery and employment growth" (quoted in Nuss, 1989 : 6). In 1985, the Nairobi Forward-Looking Strategies for the Advancement of Women came into being. The strategies which were adopted in the Nairobi Conference in the concluding year of the UN Decade for Women were comprehensive and far-reaching in their nature and dimension. The Conference emphasized the need to :

(i) Ensure that national constitutions and legislations provide for full equality between men and women with regard to their rights and obligations in the field of work, as well as in social, political and family life;

(ii) Take special measures to ratify and implement in national legislation the relevant international labour conventions and recommendations concerning the rights of women to equal employment opportunities, equal pay for work of equal value, equal working conditions, job security and maternity protection;

(iii) Extend ratification and implementation of the United Nations Convention on the 'Elimination of All Forms of Discrimination against Women';

(iv) Conceive, plan, execute and monitor programmes for eliminating unemployment and promoting job security in view of the fact that in many cases women account for a disproportionate share of total unemployment;

(v) Give greater attention, within the overall framework of policies on human resources development, to vocational and management training as well as to delivery systems for education and training; this entails identifying discriminatory practices in education and training and giving urgent consideration to young women;

(vi) Provide an adequate response to the impact of technology on labour force participation and the status of women at the work-place, notably by identifying growth sectors offering employment potential for women, diversifying women's occupations—including at a higher levels of skill, responsibility and remuneration — and increasing women's access to self-employment and co-operatives; and

(vii) Strengthen measures in relation to safety and health at work-place, working time, work organisation, maternity protection, child care facilities, population and family welfare programmes, and harmonisation of work and family responsibility (including recognition of equal rights of marriage partners and the value of house work) (Nuss, 1989 : 7-8).

Women in Education : Education is an important indicator of women's development. It is also an important instrument for attaining economic power and independence, for it opens up opportunities that are linked with various levels of formal educational attainment. However, educational opportunities available today have not been shared equally, by both men and women : as compared to men, women have been benefited much less from educational opportunities across different regions of the world.

The gaps between male and female enrolment ratios at different levels of education has been reduced from what they were in 1970 to a considerable extent in 1990 (see Table 1.1). In 1970, the enrolment ratios at first level for male and female were 95.8 per cent and 80.8 per cent respectively. These gaps were reduced considerably in 1990 : the ratios being 104.9 per cent and 92.3 per cent for male and female respectively. Similar disparities could be noticed in the enrolment ratios of male and female at second and third levels also .

However, across different regions of the world, the range of disparities varied a great deal. In the countries of Sub-Saharan Africa, Arab States and Southern Asia it could be noticed that the gaps between enrolment ratios of male and female are much more wider than in the countries of the Developed World.

The gaps between enrolment ratios of male and female in second and third levels of education are more pronounced in developing countries, and this underrepresentation ultimately influences women's capacity to

Table 1.1 : **Male and female gross enrolment ratios by level of education in 1970 and 1990**

(in percentages)

	1970						1990*					
	First level		**Second level**		**Third level**		**First level**		**Second level**		**Third level**	
	M	**F**	**M**	**F**	**M**	**F**	**M**	**F**	**M**	**F**	**M**	**F**
WORLD TOTAL	95.8	80.8	40.7	31.5	10.4	6.5	104.9	92.3	57.3	46.7	15.0	11.9
Developing countries of which :	93.1	73.5	29.6	17.8	4.2	1.8	105.5	90.4	50.3	37.5	10.1	6.5
Sub-Saharan Africa	56.7	36.0	9.9	4.4	0.8	0.2	73.5	59.9	21.2	13.8	2.8	1.0
Arab States	77.9	46.4	28.1	12.5	6.3	2.0	92.3	74.2	60.2	44.9	15.6	9.5
Latin America/ Caribbean	91.9	89.4	26.3	24.6	8.0	4.5	111.4	107.2	55.7	59.6	19.3	18.2
Eastern Asia/Oceania	107.9	94.5	33.1	23.6	1.6	1.1	124.6	114.9	58.7	47.7	7.3	4.9
Southern Asia	87.1	53.2	30.7	13.1	7.4	2.2	100.8	75.1	47.8	28.2	12.1	5.3
Developed countries of which :	104.2	103.5	77.3	76.2	27.3	19.3	102.0	101.1	93.5	93.8	37.0	36.5
Northern America	103.5	102.8	92.6	93.6	52.8	37.8	103.0	101.4	98.4	99.5	66.7	74.1
Asia/Oceania	101.7	101.4	85.5	84.8	24.6	10.2	102.2	102.4	95.9	97.8	38.8	26.6
Europe/USSR	105.6	104.5	73.8	71.6	19.4	15.0	102.5	101.7	93.2	93.1	27.6	27.0

Source : UNESCO (1991) *World Education Report, 1991*, New York.
* : Estimated

enter into paid employment which is amply demonstrated by their disproportionate share in various occupations in different regions of the world.

It may be pointed out that simple enrolment ratios do not reveal the contours of disparities between male and female in education. Because, education as such does not empower women with employment capability. There are types of education, mostly science education, which empower women with greater productive skills and employment opportunities. Unfortunately women's representation in those types of education has not yet been significant.

Table 1.2 clearly shows women's underrepresentation in various fields of science education in different regions of the world which comprise both developed and developing countries. In various parts of the world the concentration of women is in traditional areas of educational science and teacher training. It is as high as 70 per cent of the total enrolment in Eastern Europe. In engineering and agriculture, the enrolment of women is also quite low in different parts of the world. This lower proportion of enrolment of women in important branches of science results in their underrepresentation in various key occupations.

Women in Employment : In 1985, there were 2,409 million female population in the world, of which 790 million were estimated to be economically active. This constituted 32.9 per cent of the total female population. The share of the female in the total active population was 26.5 per cent. These figures clearly show the underestimation of female labour force participation. This is because many types of economic activities carried out by females are not linked directly with monetary gain. Nor inputed cost of non-monetary female labour is counted as contribution to economic activities. This understatement of female labour also speaks about the intensity of dependence of females; for it is only paid employment which empowers a person with certain amount of independence. Because, economic independence of women is, perhaps, the prerequisite for their types of independence, i.e. social, political, cultural, etc. Unfortunately in many Third World Countries the problem of women's employment has received not enough consideration from Governments. As a result, their representation in many occupations has remained insignificant. To empower women with independence for making decision for their progress employment is a must. Table 1.3 reveals participation of women in economic activities in different zones of the world.

Table 1.2: **Enrolment of women in various fields of science in different regions of the world**

(in percentages)

Regions/country	Educational science & teacher training	Social & behavorial sciences	Natural sciences	Mathematics & computer sciences	Medicine & health	Engineering	Agriculture	Total in scientific fields
Africa	30	25	20	20	30	5	15	25
Latin America and the Caribbean	60	55	50	45	50	10	20	45
Asia and Oceania	55	35	30	30	40	10	20	25
Western Europe	65	40	35	30	50	5	25	40
EasternEurope	70	60	50	45	70	25	35	45

Source : United Nations (1989) *World Survey on the Role of Women in Development, 1989*, New York.

It could be seen in Table 1.3 that in the developing countries the percentage share of economically active[1] female population from total female population and female share of the total economically active population are far less in comparison with the developed, centrally planned and market economies. But yet, in comparison with males, the percentage share of females lags far behind. This imbalance and its accompanied problems would not be easier to solve in the coming decade. "In 1985, there were 542 million women workers in the developing regions, while in 1950, there were barely 263 million working women. According to I.L.O. projections, there will be about 1 billion women workers by the year 2025. The present ecological, political and economic crisis will make it impossible for the agricultural sector of the developing world to absorb this swelling female work-force" (U.N., 1989 : 157) as most of the economically active women are employed in agricultural and allied activities (see Table 1.4).

Table 1.3 : **Female population, economically active population and crude activity rate, 1985**

World	Female population (in millions)	Economically active female population (in millions)	Curde activity rate (in %)	Female share (in %)
World	2403	790	32.9	36.5
Developing Countries	1756	542	30.9	34.7
Africa	263	71	27.0	35.7
Asia & Oceania	1290	434	33.6	35.6
Latin America	202	37	18.5	26.6
Developed Countries	-	-	-	-
Centrally Planned Economies	218	100	46.1	47.1
Market Economies	429	147	34.3	37.9

Source : International Labour Organisation (1986) *Economically Active Population Estimates and Projections, 1950-2025*, Vol.5, 3rd ed., Geneva.

1. Economic activity : The *economically active* population includes 'All persons of either sex who furnish the supply of labour for the production of economic goods and services... [The] production of economic goods and services should include all production and processing of primary products whether for market, for barter or for own consumption,... the production of all other good for the market and, in the case of households which produce such goods and services for the market, the corresponding production for own consumption' (ILO, 1989-90).

Table 1.4 : **Economically active population in agriculture and the share of women by major regions, 1988**

Region/country	Economically active population in agriculture (in thousands)	Share of females (in percentages)
Africa	1,29,210	42.3
Near East	33,657	28.1
Latin America	40,506	11.9
Far East	3,24,916	28.4
Asian Centrally Planned Countries	4,63,341	46.0
Other Developed Countries	1,448	40.5
Developing Countries	9,93,069	37.7
World	10,53,002	38.1

Source : U.N. (1989) *World Survey on the Role of Women in Development, 1989*, New York.

Women's representation in industrial labour force is quite significant and this has led to a considerable degree of independence among those who are engaged in paid employment. For emancipation of women from economic dependence, paid employment is the first step for their equal status in social setting. However, for women the entry into the industrial labour force has not always been positive. They have generally occupied jobs in industrial sector which are comparatively less remunerative.

> While there have been gains in terms of overall employment in industry, women have yet to be integrated into all occupations and sectors and to obtain conditions and content of work comparable to men's. In addition, women account for a disproportionate share of unemployment in most countries.... have more limited access than men to jobs generally (especially at the higher occupational levels) and have greater difficulty in securing adequate technical training or even information on findings and applying for available jobs (U.N. 1989 : 129).

Apart from this, women workers are ill-paid, and they are engaged in jobs which mostly require unskilled and semi-skilled workers. In addition, the works done by them are repetitive, and career prospects are dismally poor. Table 1.5 shows the share of women in manufacturing in some countries. The percentage share of women employed in manufacturing is highest in

Mauritius (62.0) followed by Barbados (54.2), and Philippines (48.7). The lowest percentage share of women employed in manufacturing could be found in India (9.5).

Most of the women industrial workers are working in units producing textiles and clothing, processed foods, chemical products, printed and published materials, and electrical machinery and apparatus. However, the major concentration of women industrial workers could be found in the textile and wearing apparel sectors.

Service sector has assumed an important place in every economy. Its growth has been rapid over the years, and it is playing a vital role in both the developed and developing economies. In service sector, a large number of women are employed. However, they are concentrated in two categories: "community, social and personal services" and "trade, restaurant and hotels". The figures in Table 1.6 show the distribution of women workers in various categories of service sector in selected developed countries. "It can be seen that community, social and personal services combined with trade, restaurants and hotels comparise about 80 per cent of the total female employment in the service sector, the former category accounting for half of the total. Financing and knowledge-intensive services account for only 10-15 per cent of female service employment. With this category, women appear largely concentrated in financial services" (U.N. 1989 : 198).

Table 1.5 : **Women's share in manufacturing**

Sl. no.	Region/country	Year	Share of women in total manufacturing (in %)
(1)	(2)	(3)	(4)
	Africa		
1.	Botswana	1985	26.7
2.	Egypt	1983	15.0
3.	Kenya	1985	9.9
4.	Mauritius	1985	62.0
	America		
5.	Barbados	1985	54.2
6.	Bermuda	1985	35.2
7.	Costa Rica	1985	31.8
7.	Cuba	1985	30.7
9.	Puerto Rico	1985	46.3
10.	United States	1985	32.3

Contd...

(1)	(2)	(3)	(4)
	Asia		
11.	Cyprus	1984	45.6
12.	Hong Kong	1985	46.5
13.	India	1984	9.5
14.	Japan	1985	39.5
15.	Korea, Rublic of	1985	38.7
16.	Philippines	1985	48.7
17.	Singapore	1985	44.3
18.	Sri Lanka	1984	37.8
	Europe		
19.	Czechoslovakia	1985	43.0
20.	Germany, F.R.	1985	29.3
21.	United Kingdom	1985	28.2
22.	Yugoslavia	1985	38.0

Source : U.N. (1989) *World Survey on the Role of Women in Development, 1989*, New York.

Table1.6: **Female service employment by sub-sectors, select developed countries**

(in percentages)

Region/country	Year	Trade, restaurant and hotels	Transport, storage and communication	Financing, insurance real estate, business & services	Community, social and personal services
Europe					
Austria	1986	37.8	4.2	9.9	44.7
Germany, F.R.	1986	30.0	4.8	11.7	50.7
Norway	1986	25.9	6.1	8.7	57.2
Sweden	1986	17.8	5.1	8.7	66.7
U.K. & North Ireland	1986	30.6	3.3	13.1	50.7
North America					
USA	1986	26.3	4.4	15.8	51.3
Canada	1986	30.1	4.6	14.8	48.4
Oceania					
Australia	1986	26.6	4.8	14.8	50.1
New Zealand	1985	30.6	7.7	14.6	44.9
Japan	1986	42.0	3.1	11.6	37.5

Source : ILO (1987) *Year Book of Labour Statistics*, Geneva.

Another important dimension of women's employment in service sector is that women are mostly employed at the lower end of the job scale as they are in the low-paid works in industrial sector. The percentage of women employed as managers and administrators is very small. Even in European countries and Japan they represent less than 3 per cent of the total employees (see Table 1.7).

The representation of women workers in service sector in the developing countries is equally dismal : only a small percentage are in categories other than "community, social and personal services". Like the developed countries the representation of women in managerial and administrative position is still marginal in the developing countries (see Tables 1.8 & 1.9).

Table 1.7 : **Distribution of economically active women by occupational groups, select developed countries**

(in percentages)

Region/country	Year	Professional, technical and related workers	Administrative and managerial workers	Clerical and related workers	Sales workers	Service workers	Agricultural animal husd. & forest workers	Production and related workers
Europe								
Austria	1986	15.3	1.7	25.5	14.0	20.0	10.2	13.1
Germany, F.R.	1984	16.1	2.1	29.5	13.5	17.1	6.7	13.1
Norway	1986	26.3	2.8	19.8	12.4	23.3	5.0	10.3
Spain	1986	12.2	0.2	15.7	15.4	28.0	13.6	14.8
North America								
USA	1986	17.4	9.6	29.3	13.1	18.3	1.1	11.3
Canada	1986	20.6	9.5	30.9	9.7	17.7	2.6	9.0
Oceania								
Australia	1986	16.6	5.4	32.7	13.5	9.3	4.0	18.5
Japan	1986	10.7	0.7	25.1	14.2	12.1	10.0	26.8

Source : ILO (1987) *Year Book of Labour Statistics*, Geneva.

Table 1.8 : **Female service employment by sub-sectors, select developing countries**

(in percentages)

Region/country	Year	Trade, restaurant and hotels	Transport, storage and communication	Financing, insurance real estate, business & services	Community, social and personal services
Africa					
Botswana	1985	25.7	2.3	6.9	63.2
Egypt	1983	19.7	3.0	4.2	63.6
Kenya	1986	8.5	3.9	6.1	78.9
Malawi	1985	20.6	7.6	8.8	58.8
Asia					
Bahrain	1982	5.4	10.2	10.9	70.1
Kongkong	1986	40.6	5.2	12.2	40.0
Indonesia	1985	61.6	0.3	0.6	36.3
Republic of Korea	1986	60.9	2.1	6.9	27.7
Philippines	1985	45.1	1.0	3.3	50.1
Singapore	1986	35.2	7.8	16.8	37.1
Sri Lanka	1984	39.9	5.0	32.7	11.0
Thailand	1984	47.6	2.3	-	46.1
Latin America and Caribbean					
Barbados	1986	33.3	4.2	4.8	55.8
Colombia	1986	35.0	2.4	8.0	53.2
El Salvador	1983	45.3	7.2	16.6	23.0
Uruguay	1986	20.2	2.7	6.0	70.0
Venezuela	1986	26.8	2.2	8.4	60.9

Sources : ILO (1987) *Year Book of Labour Statistics*. Geneva; ILO,and UN Research and Training Institute for the Advancement of Women (1985) *Women in Economic Activity : A Global Statistical Survey (1950-2000)*, Santo Domingo.

Table 1.9 : **Distribution of economically active women by occupational groups, select developing countires**

(in percentages)

Region/country	Year	Professional, technical and related workers	Administrative and managerial workers	Clerical and related workers	Sales workers	Service workers	Agricultural animal husd. & forest workers	Production and related workers
Africa								
Egypt	1983	19.7	2.0	14.9	7.7	4.1	40.8	10.8
Asia								
Bahrain	1981	30.9	0.6	27.2	1.2	28.4	-	1.8
Kongkong	1986	8.2	1.0	26.3	9.0	16.6	1.4	37.5
Indonesia	1985	3.9	-	1.9	20.9	5.9	53.4	13.4
Philippines	1985	9.8	0.6	5.9	23.5	13.6	34.9	11.8
Rep. of Korea	1986	5.6	0.1	10.7	18.1	16.6	26.2	22.7
Singapore	1986	11.4	3.4	29.2	12.2	17.6	0.7	25.2
Sri Lanka	1980	8.4	0.2	3.2	3.7	4.7	42.2	16.6
Thailand	1984	3.2	0.5	2.2	10.2	3.6	72.4	7.9
Latin America and Caribbean								
Barbados	1986	12.7	2.3	25.1	10.6	27.2	7.0	15.0
Colombia	1986	11.7	0.8	17.8	19.6	32.9	0.8	16.5
Uruguay	1986	17.6	1.7	20.9	11.8	28.1	0.5	19.3
Peru	1981	10.9	0.1	13.4	14.4	19.1	8.3	-
Venezuela	1986	21.4	2.5	20.0	14.5	28.9	0.2	11.8

Sources : ILO (1987) *Year Book of Labour Statistics*, Geneva; ILO,and UN Research and Training Institute for the Advancement of Women (1985) *Women in Economic Activity : A Global Statistical Survey (1950-2000)*, Santo Domingo.

NATIONAL LEVEL

The magnitude of effort which is required to give a due and rightful place to women in society is the reflection of the problems which act as barriers to women's participation in many development activities. The international agencies have, for the last two decades, shown considerable concern for women's development in particular and their access to education, employment and health facilities. This concern has been equally voiced at national level as well. A brief review of such efforts has been attempted here to examine various aspects of women's development efforts in India.

The position of women has been extremely marginal in Indian society. The status enjoyed by women has not yet been equal to men. Indian society is still governed by religious traditions and age-old social customs which have deprived women of equal status as that of men. In fact, Indian society has discriminated against women in every walk of life. Every religion has its own chain to enchain women. In Brahmanical system she has been given a highly derogatory status. In Christianity, Buddhism, Jainism, Islam and Sikhism — in all major religious ideologies prevalent in India — women have been oppressibly discriminated. She has been prescribed in all possible manner to be well within the four walls. Except some platitudes, which are a form of subtle conspiracy to exploit women further, there is hardly any humane attitude expressed by religious ideologies prevalent in the country.

It is being assumed that position of women was equal to men during the early phase of the Vedic period, but deteriorated in the later phases and became extremely oppressive during the medieval period. The assumption is, however, unreliable because it is not in evidence in any extant work. It has been argued that "the actual decline in the status of women ... began during the age of the *shastras, sutras* and *Epics*" (Ramu, 1989: 19). Various scriptural injuctions were against women. Women were deprived of their individual decisions and choices. They were brought under full control of men.

Their condition deteriorated further during the medieval period when their dependence on men became absolute and they became vicitims of inhuman practice of *sati* (the voluntary or coerced immolation of women). This henious crime against women continues to occur till today. A few years ago Roop Kanwar's immolation in a village in Rajasthan is a living example of this gory ritual. In other words :

> The representation of women in the post-vedic scriptures is not only contradictory but a clear manifestation of Hindu society's dualistic

> approach to nearly half of its population. For example, Manu's code has left an indelible impression on conservative sections of Hindu society even today. On the one hand, it exhorts that women be treated with love, respect and reverence; she has to be adored since she is deemed to be the source of all good. Manu declares that women must be honoured and admired by their fathers, brothers and husbands, because where women are honoured the gods are pleased; therefore, a woman is *devi* (the one who shines). On the other hand, he treats women as if they are the scum of the earth. He suggests that women be feared as embodiments of evil. Manu further recommends that, day and night, women be kept in thrall by the males of their families. In childhood, a woman must be subjected to her father, in youth to her husband, and in old age to her son; a woman must never be independent because she is innately as impure as falsehood. The Lord created woman, according to his code, as one full of sensuality, wrath, dishonesty, malice and bad conduct. Manu dictates that women be treated as slaves and strumpets because of their sensual attributes (1989:19).

Possibly, this dualistic attitudes have contributed to the degradation of women more systematically. By describing her as *'devi'*, she has been psychologically disarmed to be treated brutally later by subjugating her to the wishes and dictates of men. As a result, her contribution to many aspects of life has remained unrecognised and unaccounted. Her roles as mother and wife have been filially recognised and not materially. The resultant effect has been her underrepresentation in many areas of activities which has definitely affected the course of her life as well as others.

During the medieval period when the rulers' faith was Islamic, a new set of prohibitions was imposed on women, especially women of Islamic faith and tradition. They were consigned to hideous *Purdah* system. The Islamic religious code like its Vedic counterpart did not recognise women's status as equal to men. They were relegated to second rate status and their lives were controlled and directed by the so-called personal law which was the extension of Islamic instructions. They were virtually deprived of all their rights to stand as human beings and were also deprived of expressing themselves. Thus, the status of women both in the Vedic and Islamic religious folds deteriorated considerably and the continuation of this process was amply evident during the British colonial regime in the nineteenth and twentieth century.

However, during the British period, several social reforms were made to awaken public opinion againt *sati*, child marriage and other oppressive social evils which had harmed women colossally.

But important and far reaching efforts to emancipate women were made during the period of freedom movement in our country. It is during this movement that women made their presence felt and positively demonstrated it by participating in the movement that they were in no way unequal to men. Many women played decisive role in the freedom struggle. Moreover, the then male leaders of the freedom struggle were considerably enlightened to realise the women's potential, and as a result, the Indian National Congress recognised equality of sexes as early as in 1931.

But real breakthrough, at least in the policy formulation for the betterment of women, was made only after the Independence of the country from the British colonial yoke in 1947. The Constitution of India in Article 15 states : "The state shall not discriminate against any citizen on grounds only of religion, race, caste, sex, place of birth or any of them". The incorporation of equality before the law in the Constitution "enabled the passage of variety of laws and development of deliberate measures aimed at the improvement of the status of women in post-Independent India" (Ramu, 1989 : 21).

Various legal measures were undertaken to ameliorate the deteriorating status of women. However, women's status was not protected adequately by legal strictures.

> One of the most basic causes for the women's inferior status is the inadequacy of the legal system to keep pace with the changing needs and times and to provide her with the framework which would enable her to contribute her ability fully to society. Discrimination between sexes may stem from attitudes, customs, traditions and cultural norms. The victims of discrimination look upon law for equality and justice. Law includes not only the provisions of constitution and legislation but also judgements and governmental decisions and actions (Desai and Krishnaraj, 1987 : 311).

Before the enactment of legislations, women's life in India, almost everywhere, was governed only by the archaic and opressive male perpetuated 'personal law'. The legislation concerning amelioration of women's condition generally revolved around their : (i) marriage; (ii) divorce; (iii) family courts; (iv) dowry; (v) abortion; (vi) guardianship; (vii) adoption; (viii) maintenance; (ix) inheritance and succession; (x) prostituion; and (xi) women's labour.

Below are given some of the important laws enacted by the state to improve and protect the status of women in India :

1. The Hindu Widow's Remarriage Act, 1856.
2. The Age of Consent Act.
3. The Child Marriage Restraint Act.
4. The Hindu Women's Right to Property Act.
6. The Special Marriage Act, 1954.
7. The Hindu Succession Act, 1956.
8. The Hindu Adoption and Maintenance Act, 1961 (Amended in 1984 and in 1986).
9. The Child Marriage Restraint Act, 1976 (Amended).
10. The Medical Termination of Pregnancy Act, 1971.
11. The Suppression of Immoral Traffic in Women and Girls Act, 1956 (Amended in 1978 and 1986).
12. The Indian Divorce Act, 1936.
13. The Parsi Marriage and Divorce Act, 1936.
14. Amendment to the Criminal Law in 1983.
15. Indecent Exposure of Women (Prohibition) Act, 1986.
16. The Commission of Sati (Prevention) Act. 1987.
17. The Factories Act, 1948.
18. The Mines Act, 1952.
19. The Plantation Labour Act, 1951.
20. The Maternity Benefit Act, 1961 (Amended in 1976).
21. The Factories Amendment Act, 1976.
22. The Equal Remuneration Act, 1976.
23. The Contract Labour (Regulation and Abolition) Act, 1978.

This plethora of legislative measures though promulgated with the view to ameliorate, enhance and protect women's interest in different areas of life, yet, the *de facto* position of women in society has not changed dramatically. Their exploitation has been exacerbated by many factors of which poverty and illiteracy are most formidable and acting as the stumbling blocks which working in tandem with vested socio-economic and political intersts' camouflaged resistance. The lagislative measures did not establish conditions, like social attitudes, economic appratus as prerequisites for enforcement and execution. Moreover, the measures contained elements of paternalism. Desai and Krishnaraj highlight this point by quoting Upendra Baxi :

> Reviewing the position of the women under the Indian Constitution, Upendra Baxi feels that women have not been perceived by the founding fathers as a specially deprived and disadvantaged community like the scheduled castes, tribes and other backward classes. Women of even these scheduled groups - who are doubly depressed, first, as women and second, as women within the scheduled groups - have also not been seen as special constituent within the scheduled groups. The Constitution does not see patriarchy as problematic; it perceives it as natural. Pointing out the basic weaknesses of laws like Hindu Code Bill and Dowry Prohibition Act, he further argues that even after the independence, efforts to combat the patriarchal ideology of the law (never consciously perceived as such) have not led to even the blunting of the edge of male domination (1987 : 327-33).

In addition, the legal machinery is male dominated. The nature of deprivation undergone by women is basically the creation of men. How difficult it could be for a woman to get justice, is illustrated by the famous Shah Bano Begum case which rocked the country in 1985. Laws alone cannot guarantee protection against discrimination, precisely because the relationship between man and woman is weaved not only by socio-cultural mandates, it is commanded and determined by economic necessity. Today, like yesterday, the economic means are controlled by men and its distribution is skewed against women. Women do not, and cannot, therefore, take recourse to legal redressal of their grievances because of the *'prejudice and purpose'* of convenience.

Women and Development Policies : After independence, India adopted mixed economy framework in its development endeavour. Planning strategies and techniques were also adopted to steer the nation's economic development towards attaining a "socialist pattern of society". The First Five-Year Plan was launched in 1950-51. In each plan women's development issues, especially their economic and educational and health, received considerable attention and a number of welfare measures were undertaken to ameliorate their conditions. The First Five-Year Plan emphasised services like family planning, health care, etc. for promoting the status of women. The Second Plan paid special attention to women workers. It stipulated that :

> Women should be protected against injurious work, should receive maternity benefits, and work places should provide creche facilities for children. Nursing mothers should be entitled to paid rest intervals for feeding infants. The principle of equal pay for equal work needs to be more vigorously implemented and the tendency to scale down the job traditionally handled by women has to be guarded against. Training facilities should be provided for them so that they can compete for higher jobs. In addition, the possibility of increasing opportunities for their part-time employment should be explored (Planning Commission, 1956-61 : 584).

To look after the various welfare activities undertaken, the Union Government established the Central Welfare Board in 1953. This Board in coordination with State Social Welfare Boards also looks after state level activities.

The Third Five-Year Plan gave special attention to girls' education. The widening disparity between male and female education levels attracted the attention of the planners. They suggested : "Consequently, by far the most important objective in the field of education during the Third Plan must be to expand facilities for the education of girls at various stages" (Planning Commission, Third Plan : 592).

The Fourth Five-Year Plan laid special emphasis on women's vocational training. It also allowed voluntary agencies to undertake welfare activities. The Fifth Five-Year Plan also gave a great deal of priority to tasks considered to be ameliorating to the conditions of women. The Sixth, Seventh and Eighth Five-Year Plans also focused on various aspects of women's lives and conditions - social, political, economic, cultural and legal. Apart from these, a number of committees and commissions have been appointed, from time to time, to look into the problems detrimental to women's development (for details, see Desai & Krishnaraj, 1987; and also Nayar, 1991).

One of the important steps of the state was the appointment of a Committee on the Status of Women in 1971. This Committee made extensive study of women's problems and made some comprehensive recommendations regarding what measures should be undertaken to enhance and improve the status of women in India. The Committee submitted its report entitled *Toward Equality* in 1975. The following are some of the important highlights of the Committee's report :

(i) Child marriage especially of girl child was rampant in the country.

(ii) Demographically, the proportion of females was less than per thousand males, and the ratio was steadily declining.

(iii) Literacy rate of female as compared to male was dismally low.

(iv) Women's representation in the labour force was found to be very low.

(v) Socio-culturally, women's role was subservient to male. Majority of women "do not enjoy the rights and the opportunities guarnateed by the Constitution" (ICSSR, 1975 : 37).

(vi) Law as an instrument of social change did not change much of women's situation positively.

(vii) The state of women's participation in economic and educational activities was almost stagnant and met with resistance.

(viii) Women were empowered to vote but their participation in political activities was marginal.

(ix) Policies and programmes designed for women's welfare and development were not fully implemented.

As a result, it did not effect any *de facto* change in women's situation.

Another important step by the government was the constitution of the National Commission on Self-Employed Women. Women constitute half of the human race. But still they are deprived of many opportunities and discriminated against in many ways and counts. They play as important role as their male counterparts in every walk of life. But, the role they play is either subordinate or one as exploited. Besides, in this country, a large section of women work in unorganised sector where they are ruthlessly exploited and extremely vulnerable. A government Notification (No.9-11/85-WW, dated 5 January, 1985) prior to the constitution of the Commission voiced its concern over the disadvantaged position of women in the labour market in the following terms :

> Despite the existence of various Constitutional legal provisions safeguarding women's employment, a large number of women workers particularly in the unorganised sector suffer from various disadvantages relating to their working lives as well as their homes. The coverage of labour laws has not benefited these women workers in many crucial areas especially health, maternity and social security. With the changing social and economic conditions, women's produc-

tive roles have assumed new significance but without back-up support and services a healthy combination of women's productive and reproductive roles cannot be sustained.

This Commission made comprehensive study of women's status both at macro and micro levels. The report has been amply illustrated by specific case studies of women in various occupations. The illustrative case studies provide most telling description of female workers' problems and prospects in the vast unorganised sector in the country. On the basis of the findings, the Commission has made some of the following important observations and recommendations :

One of the important observations which the Commission made is that "all women are workers because they are producers and reproducers. Even when they are not employed, they are involved in socially productive and reproductive labour all of which is absolutely necessary for the survival of society. Women's work as home-maker must be recognised as socially economic production" (NCSEW, 1988 : 249).

The Commission recommended that :

(i) At various levels of planning, problems of women working in unorganised sector should be kept in view and appropriate strategies should be devised to protect them from exploitation to enhance their status and wellbeing. It suggested that "strategy should aim at ensuring the fulfillment of their vital requirements of life and provide them various supportive services". It further suggested that effort should be made to reach women in ever larger number.

(ii) Every agency of the government should be responsible to ensure that their planned resources and programmes benefit both men and women equally. Besides fixing this responsibilities, there be a Monitoring Cell in each agency which should be able to monitor and evaluate the utilisation of resources and the implementation of the programmes vis-a-vis women. Every agency should have this cell.

(iii) That to enlarge the areas of employment for women, to improve their working conditions, to reduce their drudgery and to provide social security, a holistic and integrated approach to be adopted. This is specially necessary since women do not perform one action and, therefore, a straight jacket approach cannot be adopted.

(iv) Apart from these broad recommendations, the Commission also made some important observations pertaining to various sectors in which women participate in greater number and where their contributions were considerable. The sectors were : (1) agriculture; (2) fuel, fodder and water collection; (3) construction; (4) industrial; and (5) credit, raw material and marketing, etc. In fact, the Commission made sweeping and comprehensive recommendations touching every aspects of working women's lives and their activities.

The Commission concluded that "since women in poverty are victims of the existing social systems, attitudes and prejudices, one of the factors which can bring about an improvement in the status, is the creation of the social will. Social will has to be created in the community, a work which has been started by voluntary action but needs to be accelerated by efforts of the government through the instruments of education, communication and research... The responsibility of the society in this context cannot be underrated. If the society and the women themselves, do not become aware and act as watchdogs of their rights, guaranteed in the Consitution and various legislations, they cannot legitimately expect the existing systems, which tend to favour the vested interest, to benefit them. Women's organisation have the responsibility of acting as pressure groups on the system and also becoming repositories through which development resources can be channelized".

Policy and Programme for Women's Education : Education plays a catalystic role in human development. It was realised before the independence. After the independence, significant effort has been made for some educational development. Since the position of women in educational map was found dismal, special policies and programmes were formulated to enhance their educational participation. The importance of education of girls was realised by the government and the Report of the Committee on Education of Women (1958-59) was a testimony. Half a decade later the Education Commission, 1964-66 also looked at the education of girls with a serious concern. It noted :

> The significance of the education of girls cannot be overemphasized. For full development of our human resources, the improvement of homes, and for moulding the character of children during the most impressionable years of infancy, the education of women is of even greater importance than that of men. The education of women can assist greatly in reducing the fertility rate. In the modern world, the role

of women goes much beyond the home and the bringing up of children. She is now adopting a career of her own and sharing equally with man the responsibility for the development of society in all its aspects. This is the direction in which we shall have to move. In the struggle for freedom, Indian women fought side by side with men. This equal partnership will have to continue in the fight against hunger, poverty, ignorance, and ill-health (238-39).

The Report of the Education Commission 1964-66 raised a number of problems and to solve them an educational policy was formulated in 1968.

National Policy on Education 1968 : The National Policy on Education, 1968 did not elaborate much on the subject of women's education. It stated that, "The education of girls should receive emphasis, not only on grounds of social justice, but also because it accelerates social transformation" (1977 : 5).

From the formulation and implementation, the problems in the educational scenario assumed more difficult dimensions. The already existing gap between male and female education remained almost same in absolute term. On this backdrop, it became imperative for the state to formulate another comprehensive policy measure. The new policy came in 1986 accompanied by a Programme of Action (POA).

National Policy on Education 1986 : The National Policy on Education, 1986 gave unprecedented emphasis on women's education, unprecedented in comparision with earlier policy in 1968. It exhorts :

> Education will be used as an agent of basic change in the status of women. In order to neutralise the accumulated distortions of the past, there will be well conceived edge in favour of women. The National Education System will play a positive, interventionist role in the empowerment of women. It will foster the development of new values through redesigned curricula, textbooks, the training and orientation of teachers, decision-makers and administrators, and the active involvement of educational institutions. This will be an act of faith in social engineering. Women's studies will be promoted as a part of various courses and educational institutions encouraged to take up active programme to further women's development (para 4.2).

Apart from this statement, the policy document laid special emphasis on the removal of illiteracy and women's increasing participation in vocational, technical and professional education at different levels, and areas of emergent technologies.

Programme of Action 1992 : The Programme of Action 1992 adopted certain strategies to achieve and accelerate women's educational development. The following lines clearly highlight various strategies and the methods for their implementation.

The Programme of Action 1992, in pursuance of National Policy on Education 1986 spelt out a wide range of actions to be undertaken to enhance women's educational opportunity. It emphasised that, for education to be the effective tool for women's empowerment, the following parameters will have to be kept in view :

(i) Enhancing self-esteem and self-confidence of women;

(ii) Building a positive image of women by recognizing their contribution to the society, polity and economy;

(iii) Developing ability to think critically;

(iv) Fostering decision-making action through collective processes;

(v) Enabling women to make informed choices in areas like education, employment and health (especially reproduction, health);

(vi) Ensuring equal participation in developmental processes;

(vii) Providing information, knowledge and skill for economic independence; and

(viii) Enhancing access to legal literacy and information relating to their rights and entitlements in society with a view to enhance their participation on an equal footing in all areas (POA 1.5.1., 1992).

The Programme of Action also envisaged a wide ranging network of organisations and institutions to achieve these parameters. It suggested a number of measures which would be undertaken to enhance women's status. Research on different socio-economic, political, and cultural aspects of development of women was also given due emphasis (for details, see POA 1992, revised).

Report of the Committee 1986 : In 1990, the Government of India appointed a Committee to review the National Education Policy 1986. With regard to women's education the Committee made some very important recommendations pertaining to the following dimensions :

(i) Access to education and quality of learning;

(ii) Content of education and gender bias;

(iii) Vocational education;

(iv) Training of teachers and other educational personnel;

(v) Research and development of women's studies;

(vi) Representation of women in educational hierarchy;

(vii) Empowerment of women;

(viii) Adult Education;

(ix) Resources; and

(x) Management.

The recommendations of the Committee were comprehensive and they touched upon many crucial issues. Due to change in the government, however, no attention was given to these recommendations.

CONCLUSION

The examination of different programmes, policies and recommendations by various agencies envisaged and formulated for the betterment of women in the society by providing opportunities of education and employment reveals that still the tilt has been toward partriarchal framework. No radical effort has been made to reverse the structural parameters to bring about equality between man and woman. In addition, it may be mentioned that in certain countries, for instance, in Iran, even already gained status has considerably been eroded by the fundamentalist forces (Afshar, 1991). This has brought a new danger to the fragile gain made in the last few decades.

Another problem which is emerging slowly is the adjustment effect coupled with recession and political instability in many of the Third World countries. All this directly affects women in many ways.

In India, political instability and recent economic problems could be found exerting its insidious influence by throwing up religious-cultural fanatical forces whose ideological apparatus is evidently retrogressive and decadent. If these forces occupy political power, the status achieved so far would undergo dramatically negative change all over again reducing further the little gain achieved towards the autonomous individual status of women.

CHAPTER TWO

WOMEN AND EDUCATION

PROLOGUE

From time immemorial, women have been discriminated against on many grounds. Their representation in many areas of life and their participation in most of the important socio-economic and political activities have been highly disproportionate to their number. In socio-cultural, political, economic and educational fields where they were disappointingly underrepresented, they did so, in most of the cases, as subordinates to and dependents of men. Socio-culturally they have been brought up to perceive man in the leadership position and this has helped men to perpetuate the discriminatory social framework.

Though their socio-economic status has relatively improved in the developed industrial countries, the conditions of women in the developing Third World countries have remained disturbingly inequitious. The large majority of them are not only discriminated against, they are also deprived of many life preparing and life sustaining opportunities. Many causes of this situation are rooted in the "gender belief system".

> The term "gender belief system" refers to a set of beliefs and opinions about males and females and about the purported qualities of masculinity and feminity. This system includes stereotypes of women and men, attitudes toward the appropriate roles and behaviours of women and men, and attitudes toward individuals who are believed to differ in some significant way from the modal pattern (e.g., homosexuals). The 'gender belief system', conceptualized in this broad manner, includes both descriptive and prescriptive elements - "beliefs about what is and opinions about what should be" (Deaux and Mary, 1987:97).

The "gender belief system" has acted as a strong barrier to women's participation in many important activities, particulary in educational and economic activities of the types which have liberating effects and which increase their access to and control of resources.

Education is a key instrument for women's development despite the fact that education could also be used to perpetuate subordinate status of women by systematically institutionalising traditional social customs and by reinforcing "gender belief system". But since education plays a dialectical role and acts as a catalyst in the long term, it has to be viewed as liberating instrument, and effort has to be directed towards removing barriers to women's access to education in general and quality education in particular.

The issue that concerned women's education was what should constitute the content? Almost everywhere society agreed that women's education should be such that severed her role as women *(Gender and Education,* Vol.4. Nos. 1-2, 1992). Wolpe (1977) argues :

> The education system is a key means of production and reproduction of the ideological structure - for this system not only in its very organisation and mode of functioning embodies the dominant ideology of the society, but also functions to reproduce this ideology in its specific form.

This being true, it is again assumed that it is education through which subordination of women has to be intellectually perceived and gradually the process of subordination has to be removed. Evidences suggest that to whatever extent women have achieved autonomous individual status today is due to their intellectual understanding and its resultant effort. In socialist countries,emancipation of women was an important agenda and in pursuance of that a great deal has been achieved. But there appeared another kind of insideous discrimination against women (Molyneux, 1991).

However, the positive contribution of education to women's liberation as autonomous individuals far outweigh its negative impact (Walker and Barton, 1983; and Smock, 1981).

Today, there are more than 996 million illiterate adults in the world. Out of this, more than 640 million are women. The disparities in educational attainment ultimately contribute to disparities in participation of women in economic and other developmental activities.

Here, in this chapter, the effort is to, first, examanine representation of women in different levels of education in India and subsequently to deal with the causes of low participation rates and its impact on labour market and participation of women in various occupations according to their educational qualifications. However, before going into the specific areas it would be appropriate to throw some light on the female literacy situation as prevailing in India today.

FEMALE LITERACY RATE

The female literacy rate in any country indicates the basic educational background of women in particular and their comparative position in relation to men's educational status in general. It also reveals the expected scenario in terms of educationally determined employment opportunities which would be available to women and the proportion of them who would indeed avail these opportunities. Table 2.1 shows the literacy rates for women at various points of time from 1901 to 1991. Over a period of nine decades, the female literacy rate increased from the insignificant 0.7 per cent in 1901 to 39.42 per cent in 1991, almost half of what was for male (63.86 per cent) in 1991. This disparity in literacy rates between females and males has been reflected in other levels of educational system : secondary and higher education.

This is indeed a highly disappointing situation in regard to female literacy in general and education in particular. Besides, literacy rates hide another important facet of educational development in India. In 1951, the absolute number of illiterates was 294.2 million which increased to a staggering 424.3 million in 1981. The situation, however, marginally improved in 1991. (see Table 2.2)

Table 2.1 : **Literacy rates in India, 1901 to 1991**

Year	Percentage of literates to total population		
	Persons	Males	Females
1901	5.3	9.8	0.7
1911	5.9	10.6	1.1
1921	7.2	12.2	1.8
1931	9.5	15.6	2.9
1941	16.1	24.9	7.3
1951	16.7	25.0	7.9
1961	24.0	34.4	13.0
1971	29.5	39.5	18.7
1981	36.2	46.9	24.8
1991	52.11	63.86	39.42

Sources : (i) *Census of India*, Various Years.
(ii) Sharma, O.P., and Robert D. Rutherford (1983) *Recent Literacy Trends in India*, Census of India, Occasional Paper No. 1 of 1983, Office of Registrar General and Census Commissioner, India.

It also hides one more fact of participation of women in education : though literacy rates among women have shown a rising trend, the absolute number of illiterate women has been rising steadily. In the race between literacy and illiteracy, the illiteracy among women has been rising still further leaving the literacy level far behind (see Figure 2.1). "During the post-independence period, the total number of illiterate women has increased from 161.9 million in 1951 to a staggering figure of 241.6 million in 1981." (NCSEW, 1988 : 22).

This is no doubt an alarming aspect of educational development in India given the already disappointing situation of women's education.

Table 2.2 : **Population, literacy and illiteracy, 1901 to 1991**

(in millions)

Year	Population	Literates	Illiterates	Increase in illiterates
1901	235.1	12.6	222.5	
1911	248.2	14.7	233.5	+11.0
1921	246.7	17.7	229.0	- 4.5
1931	273.4	26.0	247.4	+18.4
1941	312.0	50.2	261.8	+14.4
1951	353.1	58.9	294.2	+32.4
1961	428.0	102.6	325.5	+31.3
1971	533.5	157.3	376.2	+50.7
1981	665.3	241.0	424.3	+48.1
1991	843.9	352.1	234.0	+16.3

Source : *Census of India,* Various Years.

These facts provide ample evidence of the existence of an imbalanced educational growth process in India. It is clear in Table 2.2 that over the last nine decades, except 1921, the number of illiterates in absolute terms has been increasing at a faster rate and there was a spurt in the number of illiterates during the period 1961-71 where it increased from 31.3 million in 1961 to 50.7 million in 1971. In 1991, the number of illiterates in absolute terms increased by 16.3 million.

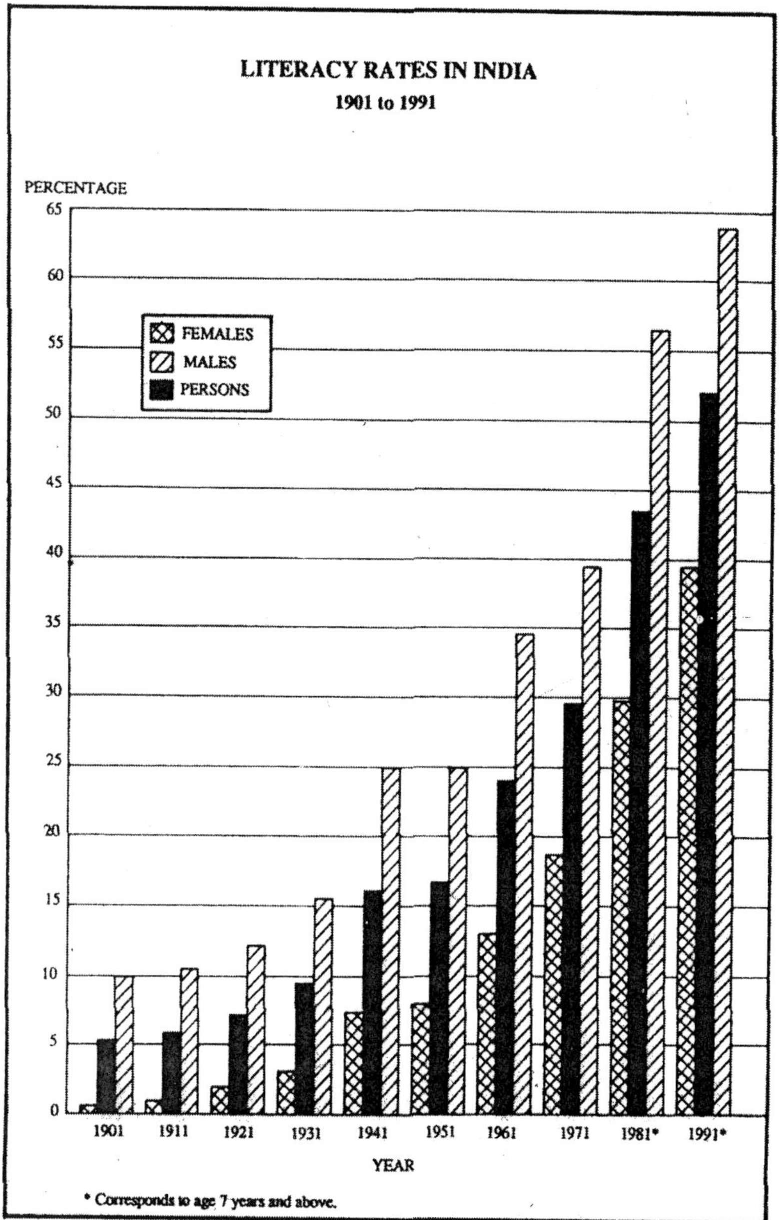
LITERACY RATES IN INDIA
1901 to 1991
PERCENTAGE
65
60
55
50
45
40
35
30
25
20
15
10
5
0
FEMALES
MALES
PERSONS
1901
1911
1921
1931
1941
1951
1961
1971
1981*
1991*
YEAR
* Corresponds to age 7 years and above.

Fig. 2.1

The dismal gaps between male and female school attendance further amplify the emerging scenario in India where participation of females in labour market requiring certified educational attainments is virtually marginal. The figures in Table 2.3 show that, in 1981, the participation of females in various age groups in education as compared to men was strikingly disporoportionate to their total number (in respective age groups). This underrepresentation of women in education results in their imbalanced representation in various employments. In 1981, only 38.3 per cent girls in the age group 6-9 were attending schools and in the age group 20-24, their attendance was only 3.0 per cent. This wide gap between the attendance rates of females in schools and colleges brings into surface the fact that, in India, a large number of females either drop out or do not participate in education, particularly in the collegiate education. Besides, the disparity between the attendance rates of females in various age groups between rural and urban areas was very high in 1981. This rate was 31.3 per cent for rural girls in the age group 6-9 and 63.6 per cent for urban girls in the same age group (see Figure 2.2). This wide gap between the attendance rates of rural and urban girls in schools and colleges has set into motion a process of building up of two parallel societies so far as education of females is concerned.

Table 2.3 : **Age-wise and sex-wise school and college attendance in India, 1981**

(in percentages)

Area	Age group	Persons	Males	Females
Rural	6-9	39.9	48.0	31.3
	10-14	44.2	57.8	29.2
	15-19	20.5	30.9	8.9
	20-24	4.7	8.2	1.3
Urban	6-9	67.1	70.4	63.6
	10-14	71.5	77.0	65.2
	15-19	42.9	50.2	34.5
	20-24	13.4	18.5	7.5
Total	6-9	45.8	52.8	38.3
	10-14	50.5	62.1	37.5
	15-19	26.4	36.0	15.5
	20-24	7.2	11.3	3.0

Source : *Census of India* (1981) Series I, India, Part-II, Special Report and Tables based on 5 per cent sample data, New Delhi, 1983.

PRIMARY AND MIDDLE LEVELS

Analysis of level-wise enrolment of girls reveals that disparities with regard to enrolment of girls is more pronounced than that of boys in 1988-89. Further, this gap in enrolment was far more pronounced among the girls belonging to the Scheduled Castes and the Scheduled Tribes communities. Table 2.4 presents data on enrolment ratios of boys and girls for the year 1988-89. It could be noted that the representation of girls in primary and middle levels was relatively less (the GER in primary and middle levels were 82.89 per cent and 42.3 per cent respectively) compared to their total number and it was still less and disappointing among girls from socio-economically disadvnataged groups such as SCs and STs (see Figure 2.3). The gross enrolment ratios of SC girls in primary and middle levels were 78.33 per cent and 30.18 per cent respectively in 1988-89 and the respective ratios of ST girls were 76 per cent and 22.73 per cent (see Table 2.4).

Table 2.4: **Stage-wise and sex-wise gross enrolment ratios (GER) in primary and middle levels in India, 1988-89**

	Boys	Girls	Total
Scheduled Castes			
Primary	121.26	78.33	100.37
Middle	58.81	30.18	44.88
Scheduled Tribes			
Primary	126.23	76.00	101.79
Middle	47.90	22.73	35.65
All Categories			
Primary	115.7	82.89	99.6
Middle	70.8	42.3	56.9

Source: MinistryofHumanResource Development (1990) *Selected Educational Statistics*, New Delhi.

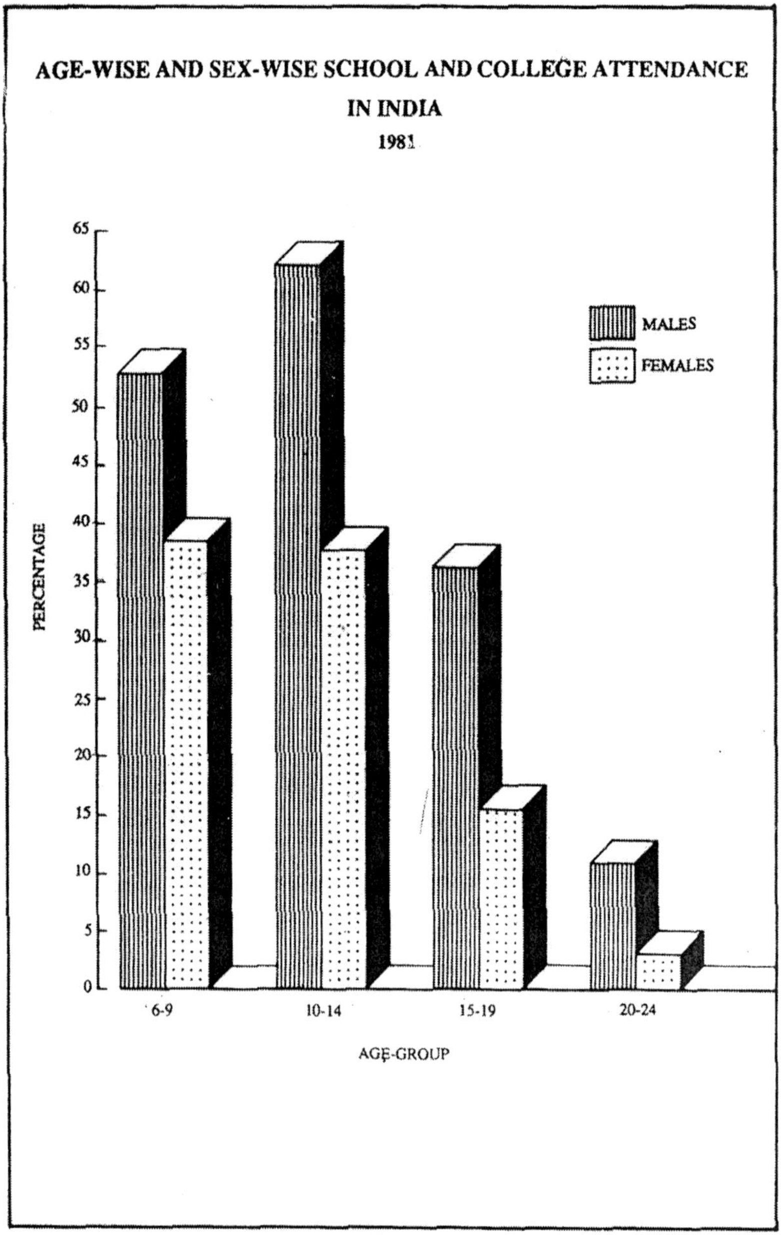
AGE-WISE AND SEX-WISE SCHOOL AND COLLEGE ATTENDANCE
IN INDIA
1981
65
60
55
50
45
40
35
30
25
20
15
10
5
0
PERCENTAGE
MALES
FEMALES
6-9
10-14
15-19
20-24
AGE-GROUP

Fig. 2.2

SECONDARY LEVEL ENROLMENT

The enrolment of girls was more disproportionate to their numbers in the secondary level in 1986. There are many causes of this underrepresentation of girls in education. First, the prevailing socio-cultural traditions in the country do not allow a girl to receive education upto the minimum level in the village primary school. Second, the relative position of a girl at home is quite unfavourable in the sense that it acts as a barrier to her entry into the school. Because a growing up girl spends more time doing household chores than a boy of the same age. Third, the low economic status of many families, particularly in rural India, discourages many families to send their girl children to schools. Since majority of the rural households live in poverty, the relative status of a girl child is much more lower than a male child in a poor household. Here again "gender belief system" dominates and, as a result, girls' participation in secondary and higher levels of education becomes gradually highly disproportionate to their numbers. The following remark clearly demonstrates the state of access and relative status of girls in the school sector in the developing countries :

> Economic realities in the developing countries often require sending boys to school while girls stay at home to care for younger children and to help their mothers in the field, gather fuel and carry water. FAO studies indicate that the girls between the ages of 10 and 14 contribute 22 per cent of family labour, while boys in the same age group contribute only 6 per cent. The fact that female skills command less pay than the comparable skills of the male is recognized by parents and tends to shape their decision not to invest in the education of their daughters. Other factors, such as distance from school, the lack of women teachers and schools for girls, the lack of toilet and other facilities, the absence of immediate pay-off and ability to meet such school expenses as clothing and transportation, are all discouraging elements (UN, 1991 : 192).

Tabel 2.5 shows that in classes IX-X the percentage share of enrolment of girls was much less (31.71) than that of the boys in 1986. In the same year, the relative share of enrolment of girls in classes XI-XII was still less - i.e. 30.77 per cent only. Underrepresentation of girls at the secondary level education is reflected in their poor participation in highr education in the country. Special efforts should be made to enhance participation of girls at primary and secondary level education. (see Rehman, 1992, for a detailed discussion on this aspect).

STAGE-WISE AND SEX-WISE GROSS ENROLMENT RATIOS IN INDIA
PRIMARY AND MIDDLE LEVELS
1988-89

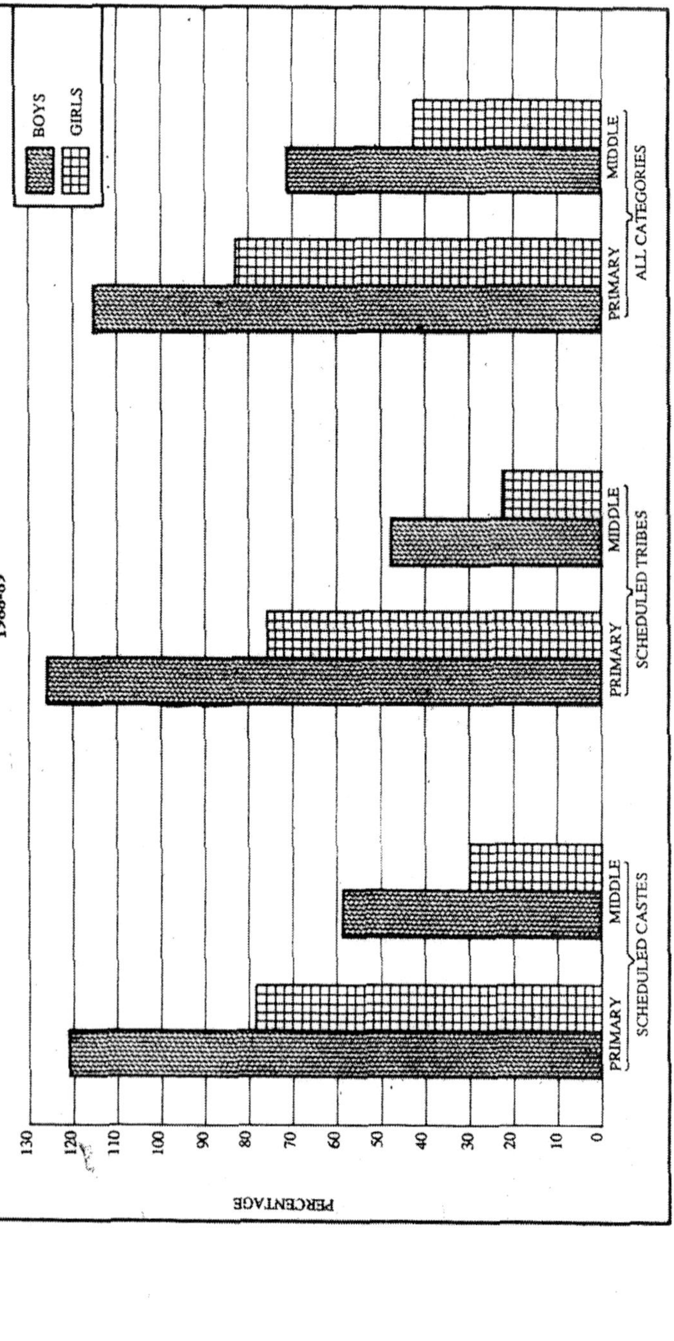

Fig. 2.3

Table 2.5 : **Girls' enrolment at second level in India, 1986**

(in percentages)

Class	Girls	Boys
Classes IX-X	31.71	68.29
Classes XI-XII	30.77	69.23

Source : NCERT (1990) *Fifth All-India Educational Survey*, New Delhi.

ENROLMENT IN HIGHER EDUCATION

Higher education is the most crucial sector in the educational system of a country. In fact, this sector is the backbone of any industrialised country. This sector not only develops human capabilities to a maximum extent possible but also empowers a person with knowledge, perceptions and ideas which help him/her to contribute to the development process of society more meaningfully and rationally. However, higher education has remained still a far cry for majority of the people in India and more so with regard to women. The participation of women in higher education is very low in the country. The percentage enrolment of women in this sector to total enrolment was 32.5 in 1991. Besides, during the last decade, the growth of women's enrollment in higher education has also been at a snail's pace. In 1979-80, the percentage enrolment of women in higher education was 26.0 which increased marginally to 32.5 per cent in 1991, even after more than a decade (see Figure 2.4). Moreover, in relative terms, during the last decade, the growth of enrolment of women in higher education was also not steady either (see Table 2.6).

Table 2.6: **Total enrolment and enrolment of women in higher education in India**

Year	Total enrolment	Women's enrolment	Percentage of women	Percentage increase over the preceding year
(1)	(2)	(3)	(4)	(5)
1979-80	26,48,579	6,88,630	26.0	-
1980-81	27,52,437	7,48,525	27.2	8.7

Contd.

(1)	(2)	(3)	(4)	(5)
1981-82	29,52,066	8,16,704	27.7	9.1
1982-83	31,33,093	8,80,156	28.1	7.8
1983-84	33,07,649	9,40,253	28.4	6.8
1984-85	34,04,096	9,92,139	29.1	5.5
1985-86	36,05,029	10,67,484	29.6	7.6
1986-87	37,54,409	11,48,349	30.6	7.6
1987-88	39,10,828	12,24,089	31.3	6.6
1988-89	40,74,676	12,91,672	31.7	5.5
1989-90	42,46,876	13,67,495	32.2	5.9
1990-91*	44,25,247	14,36,887	32.5	5.1

Source: University Grants Commission (1991) *Annual Report, 1990-91*, New Delhi.
*: Estimated.

Analysis of stage-wise distribution of women in higher education shows that, in 1990-91, the share of women in the total enrolment at graduate, post-graduate, research and diploma/certificate levels were 32.3 per cent, 34.2 per cent, 36.7 per cent and 25.5 per cent respectively (see Table 2.7). As compared to the previous year, 1989-90, the increase in the percentage share of women in various stages was insignificant in 1990-91 (see Figure 2.5).

Table 2.7 : **Percentage distribution of women's enrolment at various stages, 1989-90 and 1990-91**

Stage	Percentage of women's enrolment to total enrolment	
	1989-90	1990-91
Graduate	39.1	32.3
Post-graduate	33.6	34.2
Research	35.7	36.7
Diploma/Certificate	25.2	25.5
Total	32.2	32.5

Source : University Grants Commission (1991) *Annual Report, 1990-91*, New Delhi.

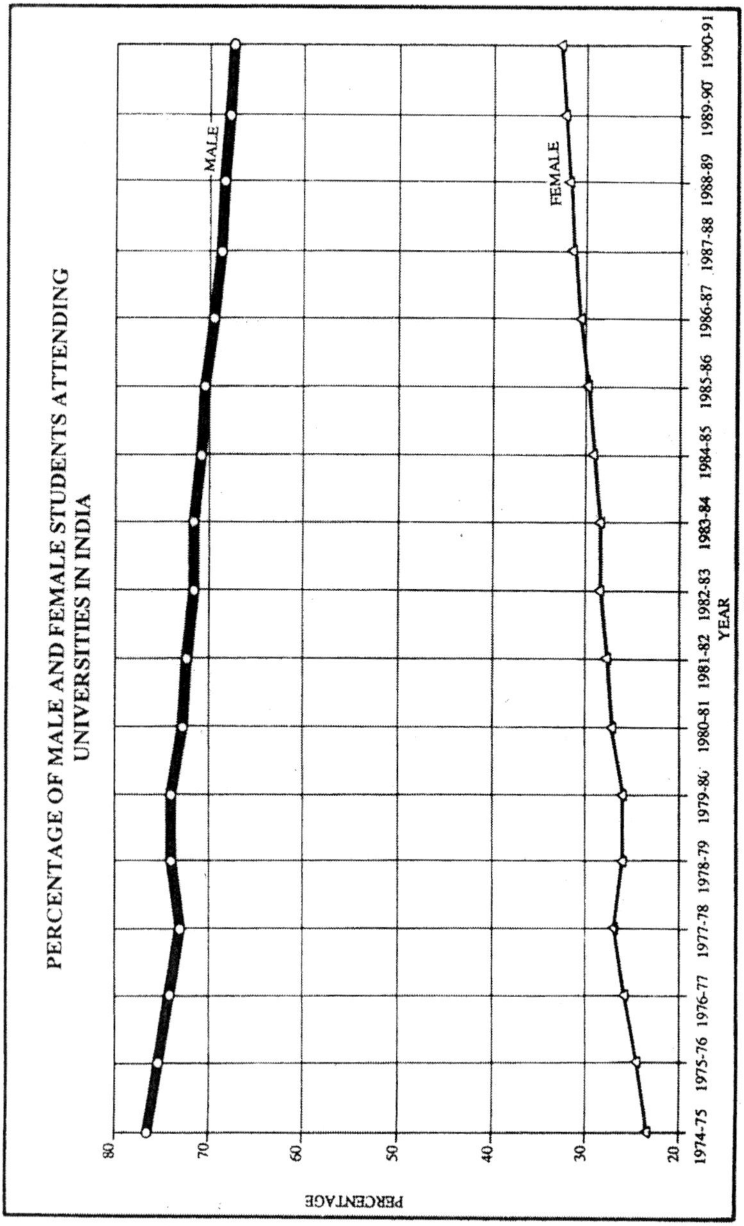
PERCENTAGE OF MALE AND FEMALE STUDENTS ATTENDING
UNIVERSITIES IN INDIA
MALE
FEMALE
PERCENTAGE
80
70
60
50
40
30
20
1974-75
1975-76
1976-77
1977-78
1978-79
1979-80
1980-81
1981-82
1982-83
1983-84
1984-85
1985-86
1986-87
1987-88
1988-89
1989-90
1990-91
YEAR

Fig. 2.4

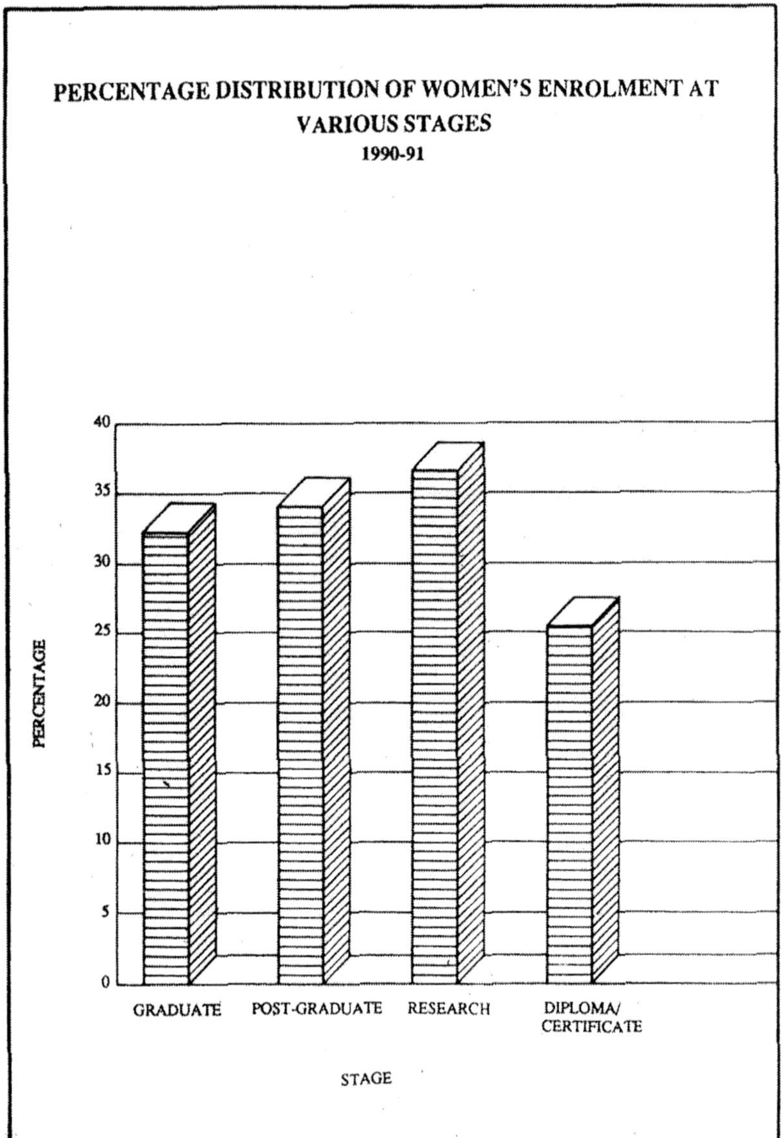
PERCENTAGE DISTRIBUTION OF WOMEN'S ENROLMENT AT
VARIOUS STAGES
1990-91
40
35
30
25
20
15
10
5
0
PERCENTAGE
GRADUATE
POST-GRADUATE
RESEARCH
DIPLOMA/
CERTIFICATE
STAGE

Fig.2.5

The point to be noted here is that, during the last decade, the growth rate of women's enrolment was relatively fast. Notwithstanding, there were only 48 women per hundred men studying in various stages in higher education in India in 1990-91.

We have seen that participation of women in higher education is highly disproportionate as compared to their male counterparts : a small number of women only reach the highest level of education in India. However, these level-wise participation rates hide a very important aspect of women's participation in higher education. The faculty-wise examination of women's enrolment reveals that women are highly underrepresented in professional courses and programmes. For instance, in 1990-91, women's enrolment in Engineering and Technical courses was 7.9 per cent, in Agriculture 7.2 per cent, and in Veterenairy Science and Law women constituted only 8.2 per cent and 10 per cent respectively. In 1990-91, women were mostly concentrated in Education (53.4 per cent) followed by Arts (44.0 per cent), Science (33.3 per cent), Medicine (32.3 per cent) and Commerce (20.8 per cent) (see Table 2.8). Moreover, the rates of growth of enrolment of women in these faculties were marginal during the last decade. In Medicine, the enrolment ratio of women does indicate a positive trend. But given the need for female medical professionals in the country women are still underrepresented in this faculty. They seem to excell only in the field of Education. Yet, there is a dearth of female teachers in rural areas. This indicates that women who are receiving higher education are from comparatively well-off families and largely belong to urban areas.

Table 2.8 : **Proportion of women studying in various courses in higher education in India**

(in percentages)

Year	Arts	Science	Commerce	Education	Engg./ Tech.	Medicine	Agriculture	Vet. Science	Law	Others
(1)	(2)	(3)	(4)	(5)	(6)	(7)	(8)	(9)	(10)	(11)
1980-81	37.7	28.8	15.9	47.3	3.8	24.4	3.3	3.3	6.9	39.8
1981-82	38.2	28.6	16.7	48.3	4.5	26.2	3.5	4.3	7.1	38.8
1982-83	38.7	28.8	17.4	47.0	5.0	27.8	4.0	4.8	7.4	36.9
1983-84	38.6	29.0	18.7	47.3	5.5	28.3	4.1	5.1	7.8	35.7

Contd..

(1)	(2)	(3)	(4)	(5)	(6)	(7)	(8)	(9)	(10)	(11)
1984-85	39.4	30.0	19.3	47.8	6.3	29.6	4.9	5.4	8.0	37.9
1985-86	40.4	30.5	19.1	49.0	5.9	29.5	4.3	4.9	8.1	38.0
1986-87	41.6	31.4	19.7	50.5	6.0	30.4	4.5	5.1	8.3	38.6
1987-88	42.7	32.2	20.2	51.8	6.2	31.1	4.6	5.2	8.5	38.9
1988-89	43.2	32.6	20.5	52.4	6.2	31.7	4.9	5.3	8.7	39.1
1989-90	43.6	32.9	20.6	52.9	7.6	31.9	6.9	7.9	9.8	39.2
1990-91	44.0	33.3	20.8	53.4	7.9	32.3	7.2	8.2	10.0	39.4

Source : University Grants Commission (1991) *Annual Report, 1990-91*, New Delhi.

ENROLMENT OF WOMEN IN STATES/UTS

The participation rates of women in higher education in various states differ considerably. In the states and union territories where enrolment rates of girls in school education are low and disproportionate to their number, the enrolment rates of women in higher education in these states and union territories are also very low. Table 2.9 demonstrates this point clearly. It could be seen in Table 2.9 that, in 1990-91, the enrolment of women in higher education was highest in Kerala (53.0 per cent) followed by Punjab (48.2 per cent), Delhi (46.3 per cent), Haryana (42.2 per cent), Meghalaya/Nagaland/Mizoram (39.0 per cent), Tamil Nadu (38.5 per cent), West Bengal/Tripura Sikkim (38.4 per cent), Jammu & Kashmir (37.6 per cent), Maharashtra (36.8 per cent), Gujarat (35.4 per cent), Madhya Pradesh (34.2 per cent), Manipur (34.1 per cent), Assam (31.0 per cent), Karnataka (29.2 per cent), Andhra Pradesh (27.7 per cent), Himachal Pradesh (26.8 per cent), Orissa (25.0 per cent), Rajasthan (24.2 per cent), Uttar Pradesh (22.6 per cent) and Bihar (16.4 per cent). In fact, as many as 15 states (in two cases, three states had been tied together) and the union territory of Delhi had percentage of women enrolment higher than the national average of 32.5 per cent in 1990-91. The lowest enrolment of women was in Bihar (16.4 per cent). The states having women enrolment in higher education less than the national average (32.5 per cent) were Bihar, Rajasthan, Uttar Pradesh, Andhra Pradesh, Himachal Pradesh, Karnataka, and Orissa. In 1990-91, the inter-state disparities with regard to growth of enrolment of women in higher education sector could perhaps be attributed to the uneven economic growth of these states.

In many cases, the existing belief system and negative attitudes of the parents as well as the relative low social weightage of women's education could partly explain this disparity in enrolment of women in higher education.

Table 2.9: **Percentage of women's enrolment to total enrolment : state-wise, 1989-90 and 1990-91**

SL no.	State/union territory	1989-90			1990-91
		Total enrolment	Women's enrolment	Percentage of women's enrolment	Percentage of women's enrolment
1.	Andhra Pradesh	2,93,768	80,459	27.4	27.7
2.	Assam	82,381	25,061	30.4	31.0
3.	Bihar	2,99,743	48,471	16.2	16.4
4.	Gujarat	2,53,316	89,605	35.4	35.4
5.	Haryana	90,034	37,216	41.3	42.2
6.	Himachal Pradesh	24,579	6,509	26.5	26.8
7.	Jammu & Kashmir	31,518	11,850	37.6	37.6
8.	Karnataka	2,80,977	80,363	28.6	29.2
9.	Kerala	1,62,347	85,484	52.7	53.0
10.	Madhya Pradesh	3,01,738	99,719	33.1	34.2
11.	Maharashtra	5,74,140	2,07,151	36.1	36.8
12.	Manipur	12,701	4,274	33.7	34.1
13.	Meghalaya/Mizoram/Nagl.	12,288	4,767	38.8	39.0
14.	Orissa	90,629	21,799	24.1	25.0
15.	Punjab	1,55,994	74,098	47.5	48.2
16.	Rajasthan	1,96,079	46,173	23.6	24.2
17.	Tamil Nadu	3,59,432	1,36,222	37.9	38.5
18.	Uttar Pradesh	5,70,023	1,27,317	22.3	22.6
19.	West Bengal/ Tripura/Sikkim	3,40,832	1,28,828	37.8	38.4
20.	Delhi	1,14,365	52,129	45.6	46.3
	Total	42,46,878	13,67,495	32.2	32.5

Source : University Grants Commission (1991) *Annual Report, 1990-91*, New Delhi.
Note : Data for years 1986-87 to 1989-90 are based on revised estimates and data for 1990-91 are based on first estimate.

A close look into the pattern of enrolment of women in higher education reveals another important aspect of their participation in various types of courses. We have already examined in this chapter the ratio of enrolment of women in terms of total enrolment. This, however, does not fully reveal the contours of disproportionate representation of women in higher education.

In Table 2.10 it could be seen that, in 1986-87, the percentage of girls in the age group 18-23 receiving higher education (general, professional and others) to total population in the corresponding age group was 2.93 while for their male counterparts it was 6.01. Across states and union territories the difference between the percentages of participation of males and females in the age group 18-23 was quite high in 1986-87. In case of girls, the participation rate ranged from a minimum of zero per cent in Dadra, Nagar Haveli and Lakshadweep to a maximum of 29.55 per cent in Chandigarh in 1986-87. In the case of boys, the participation rates varied between a minimum of zero per cent in Dadra, Nagar Haveli and Lakshadweep to a maximum of 32.13 per cent in Chandigarh in the same year. The percentage of enrolment of girls to total population in the age group 18-23 was highest in Chandigarh (29.55), followed by Delhi (11.80), Goa (5.89) Punjab (5.12), Manipur (4.87), Kerala (4.42) and Maharashtra (4.40). The lowest enrolment of girls in the age groups of 18-23 could be found in Arunachal Pradesh (0.49 per cent), followed by Sikkim (0.64 per cent), Nagaland (1.04 per cent), Bihar (1.22 per cent), Orissa (1.37 per cent), Mizoram (1.56 per cent), Uttar Pradesh (1.87 per cent) Rajasthan (1.95 per cent) and so on (see Table 2.10).

THE HIDDEN RECESSES

Though all women belong to the same gender category, they do not belong to the same class - social or economic. Women in general are deprived and discriminated against and some groups are more vulnerable and exploitable in comparison with other groups. Status-wise, women belonging to some social and economic groups are relatively better placed. However, a global picture does not show the hidden recesses of discrimination against women, particularly those belonging to disadvantaged socio-economic groups. It is, therefore, necessary to unravel the contours of hidden faces by looking at the problems of women from different social, ethnic, economic, and other group perspectives.

Indian society is highly fragmented, both socially and economically. Some social groups by dint of their access to and control over various resources in greater amount and number are better placed; and this better placement in social set-up helps them getting major benefits from educational services offered by the state. Some social and religious groups are also culturally dynamic in that they do not discourage participation of females in education.

Table 2.10: **Number of pupils receiving collegiate education (general + professional + others) - degree and above level courses and percentage coverage to population of corresponding age group, 1986-87**

Sl.	Statesd / UTs	Enrolment (Degree & above)			Projected population (In '000s)			Percentage of enrolment in colleges to population in the corresponding age group 18-23		
		Boys	Girls	Total	Males	Females	Persons	Boys	Girls	Total
(1)	(2)	(3)	(4)	(5)	(6)	(7)	(8)	(9)	(10)	(11)
1.	Andhra Pradesh	211099	82337	293436	34223	33154	67377	6.17	2.48	4.36
2.	Assam	57434	25569	83003	14112	13664	27775	4.07	1.87	2.99
3.	Bihar	254817	52751	307568	47580	43282	90862	5.36	1.22	3.39
4.	Gujarat	146985	85905	232890	24520	22788	47308	5.99	3.77	4.92
5.	Haryana	37418	20655	58073	10270	8589	18859	3.64	2.40	3.08
6.	Himachal Pradesh	16413	6413	22826	2874	2859	5733	5.71	2.24	3.98
7.	Jammu & Kashmir	17511	10973	28484	4351	3887	8238	4.02	2.82	4.46
8.	Karnataka	233744	94959	328703	25614	24265	49879	9.13	3.91	6.59
9.	Kerala	80217	76495	156712	17392	17316	34708	4.61	4.42	4.52
10.	Madhya Pradesh	208777	86187	294964	36608	32444	69052	5.70	2.66	4.27
11.	Maharashtra	383014	174345	557359	44006	39642	83648	8.70	4.40	6.66
12.	Manipur	6985	4706	11691	988	967	1955	7.07	4.87	5.98
13.	Meghalaya	4266	2689	6955	922	928	1850	4.63	2.90	3.76

Contd..

(1)	(2)	(3)	(4)	(5)	(6)	(7)	(8)	(9)	(10)	(11)
14.	Nagaland	1572	598	2170	740	573	1313	2.12	1.04	1.65
15.	Orissa	79104	23564	102668	17558	17242	34800	4.51	1.37	2.95
16.	Punjab	72681	55019	127700	11984	10756	22740	6.06	5.12	5.62
17.	Rajasthan	147229	42899	190128	24338	22155	46493	6.05	1.94	4.09
18.	Sikkim	447	149	596	284	234	518	1.57	.64	1.15
19.	Tamil Nadu	173596	94045	267641	31133	30741	61874	5.58	3.06	4.33
20.	Tripura	5812	2896	8708	1527	1486	3013	3.81	1.95	2.89
21.	Uttar Pradesh	406063	117361	523424	75637	62668	138305	5.37	1.87	3.78
22.	West Bengal	206262	136955	343217	39553	36862	76415	5.21	3.72	4.49
23.	A & N Islands	573	530	1103	152	140	292	3.77	3.79	3.78
24.	Arunachal Pradesh	974	175	1149	397	355	752	2.45	.49	1.53
25.	Chandigarh	14587	10314	24901	454	349	803	32.13	29.55	31.01
26.	D & N Haveli	-	-	-	67	71	138	.00	.00	.00
27.	Delhi	74118	54013	128131	5746	4579	10325	12.90	11.80	12.41
28.	Goa, D. & Diu	5229	4558	9787	818	774	1592	6.39	5.89	6.15
29.	Lakshadweep	-	-	-	27	22	49	.00	.00	.00
30.	Mizoram	1365	621	1986	426	399	825	3.20	1.56	2.41
31.	Pondicherry	3295	2032	5327	448	423	871	7.35	4.80	6.12
	All India	2851587	1269713	4121300	474749	433614	908363	6.01	2.93	4.54

Source : Ministry of Human Resource Development (1991) *Education in India, 1986-87*, Vol. 1(c), New Delhi.

There are some social groups which, however, are traditionally very conservative. As a result, such groups do not allow their female members to participate in education and other activities which they think might change their existing culture and tradition, specifically the relative status of women. Therefore, poverty and decadent traditions act as formidable barriers to women's participation in education in many socio-economic and ideological groups.

Here, the attempt is on to examine the participation of females of two social groups, the Scheduled Castes and Scheduled Tribes. Attempt has also been made to present the picture of participation of women belonging to different religions vis-a-vis their male counterparts.

Scheduled Caste Female Education : Traditionally, the Scheduled Castes and Scheduled Tribes constitute socio-economically and educationally the most deprived and exploited section of Indian society. An examination of literacy rates of SC and ST women in India and in its different states and union territories reveals that except in north-eastern states the literacy rates among females are disappointingly poor in comparison with women of other social groups. It could be seen in Table 2.11 that, in 1981, the literacy rate for females in the general category was 24.82 per cent in India while it was 10.93 per cent for the SC females and for the ST females it was 8.04 per cent. The literacy rates of SC and ST females in most of the states were not very promising either. In most states, the rates were below the national average while in a few states it was above it. In some states and union territories, namely, Kerala, Goa, Diu Daman, Dadra and Nagar Haveli, Delhi, Chandigarh, Gujarat, Himachal Pradesh, Jammu and Kashmir, Karnataka, Manipur, Meghalaya, Punjab, Sikkim, Tamil Nadu, Arunachal Pradesh, West Bengal, Pondichery, Mizoram, Maharashtra and Tripura, the average literacy rates for the Scheduled Caste females were well above the national average of 10.93 per cent. The lowest literacy rate for the SC females could be found in Bihar (2.65 per cent) in 1981. The highest literacy rate for the SC females was found in Mizoram 53.33 per cent in the same year. However, in the states and union territories where literacy rates for the Scheduled Caste females were higher than the national average the concentration of the SC population in these states/union territories was not comparatively very high.

Another important point is that in the states where concentration of Scheduled Caste population was higher, the number of agricultural labourers was also higher in those states, and in such states the rates of literacy among the Scheduled Caste females were also considerably lower in comparison to other states and union territories. That poverty is the single most important barrier to female participation in education is amply evidenced by the fact that most of the Scheduled Caste households in Bihar, Madhya Pradesh, Rajasthan and Uttar Pradesh are poor and their main livelihood is agricultural activities. The members of these households work as wage labourers. Besides, most of the households are also landless and semi-landless. The capacity of these households to invest in the education of the girl child is beyond their means. Most of the female members of the SC households, including children, work to eke out their living.

This situation is further influenced by social perceptions about female education. The perceptions of the male members about female's education is not congenial. Both poverty and social traditions act in tandem to undermine women's participation in education. As a result, the participation of the SC females in education was found far below the desired level in comparision with the females of other social groups in 1981. This trend in the growth of participation rates of SC women in education perhaps still continues in India.

Scheduled Tribe Female Education : Scheduled Tribes, as compared to the Scheduled Castes and other social groups, are in more disadvantageous position in India. Economically, this group (STs) are deprived of even the basic necessities of life. Geographically, they live in rural outbacks cut off from the mainstream of life. Since their habitats are in remote and in almost inaccessible and isolated areas, the present day educational facilities are neither sufficient nor congenial to their existing needs, environments, life and living patterns. Apart from these deficiencies, the tribal community lacks 'native support' which means support from within the community. Yet the tribals are far from benefitting from their own leadership and internal forces. In most of the cases, outside liberal and enlightened forces help them to organise for their rights. The excessive exploitation of the tribals at the hands of the external economic forces is reflected in their utter and abject poverty and lack of resources which can help them to sustain independently.

It has been argued many times and by many authors that tribals should be brought into the mainstream of national life. Their present pattern of living is not conducieve to modernisation. However, effort to modernise them has landed to tribal society in disastrous situation, and educational facilities provided to them did not reach in the desired manner. As a result, they have remained, more or less deprieved of education of any type. Hence efforts should be made to provide educational facilities for tribal people according to their needs.

Table 2.11:**Scheduled Castes and Scheduled Tribes female literacy rates, 1981#**

(in percentages)

Sl. no.	State/ Union Territory	General females	Scheduled Caste females	Scheduled Tribe females
1.	Andhra Pradesh	20.39	10.26	3.46
2.	Assam*	N.A.	N.A.	N.A.
3.	Bihar	13.62	2.51	7.75
4.	Gujarat	32.30	25.61	11.64
5.	Haryana	22.27	7.06	-
6.	Himachal Pradesh	31.46	20.63	12.82
7.	Jammu & Kashmir	15.88	11.70	-
8.	Karnataka	27.71	11.55	10.03
9.	Kerala	65.73	49.73	26.02
10	Madhya Pradesh	15.53	6.87	3.60
11.	Maharashtra	34.79	21.53	11.94
12.	Manipur	29.06	24.95	30.35
13.	Meghalaya	30.08	16.30	28.91
14.	Nagaland	33.89	-	32.99
15.	Orissa	21.12	9.40	4.76
16.	Punjab	33.69	15.67	-
17.	Rajasthan	11.42	2.69	1.20
18.	Sikkim	22.20	19.65	22.27
19.	Tamil Nadu	34.99	18.47	14.00
20.	Tripura	32.00	23.24	12.27
21.	Uttar Pradesh	14.4	3.90	8.69
22.	West Bengal	30.25	13.70	5.01
23.	A & N Islands	42.14	-	23.24
24.	Arunachal Pradesh	11.32	22.38	7.31
25.	Chandigarh	59.31	25.31	-
26.	D & N Haveli	16.78	44.74	8.42
27.	Delhi	53.07	25.89	-
28.	Goa, D. & Diu	47.56	27.84	18.29
29.	Lakshadweep	44.65	-	42.92
30.	Mizoram	54.91	53.33	55.12
31.	Pondicherry	45.71	21.21	-
	Total	24.82	10.93	8.04

Source : *Census of India*, 1981.

Note : No castes were scheduled by the President of India for Nagaland, A & N Islands and Lakshadweep and no tribes were scheduled in Haryana, Jammu & Kashmir, Punjab, Chandigarh, Delhi and Pondicherry.

: Literacy rate inclusive of 0-4 age group.

* : Census was not conducted in Assam.

A close look at the literacy rates among the females of the tribal social groups clearly brings into surface the disappointing educational situation of the community in India. It could be seen in Table 2.11 that only 8.04

per cent of the ST females were literates in 1981 in India which was less than one-third of what it was for the general category females in the country. The lowest literacy rate among tribal females could be noticed in Rajasthan (1.20 per cent) and the highest in Mizoram (55.12 per cent) in 1981. The highest literacy rate of females, however, does not reveal the educational scenario very clearly, because the north-eastern states are inhabited predominantly by the tribal communities, and they constitute only 7 per cent of the total tribal population in the country. The bulk of the tribal population are concentrated in the central part of India. A look at Table 2.11 reveals that the literacy rates of the female tribal population were below the national average of 8.04 per cent (for comprehensive discussion, see Rehman, 1992). It is again in Rajasthan where a considerable number of tribal population live, the literacy rate for the tribal female population was much lower in comparison with the literacy rates of the tribal females of other states in the country especially in the states of central India, in 1981. In Andhra Pradesh, the literacy rate of the tribal females was equally low (3.46 per cent). The next large concentration of tribal population is in Madhya Pradesh. Here too the literacy rate of tribal female population was alarmingly dismal (3.60 per cent). The situation was not promising in any other states either. This dismal educational scenario was largley a result of poverty and unfavourable socio-cultural traditions. The status of the tribal female population is not in any way better than women of other social groups in India. Their position as compared to men has always remained secondary.

Enrolment of SC and ST : The overall share of enrolment of the SC and ST population in the relevant age group in the school sector is relatively very small in India. Moreover, the participation rates of the SC and ST children in the school sector is still less in the rural areas as compared to that found in the urban areas. Again, the enrolment rates of the SC and ST girls are still less in rural areas compared to their counterparts in urban areas of their own community. Table 2.12 furnishes data on age specific enrolment rates of SC and ST children in rural and urban areas separately for the year 1981. In urban areas, the age specific enrolment rates of both the SC and ST females were relatively high compared to the rates found in the rural areas in 1981. Between the SC and ST girls, the comparative status of the SC girls in the school sector in rural and urban areas was high though it was much lower when compared to that of the girls of the non-scheduled communities (see Table 2.12). Thus, the low enrolment rates of the SC and ST girls at the primary level in the school sector, given the high dropout rates of the children of these communities, indicate the poor status of girls in the education sector, particularly in higher and professional education in India.

Table 2.12 : **Age specific enrolment rates of SC and ST in India, 1981**

Age	Scheduled Castes			Scheduled Tribes			Non-Scheduled		
	M	F	T	M	F	T	M	F	T
All Areas									
5	8.9	6.0	7.5	8.4	5.3	6.9	11.5	12.7	14.1
6	26.9	17.2	22.3	24.3	14.0	19.2	39.5	30.8	35.3
7	42.9	26.5	34.9	37.3	21.1	29.2	58.6	45.1	52.0
8	45.3	25.0	35.7	37.9	19.5	28.8	61.9	45.0	53.8
9	58.0	32.8	45.9	47.8	24.3	36.1	73.9	55.0	64.7
10	50.0	24.0	38.0	39.6	18.0	29.1	67.1	45.4	56.8
11	60.5	29.8	46.1	50.4	22.8	37.0	76.3	53.1	65.1
12	47.8	19.7	35.2	36.2	14.4	25.9	64.6	39.9	53.2
13	52.5	22.0	38.2	41.0	16.2	28.9	68.1	41.7	55.3
14	45.1	16.8	32.2	34.2	12.8	23.9	60.7	33.8	47.9
Rural Areas									
5	7.3	4.5	6.0	7.7	4.6	6.2	10.8	8.0	9.5
6	24.5	14.4	19.7	23.3	12.9	18.1	34.0	24.0	29.2
7	39.2	22.7	31.3	36.1	19.4	27.7	53.4	37.1	45.4
8	45.1	21.1	33.4	36.6	18.0	27.4	56.2	37.4	47.2
9	55.1	27.9	42.1	46.2	22.3	34.3	69.9	46.8	58.6
10	47.1	19.7	34.5	38.2	16.3	27.6	63.0	37.2	50.8
11	57.5	24.4	42.0	48.5	20.2	34.8	72.7	43.9	58.8
12	44.9	15.6	31.8	34.7	12.6	24.3	60.7	31.4	47.2
13	49.2	16.9	34.1	38.8	13.6	26.5	64.1	31.7	48.5
14	42.0	12.5	28.6	32.1	10.5	21.7	56.3	24.0	40.9
Urban Areas									
5	17.7	14.3	16.1	19.9	17.0	18.5	30.2	27.5	28.9
6	40.8	32.9	37.0	42.0	34.0	38.0	57.3	52.3	54.8
7	64.5	46.3	55.1	57.3	47.1	52.2	73.9	68.5	71.2
8	64.2	47.1	46.5	60.2	46.5	53.5	81.8	70.1	76.0
9	72.3	56.5	64.6	72.0	57.5	64.9	85.2	78.1	81.8
10	66.3	47.6	57.5	62.7	47.0	55.2	80.3	71.6	76.1
11	74.5	54.4	65.0	74.2	57.6	66.2	85.6	76.8	81.3
12	64.0	42.8	54.5	61.1	44.0	53.1	77.2	67.1	72.5
13	67.5	44.7	56.7	69.7	50.8	60.7	78.7	67.5	73.2
14	60.4	37.5	49.8	64.2	45.6	55.3	72.8	59.8	66.5

Source : Aggarwal, Y.P., and Sarika Sibou (1992) *Educating Scheduled Castes*. National Institute of Educational Planning and Administration, New Delhi. (mimeo).

The overall literacy rates among the SC and ST female population do not tell the whole story of their educational backwardness in India. Their participation in various stages/classes prominently magnifies the extent of their educational deprivation. An examination of the SC and ST female enrolment in various classes - from Ph.D. to primary classes - clearly shows the glaring underrepresentation of the SC and ST females in various stages of education in the country in 1988-89. In 1988-89, in Ph.D. classes, out of the total enrolment of 10,439, nearly 1.7 per cent and 0.5 per cent were the SC and ST girls respectively. These figures were highly disproportionate to the total number of the SC and ST women. Similarly, in M.A. classes, out of the total enrolment of 77,796 girls, only 4.2 per cent and 1.5 per cent were SC and ST girl students respectively. Almost the same situation could be observed in M.Sc classes also. Only 3.5 per cent and 0.6 per cent SC and ST female students were enrolled during 1988-89 in M.Sc. classes. Same level of participation of SC and ST women could be found in M.Com classes during the same year. In 1988-89, the enrolment of the SC and ST girls in the technical and professional degree courses was also very poor (4.8 per cent for SC girls and 0.9 per cent for ST girls) (see Table 2.13). The poor representation of the SC and ST women students in higher classes was partly the result of their low participation in the school sector and higher dropout rates which we have already mentioned.

Table 2.13: **Enrolment of Scheduled Castes and Scheduled Tribes by stages/classes, 1988-89**

Sl. no.	Stage/class	All	Girls	SC girls	Percentage to total	ST girls	Percentage to total
(1)	(2)	(3)	(4)	(5)	(6)	(7)	(8)
1.	Ph.D./D.Sc./D.Phil	31386	10439	182	1.7	60	0.5
2.	M.A.	201733	77796	3332	4.2	1176	1.5
3.	M.Sc.	73347	24410	873	3.5	152	0.6
4.	M.Com	75870	13983	540	3.8	88	0.6
5.	B.A./B.A. (Hons.)	1451919	568913	31962	5.6	12076	2.1
6.	B.Sc./B.Sc. (Hons.)	666405	212432	11041	5.1	1236	0.5
7.	B.Com./B.Com. (Hons.)	959780	215539	6375	2.9	1375	0.6
8.	B.E./B.Sc.(Eng.) B.A. (Arch.)	205282	16319	797	4.8	157	0.9
9.	B.Ed./B.T.	91017	40435	2196	5.4	588	1.4
10.	M.B.B.S.	80237	26261	2529	9.6	526	2.0

Contd..

(1)	(2)	(3)	(4)	(5)	(6)	(7)	(8)
11.	Intermediate/ Junior College	1981783	509423	27207	5.3	2808	0.5
12.	Pre-Degree/Pre-Univ. (2 Yr. Course)	305851	133717	12035	9.0	6999	5.2
13.	Pre-University (One Year Course)	3716	894	73	8.1	7	0.7
14.	Hr. Secondary (10+2 New Pattern)	3080591	1051564	82390	7.8	28130	2.6
15.	High/Post Basic (IX-X Classes)	13149351	4243497	435410	10.2	177074	4.1
16.	Middle/Senior Basic School	30940062	11187784	1256604	11.2	466223	4.1
17.	Primary Stage (Classes I-V)	95739976	38597251	5771002	14.9	2758778	7.1
18.	Pre-Primary/ Pre-Basic Stage	1439581	662984	66336	10.0	75917	11.4
19.	Teacher Training Sch.	100545	48850	3598	7.3	2441	4.9
20.	Polytechnical Inst.	286397	32137	2673	8.3	387	1.2
21.	Tech. Industrial, Arts & Craft School	368205	84647	7853	9.2	2842	3.3

Source : Ministry of Human Resource Development (1990) *Selected Educational Statistics, 1988-89,* Department of Education, New Delhi.

Undergraduate Level : The enrolment rates of the SC and ST girls in various undergraduate courses were not very satisfactory either though the situation was slighly better as compared to the enrolment rates in post-graduate courses and doctoral programmes. Table 2.13 shows that, in B.A./B.A. (Hons.) classes, out of the total female enrolment, the enrolment rates of the SC and ST girls were 5.6 per cent and 2.1 per cent respectively in 1988-89. In B.Sc./ B.Sc. (Hons.) courses, the enrolments of the SC and ST girls were 5.1 per cent and 0.5 per cent respectively. The situation seemed, however, to have taken a downturn in the case of enrolment of the SC and ST girls in B.Com/B.Com (Hons.) courses. The enrolment of the SC and ST girls were 2.9 per cent and 0.6 per cent respectively in these courses which were much less in comparison with other two types of undergraduate level courses, namely, B.A. and B.Com.

Table 2.13 also shows enrolment of the SC and ST girls in B.E./B.Sc. (Engg.) and B.A. (Acrh.) courses in 1988-89. The percentages of the SC and ST female enrolment were 4.8 and 0.9 respectively. Their representation in B.Ed./B.T. courses was slightly higher in comparision to professional courses like Engineering and Architecture. However, among professional courses, the representations of the SC and ST girls were comparatively high in MBBS courses. Out of the total female enrolment of 26,261 in MBBS courses, the percentages of enrolment of the SC and ST girls were 9.6 and 2.0 respectively in 1988-89. However, given the number of incentive schemes, still the representations of the SC and ST in various professional courses are much to be desired in India.

Intermediate/Pre-Degree Level : The percentage enrolments of the SC and ST females in intermediate and junior colleges show that, in 1988-89, these were only 5.3 per cent and 0.5 per cent respectively. However, in pre-degree/ pre-university (two years course) their enrolment rates were slightly on the higher side - 9.0 per cent for the SC girls and 5.2 per cent for the ST girls. Thus, the bulk of the SC and ST girl students were found in these two courses, i.e. intermediate and pre-degree courses. In pre-university (one year course) their representations were insignificant. Only 73 SC girls and 7 ST girls were found studying in this course in 1988-89.

One of the important causes of lower rate of participation of the SC and ST girls in higher level courses is that most of the educational institutions, especially institutions of higher learning, are located in urban areas while higher proportion of the SC and ST population live in rural areas. Besides, institutions of higher learning catering exclusively to women were virtually insignificant in India. In many areas socio-cultural traditions and taboos do not allow girls to attend mixed institutions i.e. institutions attended by both boys and girls. In 1987, out of 9280 institutions of higher learning only 1958 or 21.1 per cent were located in rural areas where 76.0 per cent of the total population of the country live. There were only 1270 or 13.7 per cent institutions of higher learning exclusively for women in the country in the same year. All these structural disparities contributed a great deal to the underrepresentation of the girls in general and the SC and ST girls in particular in higher education in India. Unlike other social categories, the SC, ST and backward class females experienced more barriers to their entry to the portal of higher education. First, these social classes were economically and socio-culturally disadvantaged and less enlightened about the need for education. Second, the overall educational status among the SC, ST and backward males was also not very high in 1988-89. These factors together have highly constrained the pace of female participation in higher education in India (see Table 2.13).

High/Higher Secondary Level : In 1988-89, out of the total of 10,51,564 females enrolled in higher secondary (10+2 new pattern) level, 8 per cent and 2.6 per cent were the SC and ST females respectively (see Table 2.13).

In the same year, the enrolment of the SC and ST girls in high/post-basic (IX-X classes) level were 10.2 per cent and 4.1 per cent respectively.

Middle Level : In 1988-89, the enrolment levels of the SC and ST females were not much different from that found in higher secondary and secondary levels. For the SC girls it was 11.2 per cent and for the ST girls it was 4.1 per cent (see Table 2.13).

Primary Level : In 1988-89, the enrolment rates of the SC and ST girls were relatively high in the primary level. Table 2.13 shows that the percentage of enrolment of the SC girls was 14.9 while it was 7.1 in the case of the ST females. These higher levels of participation of both the SC and ST girls in the primary levels could be attributed to the enrolment drives launched during the last decade. The steep fall in enrolment of these girls in higher classes showed that the higher rate of dropouts was the major cause of lower level of enrolment of the SC and ST girls in various higher classes and in its different courses.

In the pre-primary/pre-basic stage the enrolments of the SC and ST females were 10.0 per cent and 11.4 per cent respectively in 1988-89. What is of interest to note here is that the percentage of the ST females was higher than that of the the SC females in pre-primary/pre-basic stage (see Table 2.13).

Vocational Course : Vocational courses form an important segment of the educational system in India. The participation levels of the SC and ST females in this stream is also an important indicator of the communities' educational status in the country.

Table 2.13 shows that, in 1988-89, out of the total enrolment of girls in the Teacher Training Schools, 7.3 per cent and 4.9 per cent were the SC and ST females respectively. Similarly, in the Polytechnical Institutes, out of the total female enrolment, 8.3 per cent and 1.2 per cent were the SC and ST females respectively. However, the percentage representation of the ST girls was very low (1.2) in the Polytechnical Institutions. This could be due to the location of the Polytechnical Institutions in urban areas and also due to relative socio-economic backwardness of the ST households in the country which constraired their participation.

The overall enrolment of the SC and ST females in 1988-89 shows that they respectively constituted merely 9.2 per cent and 3.3 per cent of the total female enrolment in India.

RELIGIOUS CATEGORIES AND FEMALE EDUCATION

Religions play a very devious role in human society which not only draw demarcation lines among human beings to differentiate them with the purpose of exploitation but also to perpetuate prejudice among them. Both purpose and prejudice have shaped human society in such a manner that it has not only differentiated human beings but also sexes - male and female.

Every society, in every age, has been, more or less, under the influences of 'religion-based' ideologies, and these ideologies in their turn have perpetuated differential prejudices in various forms and measures. Over the years, the status of women in every religious category has become inferior to men. And ironically, all the founders of religions were men. The men-founders of religions promulgated instructions according to their male perceptions and especially their conveniences. Since present situation is the product of historical process, the present status of women in education and employment is also the product of past "purpose and prejudice" developed and transmitted through the historical process. Briggs clearly outlines religions' influence on women :

> Religion in Western countries had long been a primary, indeed, many would argue, the major cultural reinforcer of modern industrial patriarchy. In fact, the once pervasive and controlling influence of the Christian Churches over all aspects of social and political behaviour shrunk in the last two centuries to the role of guardian of marriage, family, and the home. Religion itself had acquired a "feminine" character : It cared for and nurtured those too tired or abused or weak to grapple with the harsh realities of the world, and much of religons' succor was provided (and still is) by the unpaid work of women in the voluntary welfare organizations of church and synagogue. The cult of domesticity in the nineteenth century always had religious undertones: The home had become a religious sanctuary and the church a second home and family. In contrast, whenever women demanded equal employment opportunities and remuneration, a fair division of labour outside and inside the home, reproductive rights and the end of the social control of women's sexuality, they began to challenge the religious legitimation of patriarchal gender roles and household arrangements (1987 : 403).

Thus, religions play dual roles : they apparently protect women but basically maintain status quo where men's position is held above women. The influence of religions has remained more or less the same everywhere in the world. An examination of women's educational status under different religious categories clearly outlines the relative position of women vis-a-vis men in both rural and urban areas in India.

Rural Areas : According to the NSS estimates, in rural areas while under Hinduism there were 514 illiterate males per thousand males, the number of illiterate females per thousand females was 750 (see Table 2.14). Similarly, while under Islam there were 582 illiterate males per thousand males, the number of illiterate females was as high as 761 per thousand females. In fact, females under Islam were more deprived of educational opportunities in comparision with females belonging to other religions in India.

Under Christianity too the number of illiterate per thousand females was also high (431) as compared to their male counterparts. Under none of the religions, namely, Sikhism, Jainism, Buddhism and Zoroastrianism the number of illiterate females per thousand females was less than their male counterparts. These facts clearly outline the retrogressive influence of religions on female education and also highlight the perpetuation of prejudice against women's equal entry into the educational system on this or that ground camouflaged by moral, physical and political shenanigans.

Primary Level : Further, while the per thousand number of rural female literates but below primary level was 118 under Hinduism, 131 under Islam, 178 under Christianity, 132 under Sikhism, 207 under Jainism. 113 under Budhism and 241 under Zorostrianism, the number of their male counterparts was relatively high in all the religious categries in 1987-88. Similar trends could be observed with regard to primary level education of rural females in different religious categories (see Table 2.14). It could be seen that, while the number of females with primary level education per thousand females under Hinduism was 75, the number of males with similar level of education was 135, almost twice the number of rural females. Under Islam, the number of females with primary level education was still less as compared to their male counterparts and in comparison with the females under Hinduism. The number of females with primary level education, per thousand females, was 69 under Islam as compared to their male counter- parts with same level of education, which was 122 per thousand.

The trend, however, varied significantly for females under Christianity, Sikhism and Jainism. Under these religious categories the number of females with primary level education per thousand females was higher than the females under other religious categories. However, relative to their co-religious male counterparts, the status of females with primary level education was not very high in these religious categories. The gap was quite wide. This again sharply outlines the religion-based bias against educating women in India (see Table 2.14).

Middle Level : Table 2.14 also presents data with regard to middle level education of females belonging to various religions in rural India in 1987-88. Under Hinduism, while there were 37 females per thousand females with middle level education, the number was 30 under Islam : in both the cases the number of females with middle level education compared to their male counterparts under corresponding religions could be noticed significantly less.

Similar situation could be observed with regard to the number of females per thousand females with middle level education under all other types of religion. The relative position of women was far below what it was for males under the corresponding religions in 1987-88.

The number of women per thousand females with middle level education was higher under Jainism (134) followed by Chiristianity (132) and Zoroastrianism (11) in 1987-88. The relative positions of females belonging to other religious categories with middle level education was, however, disappointingly less in comparison with their male counterparts. Under Islam, the number of women per thousand females with middle level education was the lowest (30) in 1987-88.

Secondary Level : We have already noted earlier that as the level of education rises, the representation of women in each subsequent higher level becomes visibly less as compared to men. Here an examination of the number of females with secondary education level per thousand females under various religious categories in rural areas points to this fact more clearly and proves the point that religious norms and beliefs have perceptibly influenced the level of female participation in education in India.

In 1987-88, the number of females under Hinduism with secondary level education, per thousand females, was only 17, while the number of their male counterparts having the same level of education was 37 (see Table 2.14). Similar situation could be noted in the case of women under Islam. Only 8 Muslim females per thousand females had had secondary level education in 1987-88. The highest number of females per thousand females with secondary level education was under Christianity (81) followed by Sikhism (60) and Jainism (47). In all religious categories the number of females having secondary level education per thousand females in rural India was only 19 persons in 1987-88. This underrepresentation of women in secondary level education prove religious discrimination against women.

Graduation and Above : The rate of participation of women, particularly in rural areas, in higher education has been highly disproportionate to their number. An analysis of religion-wise participation of women in higher education clearly reveals the unequal and low educational status of females in rural India (see Table 2.13.)

In fact, under Islam, there was not a single female per thousand females in rural areas with education upto graduation. Except under Christianity, under no religion the number of females having education upto graduation or above per thousand females was more than six.

This is perhaps due to two factors : first, the members of the rural community are very conservative, and they do not encourage the participation of women in higher education. Second, there are not many higher education institutions in rural areas and whereever they exist, they are mostly far away. These two factors discourage women to avail higher education in the rural areas of the country.

Urban Areas : Traditionally, educational facilities have always been concentrated in the urban areas. As we have mentioned earlier, in India, only 24 per cent people live in urban areas; and to provide education to these 24 per cent of the population, 79 per cent of the institutions of higher education have been located in urban areas. This spatially skewed distributional pattern of educational facilities has contributed a great deal to rural-urban divide in educational achievements of the people, particularly of women. Here, the examination of female educational status in urban India across different religious categories highlights one of the important aspects of these disparities.

Table 2.15 shows the number of females per thousand females who were illiterates, and literates but below primary level in urban areas in 1987-88. Under all religions, the number of illiterate females (441) per thousand females was higher than that of their male counterparts (277) in urban India.

Under Islam, the number of illiterate females per thousand females in urban areas was more than the females under any religion and their number was the highest followed by Budhism, Sikhism and Zoroastrianism. With regard to literates but below primarly level education, it could be noted that, under Islam, again the position of females was not very promising in urban areas in 1987-88 (see Table 2.15).

Table 2.14: **Per thousand distribution of persons by general education for each sex and household religion in rural areas, India, 1987-88**

Household religion	Illiterate		Literate and below primary		Primary		Middle		Secondary		Graduation & above		All
	M	F	M	F	M	F	M	F	M	F	M	F	
Hinduism	513	750	190	118	135	75	92	37	57	17	12	2	1000
Islam	582	761	186	131	122	69	69	30	34	8	6	-	1000
Christianity	337	431	205	178	186	160	158	132	93	81	18	15	1000
Sikhism	457	607	172	132	152	143	91	52	111	60	16	6	1000
Jainism	228	395	252	207	207	213	164	134	111	47	38	5	1000
Buddhism	529	746	171	113	176	94	70	41	47	5	7	1	1000
Zoroastrianism	439	529	137	241	101	92	135	110	143	26	46	2	1000
Others	611	794	162	93	111	57	67	33	37	18	8	2	1000
Not Recorded	518	712	220	163	132	88	81	24	28	12	4	-	1000
All Categories	516	741	190	121	135	78	90	39	57	19	12	3	1000

Source : National Sample Survey Organization (1990) *Sarvekshana*, (Special Number), July 1987-June, 1988, NSS 43rd Round, New Delhi.

Table 2.15: **Per thousand distribution of persons by general education for each sex and household religion in urban areas, India, 1987-88**

Household religion	Illiterate		Literate and below primary		Primary		Middle		Secondary		Graduation & above		All
	M	F	M	F	M	F	M	F	M	F	M	F	
Hinduism	253	422	188	172	166	150	139	103	172	107	79	42	1000
Islam	424	595	209	185	163	114	100	54	80	43	23	8	1000
Christianity	188	227	160	175	191	164	176	170	201	208	81	55	1000
Sikhism	215	303	180	164	162	156	124	111	223	195	91	70	1000
Jainism	97	154	146	195	192	264	126	84	280	204	156	93	1000
Buddhism	261	512	162	140	218	162	162	111	159	66	34	8	1000
Zoroastrianism	53	158	97	31	144	224	105	92	354	303	241	192	1000
Others	272	433	194	205	184	110	124	110	163	107	61	30	1000
Not Recorded	93	361	170	250	265	114	175	98	139	69	65	52	1000
All Categories	277	441	190	174	167	145	133	97	159	102	70	38	1000

Source : National Sample Survey Organization (1990) *Sarvekshana,* (Special Number), July 1987-June, 1988, NSS 43rd Round, New Delhi.

Primary Level : The numbers of both males and females with primary education per thousand persons each in urban India were 167 and 145 respectively in 1987-88. While 150 females under Hinduism had primary education, 166 of their male counterparts had the same level of education per thousand persons. The number of urban Muslim females per thousand females with primary education was only 114. The point which could be noted here is that the number of urban females under Jainism and Zoroastrianism having primary level education was higher than their counterparts in other religions (see Table 2.15).

Middle Level : Table 2.15 shows that the number of urban females per thousand females with middle level education was much less in comparision with the number of males having the same level of education under each religious category. However, among females across all religions, the relative position of Muslim females was insignificant thereby showing the community's utter educational backwardness even in urban areas. However, the highest number of females with middle level education per thousand females could be seen under Christianity (170) followed by Sikhism and Budhism in 1987-88.

Secondary Level : Table 2.15 also shows the number of females per thousand females across different religions with secondary level education in 1987-88. The number of urban females per thousand females with secondary level education was very less in comparison with their male counterparts in 1987-88. However, this number, if compared with the number of rural females, was significantly higher. This is precisely because of the fact that in urban areas educational facilities are well provided, besides people's attitude being relatively positive toward education, particularly toward women's education.

Among females belonging to various religious groups it could be found that the females under Islam were disproportionately underrepresented in secondary education in urban India. Only 43 females per thousand females were found to have had education upto secondary level. Another group of females who were also underrepresented in this level of education in urban areas belonged to Buddhism.

Graduation and Above : A comparsion between the figures showing the status of males and females in collegiate education sector in Table 2.15 explicitly demonstrates the fact that, in 1987-88, the number of females under all religious categories having education upto graduation and above was only 38 which was nearly half of what it was for the males having the same level of education per thousand males in urban India. The number of urban females belonging to Muslim community per thousand females having education upto graduation or above was the lowest (8) in 1987-88 and this number was highest among under women Zoroastrianism. However, the relative educational status of urban women under each religious category was much higher as compared to rural women under corresponding religious categories.

RELIGION-WISE ATTENDANCE

Rural Areas : The analysis of the level of attendance of population of various age group in educational institutions in rural India under different religious categories highlights another aspect of the dismal educational scenario of females. It could be seen in Table 2.15 that in the age group 0-4 the number of girls per thousand girls attending educational institutions was comparatively less than that of the boys in the same age group. Under Islam, it could be noted that the number of girls in the age group 0-4, per thousand girls attending educational institution, was comparatively less than that of the boys in the same age group. In comparision with attendance of girls under other religions it could be found that under Islam, the number of girls in the age group 0-4 per thousand girls attending educational institution was lowest in 1987-88. The highest number of rural girls in this age group attending educational institutions could be found under Jainism followed by Christianity, Sikhism and Hinduism.

The analysis of the attendance rates of females in the age group 5-9 in educational institutions also reveals that their number per thousand females was disproportionately lower than their male counterparts. Similar trends could be observed with regard to the attendance of girls in age groups 10-14, 15-19, 20-24 and 25 and above in educational institutions in rural India. As compared to other religious categories the attendance rates of females belonging to Muslim and Buddhist communities were disappointing in rural areas in 1987-88 (see Table 2.16).

Urban Areas : Table 2.17 depicts the levels of attendance of both males and females per thousand persons in educational institutions in urban India in 1987-88. The number of females in various age groups attending educational institutions was high compared to that of the rural females per thousand females in 1987-88. However, the numbers of such females in comparison with their urban male counterparts were far less.

Table 2.16 : **Number of persons currently attending educational institutions per thousand persons by age group and household religion for each sex in rural areas, India, 1987-88**

Household religion	Age group													
	0-4		5-9		10-14		5-15		15-19		20-25		25 & above	
	M	F	M	F	M	F	M	F	M	F	M	F	M	F
Hinduism	26	22	535	406	669	413	598	409	377	126	84	15	4	3
Islam	14	13	421	328	566	370	486	347	269	88	70	12	4	2
Christianity	69	51	674	669	756	701	716	685	477	433	131	98	9	6
Sikhism	57	50	644	588	730	575	690	581	303	176	31	17	1	2
Jainism	102	98	935	831	936	858	935	847	560	276	83	38	-	-
Buddhism	9	16	540	555	839	597	691	575	394	166	166	3	1	6
Zoroastrianism	304	-	743	256	-	1000	743	530	-	-	-	-	-	-

Source : National Sample Survey Organization (1990) *Sarvekshana*. (Special Number), July 1987-June, 1988, NSS 43rd Round, New Delhi.

Table 2.17 : **Number of persons currently attending educational institutions per thousand persons by age group and household religion for each sex in urban areas, India, 1987-88**

Household religion	Age group													
	0-4		5-9		10-14		5-15		15-19		20-25		25 & above	
	M	F	M	F	M	F	M	F	M	F	M	F	M	F
Hinduism	88	77	763	707	832	746	797	726	561	424	210	96	8	6
Islam	48	35	560	521	636	536	597	528	348	193	113	43	8	4
Christianity	126	141	892	861	933	900	913	881	606	571	169	166	13	4
Sikhism	157	173	867	889	861	879	864	883	459	558	153	97	6	5
Jainism	118	270	925	986	904	960	914	971	811	557	199	53	13	-
Buddhism	20	63	742	722	902	876	816	799	669	514	367	133	11	-
Zoroastrianism	-	32	1000	1000	877	690	928	868	786	737	1000	564	-	4

Source : National Sample Survey Organization (1990) *Sarvekshana*, (Special Number), July 1987-June, 1988, NSS 43rd Round, New Delhi.

In urban areas, the number of females in the age group 25 and above, in almost all religious, categories was marginal in 1987-88 thereby indicating the low rate of participation of females in higher education in India, even in urban areas.

FAMILY BACKGROUND OF COLLEGIATE STUDENTS

One of the important features of participation of women in higher education in India is that mostly they have a sound socio-economic background - i.e. the socio-economic status of their families is relatively high. In 1991, our study in a college in Haryana, which was located in the periphery of Delhi, showed that out of 151 female undergraduate students interviewed, there was not a single student from an agricultural labour household (see Table 2.18). The highgest number of female students (33.11 per cent) were from the households in which the fathers of the students were either government, or private servants, followed by traders (19.86 per cent) shopkeepers (13.24 per cent), school teachers (13.24 per cent), college teachers (6.62 per cent), army personnels (3.97 per cent), cultivators (3.31 per cent), skilled workers (3.31 per cent), household workers (1.98 per cent) and professionals (1.32 per cent). It is to be noted here that the percentage of girls whose fathers were professionals was the lowest in this college. This is because of the fact that most of the girls from professional households, instead of going for general education, opt for professional courses and hence their rates of participation in most of the courses of general education are usually low. Besides, the place where the college is located is not a big town, and consequently professionals are not usually found in large numbers. Though the data base of this study is not wide enough to generalise anything, we can only say that the occupational background (which is important in determining the relative socio-economic status of the family) of the parents of girls is one of the important factors determining their participation rates in higher education, particularly in arts, science and commerce courses. This is also equally true in the case of girls participating in professional courses such as engineering in India, as found in a study conducted by Indian Institute of Technology, Bombay, in 1992 (see Chapter 3).

Study of parents' occupational backgrounds of students celarly establishes the fact that both male and female students mostly belong to families with comparatively well-off families. For majority of our people, as a result, the benefit of education is not reachable. This is particularly more true for females in the country.

Table 2.17 : **Occupational background of fathers of undergraduate female students in a college in Haryana**

Sl. no.	Occupation of father	Number of female students	Percentage of female students to total
1.	Agricultural Labourer	-	-
2.	Skilled Worker	5	3.31
3.	Household Worker	3	1.98
4.	Shopkeeper	20	13.24
5.	Cultivator	5	3.31
6.	Trader	30	19.86
7.	Office Worker	50	33.11
8.	School Teacher	20	13.24
9.	College Teacher	10	6.62
10.	Army	6	3.97
11.	Professionals (Doctors, Engg., Lawyers)	2	1.32
	Total	151	100.00

CONCLUSION

Here, in this chapter, the discussion on the relative educational status of girls and women has made it clear that sex disparities exist in India in most virulent form, and these disparities are more pronounced in rural areas and between various socio-economic and demographic groups. However, it should be noted here that the levels of enrolment of women in various stages and courses in the school and collegiate sectors in India in any particular point of time do not tell us the true story of educational development. If the dropout rates of girls and women are taken into account, their relative educational status would get further marginalised. Besides social, economic, political, geographic and demographic factors, sex disparities in education in India can primarily be attributed to existence of unfavourable cultural factors. However, given the evidences (backed by the data collected by various agencies) and unequal participation levels of girls and women in school and higher education sectors, we can deduct the following propositions which can be fitted into the explanations of the existence of sex disparities in India.

The lower female enrolment ratios, particularly in SC, ST, religious and other socio-economically disadvantaged communities, are indicators of low overall participation rates (for both boys and girls) in school as well as collegiate sectors or the existence of deep rooted religious and/or other cultural factors which still strongly resist equality of education for girls and women in India (as is found in many Muslim and traditional conservative Hindu communities). Conversely, a rapid growth in overall enrolment both in school and collegiate sectors increases the relative participation rates of girls and women in these sectors. As we find that the comparative educational status of women in urban and semi-urban areas in India has been improving over the years, we can perhaps infer that urbanisation has a positive effect on the growth of enrolment of girls and women irrespective of their socio-economic and religious backgrounds.

Our dicussion on the patterns of participation of girls and women in various stages of education in India reveals that where significant female disparities exist, they are always greatest in higher and professional education, with few exceptions such as in education and nursing. These disparities in general higher and professional education levels are invariably rooted in inequalities at the secondary level, where the base of the college and university-bound students is formed. Similarly, disparities at the primary level feed the sex disparities at the secondary level. It follows, therefore, that untill and unless we reduce sex disparities at primary and secondary levels, the gaps in the participation of girls and women at higher and professional education levels are bound to remain still larger in India.

In India, at higher education level, it is found that females are mostly crowded into courses such as education, arts, humanities, nursing and home science whereas males are crowded into courses like physical sciences, mathematics, engineering, medicine, law, architecture and the like. To minimise sex disparities within the higher and professional education sectors, these inter-faculty disparities need to be reduced first.

Moreover, the disproportionate participation of girls and women in various fields of study in higher education can partly be attributed to the discriminatory hiring practices of employers in the Indian labour markets. Women are not preferred in certain types of jobs (at least from the employers' point of view) and accordingly the employment markets in India have been segmented into various sub-markets and entry of women into some of these sub-markets has been marginal. Such a behaviour of the Indian labour market is reflected in the unequal participation rates of women in various fields of study in the higher education sector (see Box 2.1).

Box 2.1: **The state, education and labour market status of women**

If women had greater levels of education, they could be more productive in the labour market. several studies reveal that the rates of return to women's eduation are as high as those of me and even that their levels of primary eduation have an impact on economic development (measured in terms of GNP per capita) greater than that of men (Benavot, 1989). But if more women entered the labour market, they would come into competition with men and, given the existing sexual division of labour, families would go unattended. In the latter case, the problem is not so much that women could not be replaced in the home but to do so would necessitate funding - men would certainly expect to be paid for tasks that go against their nature to perform - and would introduce an element of instability because the supply of women for mothering would be less predictable.

The examination of the state's provision of literacy and higher education shows that there is a strong material basis for women's subordfination. But the maintenance of this pattern is not justified on a crude rationale. The state has grown sophisticated and elegant in its discourse. Thus material reasons are cast in 'self-evident truths', the key ones being that motherhood is an innate ability of women and thus their main responsibility must be to husband and children, within the context of a nuclear family - which in turn is upheld as the basic pillar of society.

There seems to be a complicit behaviour between men and women of upper classes regarding women of lower social classes. It emerges in the exercise among upper class women of special preorgatives when it comes to higher education. This understanding between upper class men and women ensures the emergence of 'educated' and satisfied women - which gives men companions and which makes a few women (the most influential) feel that the social system is fair. All states endorse the principle of equality but few endorse equality specifically for woemn. Therefore, there is a wide disparity between the spirit of the discourse and the practices institutionalized by the state. This disparity is largest among women with limited access to resources. Hence, there will be a wider gap between policy and practice in literacy than in tertiary education.

Source: Stromquist, N.P. 1991. Educating women: The political economy of patriarchal states. *International Studies in Sociology of Education* 1.

The most important proposition relating to the existence of sex discrimination in education in India is that sex disparities in education have grown primarily out of traditions, cultures, customs and taboos in our society. The defined sex roles within the family and the relative perceptions of the members of particular social, religious, and demographic communities about women's roles have shaped the individual attitudes and behavioural patterns towards girls and women. And it is quite natural, in this context, for these sex attitudes to carry over into education in India.

However, inso far as India is concerned, it is now widely recognised that the education of women holds the key to all other elements on which the development of our society depends - i.e. population control, family health, nutrition, receptivity to innovations and educational motivation of children. To transform Indian society, there is the need to reduce sex discrimination in education. The sex disparities can only be minimised by focusing on the policies and programmes which could favourably change the cultural and religious attitudes of people thereby increasing the participation rates of girls and women in education, particularly in the school sector. In other words, the existing sex roles and gender stereotypes in Indian society must undergo a change to have a balanced educational development. This does not, however, mean that the policies and programmes relating to higher education of women should be overlooked. Efforts have to be directed towards narrowing the gap between men's and women's participation in higher education by formulating and designing policy measures which would ultimately lead to a greater level of women's entry into labour market that require education and skills of higher levels.

CHAPTER THREE

WOMEN AND EMPLOYMENT

PROLOGUE

Development process of society affects different sections of its population differentially. On the same line of argument, the development process of the Indian society has also affected its different sections, especially men and women, differentially. During the last three decades, the Indian economy has witnessed a structural transformation, broadly in favour of the industrial sector, and that again in favour of the manufacturing and and service sectors. The industrial employment has increased at a faster rate than the historical rate of developing countries, though the annual labour absorpotion capacities of the various sub-sectors of the industrial sector in India have not increased at the desired rate.

However, the development process, instead of benefiting women, has put more burden on them i.e. they now have to do a multiple of jobs starting from production, reproduction to a number of out-of-home jobs. Besides, this development process has further sharpened the segmentation of the labour force in the economy on gender lines. Though the sexual division of work existed during the early days of independence, the degree of the gender based division of jobs has, however, become more pronounced in the recent years.

It should be noted here that 'sex' is an inherent characteristic of an individual while 'gender' is a socially constructed characteristic. The institutional and social factors in our society have given new dimensions to gender, particularly gender specified jobs in our economy, which is reflected in the disproportionate representation of women across occupations and the corresponding differential status enjoyed by them in the labour market. The common denominator of gender is female subordination which has its origin at home, and this concept of gender has been transmitted outside the home over to various sectors of our economy - i.e. education, employment, etc. Therefore, understanding of the gender differences in representation and status of individuals in various sectors in the country calls for understanding the dynamics of gender differentiation within the family first. Now, jobs in our economy have been clearly segregated on the lines of sex, caste, place of origin and the like. Men are found concentrated in many high status and well-paid occupations thereby pushing aside women to occupy peripheral low status and under-paid jobs in the labour market. However, the unfortunate part of many studies on women is that, so far, not many empirical research have been undertaken to examine and provide clearcut evidence of women's marginal position in the labour market. But one thing is clear that girls and women are crowded into particular segments of the labour market having distinct characteristics like mobility patterns, reward structures, relative security and regularity of employment and the like. This kind of the behaviour of the employment market in our economy clearly demonstrates the existence of socially and institutionally induced distortions in the labour market.

Women are discriminated against on many grounds in the labour markets of developing countries as well as in developed countries. For a country like India this is now more prononunced due to several socio-economic and cultural factors. However, discrimination against women in the labour market is not a new phenomenon, for with the advancement of the economy the discriminating behaviours of individuals and groups have become more transparent in recent years. A brief review of some of the literature on discrimination would make this phenomenon more clear.

John Stuart Mill, way back in 1848, raised the issue of discrimination on the basis of sex in the labour market while explaining the earnings differentials between men and women for employment of equal skills and equal disagreeableness. While conceptualising the problem of discrimination on the basis of sex he observed :

> In the occupations in which employers take full advantage of competition, the low wages of women as compared with the ordinary earnings of men are a proof that the employments are overstocked : that although so much smalled number of women, than of men, support themselves by wages, the occupations which law and usage make accessible to them are comparatively so few that the field of their employment is still more overcrowded (1848, II. XIV : 5).

Thus Mill, nearly one and a half century ago, was referring to the phenomenon of 'overcrowding' of women in particular jobs in the labour market in almost all the countries. Women and girls are also discriminated against both at the point of entry into various employments and with regard to wages even when they are employed in the same job as that of men which can be attributed to factors such as : (i) customs and public opinion; (ii) lower demands from women, partly because lower standard of living, and partly due to their family situation i.e. being economically supported by their family or husband; (iii) lower productivity of women caused by insufficient human capital, on-the-job training, lack of strength and institutional and social restrictions; and (iv) lack of protective power, adaptability, limited number of alternatives and greater immobility, both between places and between jobs. (Webb, 1891). Thus, institutional factors such as legislations, traditions, the educational system, the family structure and the like, to a great extent, condition the labour market opportunities and relative status of women in almost all the societies, particularly in developing societies. The lower representation of girls and women in certain specific occupations has also been attributed to lack of trade unions to protect their interests in the employment markets (Rathbone, 1917). Moreover, existence of male trade unions in the labour market also negatively affect the employment opportunities and status of girls and women in the labour market. These male dominated trade unions, particularly in the private sector, limit the occupational choice of women in several ways, especially by indirectly raising the level of competition among the existing reserve army of unemployed girls and women. This ultimately leads to occupational segregation which is followed by wage discrimination between segments and within the crowded segment itself (Fawcett, 1917). It has also been argued that differences in representation of women in various occupations and the relative differences in wages between males and females arise because of the fact that men and women are not of equal value to the employers (at least, in terms of productivity differences, differences in personnel turnover and many other factors) and, therefore, these groups are rated differentially in the labour market (Brown, 1977). Moreover, in some cases, the exploitation and unfair treatment of girls and women in the labour market has been explained in terms of existence of monopsony power with the employers and the relative low elasticity of supply of female labour (Madden, 1975). It has also been argued that prejudice, which can be labelled as a 'taste for discrimination' affects the decision-making of employers, employees and consumers within the free and competitive market (Becker, 1971). Thus, discrimination against girls and women is manifested as a desire to avoid certain economic transactions with the member of this particular group.

According to segmentation theorists (Gordon, 1972; Deoringer and Piore, 1971; Osterman, 1975; Reich, 1981) the labour market is divided into distinct segments such as primary independent, primary subordinate, secondary and crafts, out of which the latter two segments are characterised by low status of employment, less wages, occupational immobility, irregularity of employment and less provision of on-the-job training. Given such a segmented labour market, girls and women are found to be crowded into the secondary segment where their relative human capital is not proportionately rewarded. Both vertical and horizontal mobility prospects of this particular gender group are limited in this segment. According to these theorists, a host of political, economic, social and institutional factors act and interact in the labour market to condition the labour market status of women and girls. According to radical economists (Carnoy, 1976; Rumberger, and Carnoy, 1980; Rosenberg, 1980) employers try to segregate jobs on the line of sex to have control over the labour force - i.e. to make the bargaining power of trade unions ineffective so as to enable them to discriminate more effectively. The gender theorists (Vanek, 1974; Bodrovia & Anker, 1985) argue that the relative position of women in the labour market should be seen as a part of a whole social system where women are subordinate to men. One of the key issues raised by these theorists is the allocation of domestic work, especially child care, to women. Thus, women's handicap in the labour market, particularly in urban areas has been increasing because of increase in the degree of domestic work responsibility, specifically in the context of an extended family structure - i.e. a shift toward nuclear type of families. Some theorists maintain that sexual harassment is a major factor contributing to high turnover among women workers particularly in developing countries (Farley, 1978). In fact, job segregation by sex is to a large extent maintained by sexual harassment at the work place. Moreover, mostly women's jobs in the labour market are mere extensions of their domestic jobs - viz. teaching, nurshing, cleaning, serving, etc.

The literature reviewed here, more or less, indicate that discrimination on the basis of sex exists in almost all types of societies - industrial and industrialised. A number of economic, social, cultural, institutional and political factors act and interact with each other in any particular society thereby evolving ways and means to discriminate against girls and women, both at the pre-market and in-market situations. Thus, one of the important propositions with regard to participation of girls and women in the labour market is that they are crowded into particular occupations.

In this chapter, our main objective is to show, by using available secondary data, that the 'crowding hypothesis' is still applicable to the Indian labour market, rather the relative applicability of this hypothesis in analysing the Indian labour market has gone up over the years.

In a male dominated society, perceptions about everything is from the male point of view. This bias is clearly reflected in the case of defining who is a 'worker' and who is not and whose work is 'economic' and whose not. Though nearly half of the population in any society is female, and their contribution to sustaining life process is as equal and important as that of men, still majority of women have not been considered as economically productive. In every country's census enumeration a small proportion of them has been included in the category of economically active population. This downright discriminatory bias against women could be seen reflected in the Indian census enumeration of men and women workers. Here, in this chapter, the attempt is to examine these aspects from several dimensions to highlight the contours of discrimination against women in the context of their being recognised as workers.

WORK PARTICIPATION

In every ten years, census enumeration is done in order to determine, inter alia, the work participation rates of males and females in our country and from census to census, the definition of a 'worker' has been changed. Similarly, the criteria for categorisation of workers have also been changed in different census enumerations. Such manipulations in definitions in different census enumerations have always undermined the work participation rate of women in India. This bias against women could be clearly seen in Table 3.1. The work participation rates of females in various censuses, upto 1961, show that the rates of work participation of females were almost half of that of males. After the 1961 census and upto 1981 census, females' work participation rates were nearly one third of that of males. Could this be true? It seems rather unusual given the ground level reality. By defining various activities as 'economic' and 'uneconomic' according to male purposes and prejudices, and by assigning the socalled uneconomic activities which have no exchange value, women have been pushed out of the category of workers. This point has been well argued by Groot :

> Gender-blind theory and practice were reinforced by the establishment of modern methods and languages for social science research and writing (impersonal, 'objectives', quantitative and technical) which marginalised women not through overt prejudices or stereotypes but through the 'scientific' use of neutral, abstract concepts and assumptions. This could be seen in British government statistics or in Marxist approaches to 'class' the universal 'he/him' to describe groups which include men and women, or in the obscuring of women's reproductive and domestic work. Moreover, changes in women's situation, whether through legal and social reforms in the west or decolonisation in Asia and Africa, encouraged the view that emancipation and equality, or at least 'progress' for women, had been or was being achieved, and was not a contentious issue (1991 : 119).

Table 3.1 : **Work participation rates in India, 1901-1981**

(in percentages)

Year	Total	Males	Females	Women's work participation as % of men's work participation rate
1901	46.1	60.8	31.7	58.1
1911	48.1	62.0	33.7	54.3
1921	46.9	60.4	32.6	53.9
1941	43.8	58.1	28.8	49.5
1951	39.1	53.9	23.4	43.8
1961	43.1	57.3	28.0	48.8
1971	34.2	52.7	14.2	26.9
1981*	33.4	51.6	14.0	27.1

Source : *Census of India,* Various Years.
* : Census in Assam and Jammu and Kashmir was not conducted.

Rural-Urban Divide : The bias against women could further be seen reflected in the worker population ratios in rural-urban context. Table 3.2 shows that, in 1981, the ratio of women workers as compared to that of males in rural areas was less than fifty per cent. In urban areas, this ratio was even less than one third of that of men. Though majority of women in comparable age groups of men are engaged in work, but since many works performed by women within the household sector do not have pecuniary value, they have been excluded from worker status, and the bias is more pronounced in urban India.

Table 3.2 : **Worker population ratios in rural and urban India, 1981**

(in percentages)

Area	Persons	Males	Females	Women's work participation as % of men's work participation rate
Rural	39.4	54.3	23.9	44.0
Urban	31.4	49.7	10.7	21.5

Source : *Census of India,* 1981.

Age-wise Divide : Another dimension of employment of females is their age specific participation in both urban and rural areas in India. Table 3.3 shows that, according to 1981 census, for all age groups, the participation rates of women were 16 per cent and 7.28 per cent in rural and urban areas respectively. In the age group 0-14, it was 3.53 per cent and 0.88 per cent in rural and urban areas respectively. Similarly, in the age groups 15-19, 20-24, 25-29 and so on, the participation rates of females in comparison with their male counterparts were highly disproportionate to their numbers in 1981. In the age group 40-49, the work participation rates of women, both in rural and urban areas (i.e. 28.90 per cent and 15.34 per cent respectively), were the highest. The unfavourable definational aspects of women's work participation have serious policy implications. First, by excluding majority of women from proper work status as that of men, a sort of psychological inferiority complex is created, besides grossly underestimating the truth. Secondly, policy measures formulated on such faulty and one sided interpretation of women's participation in work do not reflect women's actual position in the labour market and their contributions to development of our society. The various census figures thus not only underestimate women's work but also do not recognise women's contirbutions to productive activity.

Table 3.3 : **Work participation rates in rural and urban areas by sex and age in India, 1981**

(in percentages)

Age group	Rural		Urban	
	Males	Females	Males	Females
All Ages	52.62	16.00	48.54	7.28
0-14	6.30	3.53	2.46	0.88
15-19	58.19	22.77	31.54	6.19
20-24	82.71	24.29	63.35	9.25
25-29	92.79	26.14	86.78	12.17
30-39	96.71	28.45	94.93	15.14
40-49	97.25	28.90	95.49	15.34
50-59	94.08	23.94	86.86	12.42
60 and above	67.59	11.29	47.49	5.75

Sources : Office of the Registrar General and Census Commissioner (1988) *Census of India*, 1981, and *Occasional Paper*, No. 8, New Delhi.

Similary, Table 3.4 also clearly highlights the underestimation of women's work participation rates by categorising women into : (i) main workers; and (ii) *marginal* workers. It could be noted from Table 3.4 that, in both rural and urban areas, the participation rates of females in both the categories were much less than that of their male counterparts in 1981 (see Figure 3.1). The gap between the work participation rates of female main workers in rural (16 per cent) and urban areas (7.28 per cent) was very wide as compared to that of female marginal workers in 1981 (see Table 3.4).

Table 3.4 : **Work force participation rates in India by sex, rural and urban areas, 1981**

(in percentages)

Category	Total			Rural			Urban		
	P	M	F	P	M	F	P	M	F
Main Workers	33.45	51.62	13.99	34.76	52.62	16.00	29.23	48.54	7.28
Marginal Workers	3.32	1.03	5.77	4.11	1.19	7.18	0.77	0.53	1.04
Total Workers	36.77	52.65	19.76	38.87	53.81	23.18	30.00	49.07	8.32

Sources :(i) *Census of India, 1981*, Series I - India, Part-II, Special Report and Tables based on 5 per cent sample data, New Delhi, 1983.
(ii) *Census of India, 1981*, Vol. I, Part II B (I), General Economic Tables, Table B-I, New Delhi, 1985.

Tables 3.5 and 3.6 furnish figures on some of the important dimensions of women's work participation such as the distribution of female workers in primary, secondary and tertiary sectors, and by types of activity in India in 1981.

In 1981, in all age groups, women's work participation rate was highest in the primary sector (81.59 per cent) followed by the tertiary (9.47 per cent) and the secondary (8.94 per cent) sectors. In the age group 0-14, this rate was highest in the primary sector (86.39 per cent) followed by the secondary (9.70 per cent) and the tertiary (3.91 per cent) sectors. In the age groups 15-59 and 60 and above, the trends of workforce participation rates of women were the same - i.e. highest in the primary sector followed by the tertiary and the secondary sectors. In the secondary sector, women in the age group 0-14 had the largest share in the total workforce. However, in the tertiary sector the situation was different - i.e. women in the age group 15-59 had the highest rate of workforce participation (10.02 per cent). Thus, in 1981, more than 80 per cent of women were engaged in the primary sector occupations thereby clearly demonstrating the marginal occupational status of Indian women, even after more than 30 years of independence.

Table 3.5 : **Percentage distribution of main workers in primary, secondary and tertiary sectors by age groups and sex in India*, 1981**

Sector	Age group	Males	Females
Primary	All Ages	66.22	81.59
	0-14	84.63	86.39
	15-59	64.15	80.99
	60 and above	79.64	84.29
Secondary	All Ages	13.91	8.94
	0-14	9.18	9.70
	15-59	14.59	8.99
	60 and above	8.80	6.65
Tertiary	All Ages	19.87	9.47
	0-14	6.19	3.91
	15-59	21.26	10.02
	60 and above	11.56	9.06

Source : *Census of India, 1981*, Series-I, Part-II, Special Report and Tables based on 5 per cent sample data.

Note : The percentages in the age groups have been calculated on the basis of the respective population of workers in that particular age group.

: Figures exclude Assam.

In Table 3.6, an area-wise analysis of women's participation in various types of occupations reveals that, in 1981, the percentage of women working as agricultural labourers was the highest (i.e. 6.46) whereas most of the males were also engaged in cultivation. The percentage of women working in the household industry was the lowest - i.e. 0.64. In rural areas, most of the women (8.03 per cent) had the occupational status as agricultural labourers whereas in urban areas they were largely engaged in other activities (4.97 per cent). The relative percentage share of women as main workers was higher in rural areas as compared to that in urban areas in 1981.

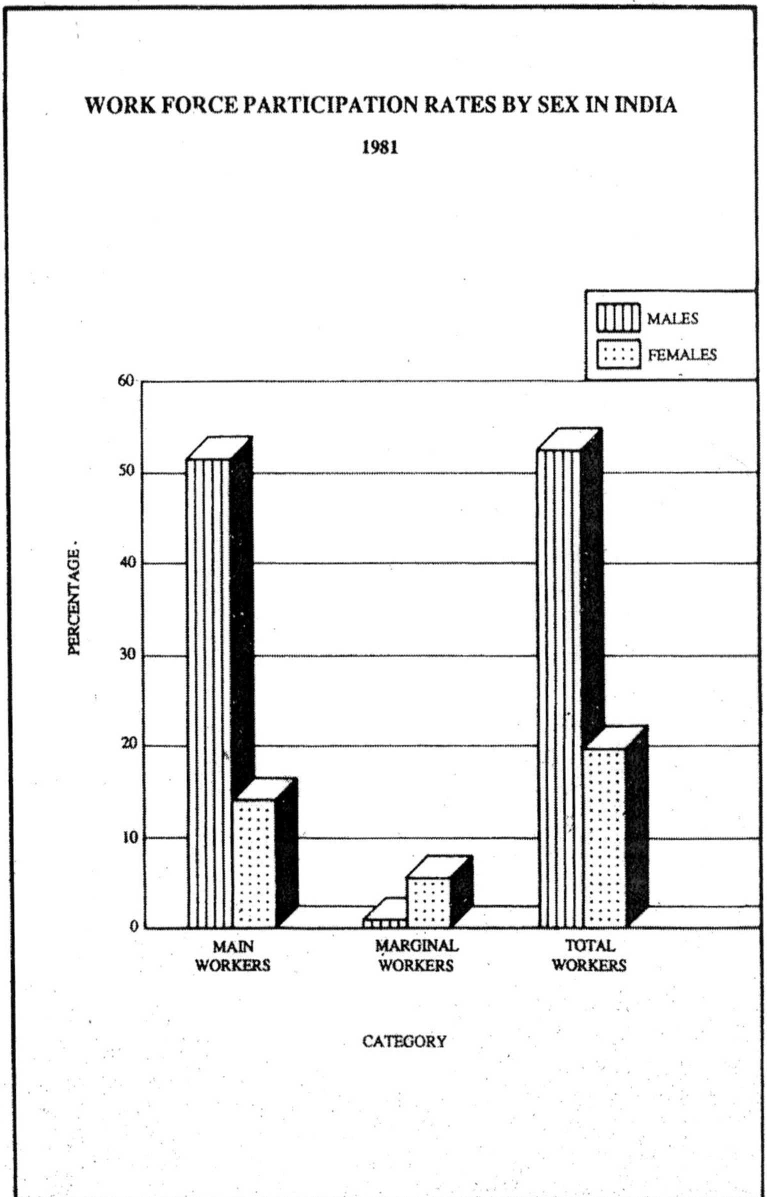
WORK FORCE PARTICIPATION RATES BY SEX IN INDIA
1981
MALES
FEMALES
PERCENTAGE
60
50
40
30
20
10
0
MAIN WORKERS
MARGINAL WORKERS
TOTAL WORKERS
CATEGORY

Fig. 3.1

Table 3.6 : **Percentage of main workers by area, sex and type of activity to total population in India, 1981**

Area	Sex	Total main workers	Culti-vators	Agricult-ural labourers	Household industry workers	Other workers
All Areas	Persons	33.45	13.91	8.34	1.16	10.04
	Males	51.62	22.56	10.10	1.64	17.32
	Females	13.99	4.65	6.46	0.64	2.24
Rural	Persons	34.76	17.76	10.39	1.07	5.54
	Males	52.62	29.02	12.63	1.51	9.46
	Females	16.00	5.93	8.03	0.61	1.43
Urban	Persons	29.23	1.50	1.77	1.45	24.51
	Males	48.54	2.52	2.26	2.05	41.71
	Females	7.28	0.34	1.21	0.76	4.97

Source : *Census of India, 1981*. Series-I, Part-II-B (i), Primary Census Abstract, GeneralPopulation.

Notes : (i) The 1981 census figures exclude Assam as no census was taken due to disturbed conditions prevailing there at the time of census enumeration.

(ii) The term "main worker" (one who has worked for more than 183 days in the preceding year, usual status) was used for 1981 census.

(iii) Household industry includes manufacturing, servicing and repair.

(iv) 'Other workers' include factory workers, plantation workers, those in trade, commerce, business, transport, mining, construction, political or social work, all government servants, municipal employees, teachers, priests, entertainment artists, etc.

In Table 3.7, analysis of the share of women workers to total population by their educational level, both in rural and urban areas in 1981, reveals that, as a whole, irrespective of their relative educational status, the percentage of women main workers in urban India was relatively less than that was found in rural areas. This trend can be found in various categories of women main workers having different levels of educational achievements. Moreover, as educational levels of main workers go on increasing, the percentage share of women in the total main workers goes on decreasing. In rural areas, not a single woman main worker having technical or post-graduation degree was found in 1981. All these reveal that, relative to men, women's educational status is very low and whereever they have equal educational status they have been underrepresented in total main workers, both in rural and urban areas.

Table 3.7 : **Percentage of main workers to total population by educational level and sex in urban and rural areas, India, 1981**

Educational level	Total oopulation (in '000)				Percentage of total main workers			
	Urban		Rural		Urban		Rural	
	M	F	M	F	M	F	M	F
(1)	(2)	(3)	(4)	(5)	(6)	(7)	(8)	(9)
All India*	83,876	73,803	260,054	247,537	48.54	7.28	52.62	16.00
Illiterate	28,657	38,508	153,988	203,103	38.50	7.95	51.21	17.22
Literate (without educational level)**	12,075	9,501	37,570	18,262	29.92	2.98	42.46	8.59
Primary	13,175	10,095	33,595	15,982	53.09	3.99	60.81	11.81
Middle	10,354	6,680	18,507	6,660	55.94	3.61	59.14	9.17
Matriculation /Secondary	9,930	4,969	10,446	2,541	68.03	10.63	66.10	12.64
Higher Secondary/ Intermediate/ Pre-Univ.	4,179	1,857	3,246	539	54.12	9.07	55.31	9.99
Non-Technical Diploma or Certificate not equal to Degree	36	37	71	30	69.88	38.41	75.47	45.79
Technical Diploma or Certificate not equal to Degree	578	151	474	123	79.16	61.52	77.31	69.72
Graduate Degree other than Technical Degree	3,274	1,338	2,147	312	74.01	20.71	70.90	31.38
Post-Graduate Degree other than Tech. Degree	836	371	-	-	81.73	33.22	-	-

Contd..

(1)	(2)	(3)	(4)	(5)	(6)	(7)	(8)	(9)
Technical Degree or Diploma equal to Degree or Post-Graduate Degree								
(i) Engineering and Technology	334	7	-	-	86.87	47.35	-	-
(ii) Medicine	177	49	-	-	82.09	72.24	-	-
(iii) Agriculture and Dairying	26	1	-	-	81.91	46.95	-	-
(iv) Veterinary	8	0.3	-	-	88.45	56.98		
(v) Teaching	233	238	-	-	88.45	56.98		
(vi) Others	2	0.7	-	-	74.41	37.12		

Source : *Census of India, 1981*, Series-I, Part-III-A (1), General Economic Tables (Tables B-1 to B-5).

Note : Total in each category may not tally because of rounding of figures.

* : All India excludes Assam.

** : Includes figures for educational levels not classifiable.

Another Aspect of Disproportionate Underrepresentation : The uneven representation of women having varying educational status can be found by analysing DGE & T data on job-seekers on the live registers of employment exchanges in India in 1984 (see Table 3.8). In 1984, the percentages of female job-seekers having matriculation, higher secondary, graduate and postgraduate degrees, and who had registered themselves in the live registers of employment exchanges, were 20.2, 17.8, 31.2 and 29.3 respectively. Nearly one third of the applicants having graduate and post-graduate degrees were women thereby clearly indicating the low participation rate of women in the labour market.

Besides, among graduate applicants, the percentage of women having degree in education was the highest in 1984. Moreover, the percentages of females having professional degree who were looking for jobs were relatively low, in some cases, one-tenth of that of their male counterparts. This trend was also found among the applicants having post-graduate degree in different subjects. Thus, it is clear now that most of the women are concentrated in arts subjects, particularly in Education. This is the reason as to why some subjects have probably been termed as women's field of study in India.

Table 3.8 : **Number of applicants (matriculates and above) by sex and level of education on the live registers of employment exchanges in India, 1984**

Sl. no.	Educational level	Total (in '000)	Females (in '000)	Percentage of females
1.	Matriculation	7,301.2	1,475.8	20.2
2.	Persons who passed Higher Secondary (including Intermediate/ Undergraduate)	3,075.5	549.3	17.8
3.	Graduate	1,393.3	435.6	31.2
	(i) Arts	901.1	209.2	23.2
	(ii) Science	416.6	82.4	19.7
	(iii) Commerce	355.2	37.7	10.6
	(iv) Agriculture	18.9	0.3	1.5
	(v) Education	177.3	92.8	52.3
	(vi) Engineering	26.6	2.0	7.5
	(vii) Law	8.4	0.7	8.3
	(viii) Medicine	20.6	5.1	24.7
	(ix) Veterinary Sc.	0.7	Neg	Neg
	(x) Others	13.9	5.4	38.8
4.	Post-Graduate	219.9	64.4	29.3
	(i) Arts	119.9	37.3	31.1
	(ii) Science	43.5	13.0	29.8
	(iii) Commerce	28.6	2.0	6.9
	(iv) Agriculture	1.2	Neg	Neg
	(v) Education	18.8	9.5	50.5
	(vi) Engineering	0.5	Neg	Neg
	(vii) Law	0.2	Neg	Neg
	(viii) Medicine	0.8	0.2	25.0
	(ix) Veterinary Sc.	Neg	Neg	Neg
	(x) Others	6.4	2.4	37.5
	Total	12,535.9	2,525.1	20.14

Source : Directorate General of Employment and Training, Ministry of Labour, *Employment Review*, Government of India, New Delhi.

Note : Neg = Negligible.

Apart from this, analysis of data on job-seekers furnished by the Labour Bureau, Chandigarh, reveals that, in 1984, most of the female job-seekers having differential educational status - i.e. below middle, middle and upto matriculation, matriculation, undergraduation and graduation - were in the age group 20-24. But, the number of women having post-graduate degree and who were looking for placement was highest in the age group 25-29 in the same year.

Table 3.9 : **Number of women job-seekers, classified by age, sex and educational levels in India, as on the 31st December, 1984**

(in '000)

Age group	Total/ women	Below middle standard	Middle standard and upto matriculation	Matriculation	Under-graduate	Graduate	Post-graduate
Upto 14	Total	28.2	60.7	112.6	57.4	-	-
	Women	5.2	6.9	29.4	18.8	-	-
15 - 19	Total	852.3	1130.2	1831.3	689.9	211.4	7.0
	Women	98.2	173.5	400.5	129.7	51.8	1.5
20-24	Total	1786.2	2246.9	2859.2	1244.2	818.1	85.3
	Women	203.4	316.8	572.3	2231.1	178.8	23.4
25-29	Total	1492.5	1505.7	1659.1	751.8	639.6	85.5
	Women	169.5	224.5	303.6	121.7	136.0	24.5
30-34	Total	629.2	632.0	613.6	247.7	204.9	30.1
	Women	82.2	93.7	123.9	40.6	48.2	10.6
35-39	Total	245.5	244.0	183.3	70.8	53.9	9.4
	Women	35.2	43.0	36.7	11.0	15.3	3.4
40-49	Total	73.6	65.9	37.7	11.4	9.8	2.5
	Women	10.3	11.6	8.5	2.8	4.6	0.9
50-59	Total	10.3	6.3	3.9	2.0	1.4	0.2
	Women	1.5	1.2	0.9	0.5	1.0	0.1
60 & above	Total	1.1	0.5	0.6	0.4	0.1	0.0
	Women	0.2	0.1	0.1	0.2	0.1	0.0
All Age	Total	5118.7	5892.1	7301.3	3075.5	1939.3	219.9
Groups	Women	605.7 (11.83)	871.2 (14.79)	1475.8 (20.21)	549.3 (17.86)	435.6 (0.22)	64.4 (29.29)

Source : Labour Bureau (1990) *Statistical Profile on Women Labour,* (Third issue), of Labour, Government of India, Chandigarh.

Notes : (i) Total of all age groups may not tally due to rounding off.

(ii) Figures in parentheses show the percentage share of women work-seekers to total work-seekers in all age groups.

An analysis of DGE & T data in Table 3.10 also reveals that, except for the years 1985 and 1986, the percentage of women work-seekers to total work-seekers on the live register of the employment exchanges had been constantly increasing since 1971. However, during this period, the percentage of women who had been provided placements to total women work-seekers had been steadily declining thereby probably implying a relatively lower demand for women in the organised sector. On the one hand, the supply of women labour has gone up during the last two decades and, on the other, the demand for such labour has gone down during this period which has created a large pool of 'reserve army' in our organised sector. Such a behaviour of the organised labour market in the country had made the magnitude of educated unemployment, particularly of educated women, relatively more pronounced in the late 1980s.

Table 3.10 : **Number of work-seekers and their placements for the years 1971, 1974 and 1980 to 1987**

(in lakhs)

Year	Total number of work-seekers on live register**			Total number of placements effected during the year		
	Total	Women	Percentage to total women	Total	Women	Percentage to total women
1971	51.00	5.83	11.4	3.99	0.48	8.2
1974	84.33	9.73	11.5	3.97	0.57	5.9
1980	150.03	22.64	15.1	4.03	0.57	2.5
1981	174.24	26.68	15.3	4.11	0.51	1.9
1982	197.50	31.38	15.9	4.73	0.63	2.0
1983	219.53	35.81	16.3	4.86	0.66	1.8
1984	235.47	40.02	17.0	4.07	0.56	1.4
1985	262.70	44.47	16.9	3.89	0.55	1.2
1986	301.31	50.98	16.9	3.51	0.51	1.0
1987	302.47	53.73	17.8	3.34	0.45	0.8

Source : Labour Bureau (1990) *Statistical Profile on Women Labour*, (Third issue), Ministry of Labour, Government of India, Chandigarh.

* : For the year 1971 the total number of placements effected related to the period April to December and for the years 1980 and 1981 this period related to January to October.

** : For the years 1980 and 1981 (the total number of work-seekers on live registers) the period related to October to October.

In Table 3.11, a break up of the number of women work-seekers to whom placements were made in 1984 according to their levels of educational achievements provides an idea about the disproportionate demand for women labour having different types of educational background and achievements. In 1984, only 21.5 per cent of women who had registered themselves in the live registers of employment exchanges provided with jobs, whereas the percentage of men who had had the placement facility, was 38.3. So far as the placement of graduate women was concerned, the largest number of women having degree in Education (37.3 per cent) had been given employment followed by women having degree in Medicine. The same trend was there with regard to placement of women work-seekers having post-graduate degree. However, the most important point is that the percentages of women work-seekers having professional degrees such as Law, Engineering, Veterinary, Agriculture and to whom placements were made were negligible in 1984. Thus, the above analysis brings into surface the distinct pattern of employment of women in the organized sector in India and their disadvantaged position in the labour market.

Table 3.11 : **Number of applicants (matriculates and above) by sex and level of education for whom placements were made by employment exchanges in India, 1984**

(in lakhs)

Sl. no.	Educational level	Total (in '000)	Females (in '000)	Percentage of females
(1)	(2)	(3)	(4)	(5)
1.	Matriculate	89.1	17.6	19.7
2.	Persons who passed Higher Secondary (including Intermediate/ Undergraduate)	42.0	8.7	20.7
3.	Graduate	41.8	10.3	24.6
	(i) Arts	12.2	3.4	27.8
	(ii) Science	6.7	1.1	16.4
	(iii) Commerce	5.2	0.6	11.5
	(iv) Agriculture	1.7	0.1	5.1
	(v) Education	12.3	4.6	37.3
	(vi) Engineering	2.3	0.1	4.3

Contd..

(1)	(2)	(3)	(4)	(5)
(vii)	Law	Neg	Neg	Neg
(viii)	Medicine	0.8	0.2	25.0
(ix)	Veterinary Sc.	0.3	-	-
(x)	Others	0.3	0.2	66.0
4.	Post-Graduate	4.7	1.7	16.1
(i)	Arts	1.7	0.7	14.8
(ii)	Science	1.1	0.4	36.3
(iii)	Commerce	0.4	0.1	25.0
(iv)	Agriculture	0.1	-	-
(v)	Education	1.2	0.5	41.6
(vi)	Engineering	Neg	Neg	Neg
(vii)	Law	Neg	Neg	Neg
(viii)	Medicine	0.1	Neg	Neg
(ix)	Veterinary Sc.	-	-	-
(x)	Others	0.1	Neg	Neg
	Total	177.6	38.3	21.5

Source : DGE & T, *Employment Review*, Ministry of Labour, Government of India, New Delhi.

Note : Neg = Negligible.

WOMEN IN ORGANISED SECTOR :

The organised public and private sectors employ a large number of women in India. However, the relative proportion of women employed in various types of industries and/or services is highly disproportionate to their numbers, and as compared to their male counterparts they are underrepresented in many important occupations. The figures in Table 3.12 clearly show the proportion of women employed in various types of industries and services in India in 1984-85. It could be seen that in agriculture, hunting, etc. the number of women employed was 0.36 lakh out of a total of 5.00 lakh which accounted for only 7.2 per cent of the total in the public sector. However, in private sector the proportion of women in the above type of industry was quite high, i.e. 50.4 per cent.

The relative share of women could be found considerably higher in community, social and personal services categories under both public and private sectors in 1984-85. Women constituted 16.5 per cent and 26.7 per cent respectively of the total employed persons in these occupations under public and private sectors. In public sector, the percentage of women employed in financing, insurance, real estate, etc. was relatively high

(10.5) as compared to 7.8 per cent in private sector. Besdies, women were relatively more concentrated in construction industry in private sector (10.8 per cent) in 1984-85.

The share of women employees in the public sector manufacturing industry was 5.9 per cent, while in the same industry 10.7 per cent of the total employees in private sector were women. Between these sectors, women's share was found to be relatively high in industries/services in the private sector (18.25 per cent) in 1984-85. This distributional pattern of employees perhaps indicates a relative preference for women employees in the private sector.

Table3.12: **Number of employees by sex in major industries/ services in organised sector in India, 1984-85**

(in lakhs)

Sl. no.	Type of industry/ services	Public sector		Private sector	
		Total	Women	Total	Women
1.	Agriculture, Hunting etc.	5.00	0.36 (7.2)	9.16	4.62 (50.4)
2.	Community, Social and Personal Services	80.41	13.30 (16.5)	12.86	3.43 (26.7)
3.	Construction	11.32	0.51 (4.5)	0.65	0.07 (10.8)
4.	Electricity, Gas and Water	7.51	0.20 (2.7)	0.40	0.01 (2.5)
5.	Financing, Insurance Real Estate etc.	9.39	0.99 (10.5)	2.17	0.17 (7.8)
6.	Manufacturing	17.21	1.01 (5.9)	43.23	4.61 (10.7)
7.	Mining and Quarrying	9.63	0.66 (6.9)	1.11	0.20 (18.0)
8.	Transport, Storage and Communications	28.78	1.05 (3.6)	0.56	0.03 (5.4)
9.	Wholesale and Retail Trade etc.	1.25	0.08 (6.4)	2.75	0.16 (5.8)
	Total	170.50	18.16 (10.65)	72.89	13.30 (18.25)

Source: DGE & T, *Employment Review*, Ministry of Labour, Government of India, New Delhi.
Note : Figures in parentheses show percentages to total.

Occupational Pattern of Women : Till today, women's participation in education and employment is dismal and highly disproportionate in India. They are underrepresented in education and in different paid and well-provided employments. Their status in the labour market is marginal. Their contribution to production activities still go unrecognised. The perception about their nature of work has not yet been economically termed. Though they work harder than their male counterparts and the total hours of a day they work is more than that of men, so far, no effort has been made to develop such indicators which would measure their share in the processes of production, distribution and consumption. The irony is that they are termed as non-workers if they are not earning money wages or salary. In other words, they have been discriminated against both outside and within the labour market in India. Within the labour market, they are discriminated against at the point of entry into well paid and high status occupations, though no one has yet proved the so-called proposition of less productivity of women in some jobs in which they are underrepresented (see Banerjee, 1991). The differential occupational pattern of women in the organised sector becomes clear if we look into the available data furnished by various government departments in India (see Table 3.13).

Table 3.13 : **Occupational pattern of women employees in public sector, 1982**

(in lakhs)

Occupational division	No. of women employees	Percentage of all occupations	Total employment	Percentage of women to total
Professional and Related Workers	5.27	54.1	25.43	20.7
Administrative, Executive and Managerial Workers	0.08	0.8	2.74	2.9
Clerical and Related Workers	2.25	23.1	28.55	7.9
Sales Workers	0.02	0.2	0.34	6.0
Service Workers	1.08	11.0	10.67	10.1
Farmers, Fishermen, Hunters, Loggers and Related Workers	0.10	1.0	2.03	4.7
Production and Related Workers, Transport, Equipment Operators and Labourers	0.95	9.8	22.69	4.2
All Occupations	9.75	100.0	92.45	10.6

Source : Directorate General of Employment and Training (1987) *Occupational Educational Pattern in India (Public Sector-1982)*, Ministry of Labour, Government of India, New Delhi.

Public Sector : Public sector as we have noted earlier, is one of the largest employers in India. In 1982, there were 1,15,504 establishments in the public sector out of which 85,246 establishments furnished data of 92.45 lakh employees. Analysis of the occupational patterns of employees in this sector reveals some intersting insights. In Table 3.13, in terms of percentage of all occupations, it could be seen that, among various occupational divisions, women were highly concentrated in professional and related occupations (54.1), followed by clerical and related jobs (23.1), services (11.0) and production and related jobs, transport, equipment operation and as labourers (9.8). The share of women in administrative, executive and managerial occupations was marginal (0.8 per cent) in 1982.

In terms of percentage of women employees to total employees in respective individual occupations, the distributional pattern of women employees among various occupations was different from the above mentioned pattern in 1982. In this case, relatively large number of women were found in professional and related occupations (20.7 per cent), followed by services (10.1 per cent), clerical and other related occupations (7.9 per cent) and sales (6.0 per cent). However, women's share in the administrative, executive and managerial occupations was the minimum (2.9 per cent) in the same year (see Table 3.13).

Private Sector : Table 3.14 provides data on employment pattern of women in various occupations in the private sector in India. In 1983, out of 50.80 lakh employees, 9.22 lakh employees were women (18.15 per cent). The data on the patterns of employment of women in various occupations show that, in 1983, women constituted slightly more than one-third of the total employees in occupational categories of: (i) farming, fishery, hunting, logging and related jobs; and (ii) production and related jobs, transport equipment operating and wage labour. The important point to be noted here is that the proportion of women employees was more in these two categories of occupations in the private sector in comparison to their proportion in the corresponding occupations in the public sector. In the private sector, the representation of women in other professions was virtually insignificant in 1983. In terms of percentage of women to total employees in respective individual occupations in 1983, women were found to be more concentrated in agriculture, fishery, hunting, logging and related jobs (48.5), followed by professional and related occupations (28.11), production, transport and related jobs (12.2), services (7.8) and clerical and related jobs (7.5). It is important to note that the relative percentage of women to the total employees in the administrative, executive and managerial occupations in the private sector was relatively high (3.7) compared to that found in the public sector (2.9).

Table 3.14 : **Distribution of women employees according to professional and technical operations in private sector in India, 1983**

Occupational division	No. of women employees (in lakhs)	Percentage of all occupations	Total employment (in lakhs)	Percentage of women to total
Professional and Related Workers	2.35	25.4	7.92	28.11
Administrative, Executive and Managerial Workers	0.04	0.4	1.06	3.7
Clerical and Related Workers	0.54	5.9	7.11	7.5
Sales Workers	0.01	0.1	0.50	2.0
Service Workers	0.20	2.2	2.56	7.8
Farmers, Fishermen, Hunters, Loggers and Related Workers	2.94	32.0	6.06	48.5
Production and Related Workers, Transport, Equipment Operators and Labourers	3.14	34.0	25.59	12.2
All Occupations	9.22	100.0	50.80	18.15

Source : Directorate General of Employment and Training (1987) *Occupational Educational Pattern in India (Private Sector-1983)*, Ministry of Labour, Government of India, New Delhi.

PROFESSIONAL AND TECHNICAL OCCUPATIONS

Professional and technical occupational category is an important constituent of overall occupations in any country. Though it occupies the middle level status in the hierarchy of occupations, it forms the core of the white collar job market in India, and in most of the developing and developed countries the tastes and aspirations of the rising middle class are geared to these occupations. In India, over the years, this occupational category has gained considerable importance and momentum.

The distribution of women employees among various occupational divisions in this category shows that the largest segment of women employees both in public and private sectors was constituted by teachers, and their relative percentage is high in the private sector (see Table 3.15). The second most important division in which women could be seen in considerable proportion, in terms of their total representation, was medicine, and their percentage was relatively more in the public sector (23.6). As social scientists, women were mainly concentrated in the public sector (2.6 per cent). However, women's share in engineering and other related technical occupations including physical sciences was quite marginal in 1982. Similar situation could also be found in the U.K. and other developed countries (see Carter and Kirkup, 1990; and Silverstone and Ward, 1980).

The pattern of distribution of women employees among various divisions of professional and technical occupations in both private and public sectors perhaps indicates the fact that such a distributional pattern is the outcome of existing social traditions and policy directions of the government.

Table 3.15 : **Distribution of women employees according to professional and technical occupation in India**

Sl.no.	Occupational category	Public sector, 1982		Private sector, 1983	
		No. of women employees	Percentage to total	No. of women employees	Percentage to total
1.	Engineering Personnel	6,447	1.2	1,371	0.6
2.	Medical Personnel	1,24,015	23.6	21,075	9.0
3.	Physical Scientists and Physical Science Technicians	1,298	0.2	1,131	0.5
4.	Social Scientists and other Related Workers	13,441	2.6	1,785	0.7
5.	Teachers	3,64,829	69.3	2,03,341	86.7
6.	Others	16,548	3.1	5,889	2.5
	Total	5,26,578	100.0	2,34,592	100.0

Sources : (i) Directorate General of Employment and Training (1987) *Occupational Educational Pattern in India (Public Sector-1982)*, Ministry of Labour, Government of India, New Delhi.

(ii) Directorate General of Employment and Training (1987) *Occupational Educational Pattern in India (Private Sector-1983)*, Ministry of Labour, Government of India, New Delhi.

The existing socio-cultural patterns and traditions influence policy directions and policy directions in turn influence individual aspirations and choices. This is reflected in the country's First Five-Year Plan document :

> The main point of difference to be stressed is that there are particular spheres of life in which women have a distinctive role and in which they can make a special contribution. It is now universally recognised that in the management of the household, in bringing up children, in the field of social service, in the nursing and midwifery, in teaching, especially in elementary schools, in certain crafts and industries like knitting, embroidery, etc., and in the field of fine arts, women have, by instinct, a better aptitute. This does not, however, mean that women should, whatever be their individual aptitudes and ambitions, be confined to these few spheres. They must have the same opportunities as men for taking to all kinds of work and this presupposes that they get equal educational facilities so that their entry into the professions and public services is in no way prejudiced (557).

This statement clearly emphasises the sextyping of jobs and ambivalently sermonises the need to allow women to enter into other important professions and services. The higher share of women employees in teaching and medical professions hence is the result of systematic emphasis on the assumption that women have natural aptitude for certain jobs like teaching, midwifery and nursing, etc. These jobs have been basically considered as women's jobs. While engineering and other technical occupations have been considered as men's occupations and as a result the representation of women in these occupations has remained pitifully poor. (We have discussed representation of women in teaching profession separetely in this chapter).

Medical and Para-Medical Occupations : By nature and character medical profession is highly differentiated—the physicians and surgeons are on the top, and at the bottom level of the hierarchy, are the nurses, dieticians, health technicians, etc. While, as could be seen in Table 3.16, the percentages of female physicians and surgeons were only 4.9 in the public sector in 1982 and 8.2 in the private sector in 1983, the bulk of the medical personnel was consituted by dieticians, pharmacists, physio-therapists, medical and health technicians (32.6 per cent), nurses (31.9 per cent) and midwives and health visitors (30.6 per cent) in the public sector. The same pattern of distribution could also be found in the private sector. What this indicates is that women are still underpresented in high status medical professions such as physicians and surgeons. This category of occupations is still dominated by men.

Table 3.16 : **Distribution of women employees in medical and para-medical occupations in India**

Sl.no.	Occupational category	Public sector, 1982		Private sector, 1983	
		No. of women employees	Percentage to total	No. of women employees	Percentage to total
1.	Midwife and Health Visitor	37,863	30.6	2,698	12.8
2.	Nurse	39,603	31.9	10,378	49.2
3.	Physician and Surgeon	6,112	4.9	1,724	8.2
4.	Others (Dietician, Pharmacist, Physiotherapist, Medical and Health Technician)	40,437	32.6	6,275	29.8
	Total	1,24,015	100.0	21,075	100.0

Sources :(i) Directorate General of Employment and Training (1987) *Occupational Educational Pattern in India (Public Sector-1982)*, Ministry of Labour, Government of India, New Delhi.

(ii) Directorate General of Employment and Training (1987) *Occupational Educational Pattern in India (Private Sector-1983)*, Ministry of Labour, Government of India, New Delhi.

Clerical Occupation : The distributional pattern of women employees in various types of clerical jobs in Table 3.17 shows that the clerical and related workers made up 34.4 per cent in the public sector, and 33.7 per cent in the private sector of the total number of women employed in clerical occupations. It could further be seen that, in the public sector, 14.2 per cent were book-keepers, cashiers and related workers. In the private sector, it was, however, only 9.4 per cent. The other important divisions of clerical occupation, where women employees could be found concentrated, were clerical supervisors and superintendents, head clerks and office assistants (15.5 per cent and 9.3 per cent respectively) in public and private sectors, followed by stenographers, typists, etc. and office attendants, (11.7 per cent in the public sector and 22.8 per cent in the private sector). In the private sector, relatively a large number of women were found working as stenographers, typists, card and tap punching machine operators and office attendants.

Table 3.17 : **Distribution of women in clerical jobs in India**

Sl.no.	Occupational category	Public sector, 1982		Private sector, 1983	
		No. of women employees	Percentage to total	No. of women employees	Percentage to total
1.	Book-Keepers, Cashiers and Related Workers	31,974	14.2	5,070	9.4
2.	Clerical Supervisors and Superintendents, Head Clerks, Office Assistants	34,997	15.5	5,009	9.3
3.	Clerical and Related Workers (Misc.)	77,503	34.4	18,243	33.7
4.	Office Attendants	36,895	16.4	11,387	21.1
5.	Stenographers, Typists, Card and Tape Punching Machine Operators	26,325	11.7	12,324	22.8
6.	Telephone Operators	9,010	4.0		
7.	Others	8,552	3.8	1857	3.4
	Total	2,25,256	100.0	53,890	100.0

Sources :(i) Directorate General of Employment and Training (1987) *Occupational Educational Pattern in India (Public Sector-1982)*, Ministry of Labour, Government of India, New Delhi.

(ii) Directorate General of Employment and Training (1987) *Occupational Educational Pattern in India (Private Sector-1983)*, Ministry of Labour, Government of India, New Delhi.

Administrative and Management Jobs : The administrative, executive and managerial jobs are still predominantly occupied by men in India. In terms of relative status in the labour market, these jobs are on the highest point of the professional ladder. There were 8,004 women employees in administrative, executive and managerial occupations in the public sector in 1982. This constituted only a marginal 0.8 per cent of the total women employees in various occupational categories and 2.9 per cent of the total employees in these occupations. These figures clearly indicate that women as directors, managers, administrative and personnel officers are still insignificant and highly disproportionate to their numbers in the public sector. In 1983, in the private sector, women employees in administrative, executive and managerial positions constituted only 3.7 per cent of the total employees in these jobs. In this sector, women's relative share in administrative, executive and managerial occupations was relatively higher as compared to that found in the public sector. The lower share of women in these occupations reflects policy biases and women's choices which have been conditioned by social and cultural traditions, and which have made them to pursue a career which provides 'best of both the worlds' i.e. home and work place.

Apart from this, decision-making and implementation are sensitive areas and are related to jobs having differential labour market status. And in all decisions — business, social and cultural — women as a group is an affected party in that their lives are mostly influenced by people who are in high places of administrative and executive machinery. This area being male dominated and males are still the major controllers of various means and resources, they generally do not allow women who are still underprivileged on many counts to enter into these occupations. This is rather a subtle and apparently innocent social conspiracy against a gender group whose control has been at the best advantage of the males of our society.

Similar situation could be observed in the private sector as well with regard to women's position as managers, administrators and executives. It was clearly recognised by the Education Commission (1964-66) which states that :

"Shortages of educated women available for taking up positions of directional and organizational responsibilities in various professions and occupations, however, point to the need for special efforts to expand women's education at the college and university stage" (569). The Commission in order to enhance women's representation suggested that

> In the Third Five-Year Plan, there was a scheme to set up a National Institute for Women for giving high-level training to women candidates in organization, administration and management to enable them to take up responsible positions. Women trained in these lines would be needed for implementing many national plans and projects, particularly in social services to meet the requirements of voluntary organisations and to provide competent personnel to take up positions that are becoming increasingly available to them in the industrial sectors (572).

These observations and suggestions made by the Education Commission (1964-66), have, however, still remained more or less on paper. The share of women in many important occupations has remained dismally disproportionate compared to their male counterparts in these occupations.

Service Sector : Women's participation in the service sector is quite traditional, first, because employment in this sector and in its various divisions does not require much advanced educational preparation nor it requires very high level of professional or technical skills. Table 3.18 shows that, in 1982, out of a total of 1,07,577 women service workers, 84.4 per cent were in building caretakers and related workers category; 5.8 per cent were working as protective service workers; and 5.2 per cent were maids and housekeeping service workers in the public sector. Most of these workers were under-paid in this sector. Besides, they were not, status-wise, in better positions as compared to employees in other occupational categories. Because "Both gender-segregated and segmented labour markets have complex effects on levels of employment for both sexes. Women's confinement to primary and low value-added segments may mean that they are protected in some areas of employment, but this is at the cost of low wages and vulnerability to technical substitution" (Hillary, 1992: 73).

Table 3.18 : **Distribution of women in service sector in India**

Sl.No.	Occupational category	Public sector, 1982		Private sector, 1983	
		No. of women employees	Percentage to total	No. of women employees	Percentage to total
1.	Building Caretakers and Related Workers	90,791	84.4	10,581	53.1
2.	Cooks, Waiters Bartenders and Related Workers	3,631	3.4	2,407	12.1
3.	Maid and Related House Keeping Service Workers (Not elsewhere classified)	5,679	5.2	3,361	16.9
4.	Protective Service Workers	6,214	5.8	1,947	9.8
5.	Others	1,262	1.2	1,607	8.1
	Total	1,07,577	100.0	19,903	100.0

Sources :(i) Directorate General of Employment and Training (1987) *Occupational Educational Pattern in India (Public Sector-1982)*, Ministry of Labour, Government of India, New Delhi.

(ii) Directorate General of Employment and Training (1987) *Occupational Educational Pattern in India (Private Sector-1983)*, Ministry of Labour, Government of India, New Delhi.

In the prviate sector, in 1983, 53.1 per cent of the 19,903 women workers were building caretakers and related workers; 12.1 per cent were cooks and waiters and other related workers; and 16.9 per cent were maids and related housekeeping service workers.

The figures in Table 3.18 also show that 5.8 per cent and 9.8 per cent of the women employees were protective service workers in public and private sectors respectively. In the public sector, women were mainly concentrated in building caretaking and other related jobs (84.4 per cent) thereby making these the women's jobs.

The interesting point to note here is that, at home women are the only cooks but when it comes to cooking as paid occupation, women are very much conspicuous by their total absence. As an occupational category, this is still a male dominated occupation. Despite women's traditional skills, they are far outnumbered by male professionals in many of the activities in the service sector.

Production and Related Sector : A close look into the data in Table 3.19 reveals that, in 1982, the largest number of women employees, in production and related works in the public sector, were constituted by the unskilled women labourers. They comprised of 56.9 per cent of the total 95,535 workers. This was follow by their concentration in the jobs such as food and beverage processing (20.3 per cent), spinning, knitting, weaving and dying (6.4 per cent), mining, quarrying and drilling (3.7 per cent) and material handling, equipment operation, loading and unloading (3.2 per cent). The smallest number of women were found working as brick layers and other construction workers in the public sector in 1982. In other jobs their representation was marginal in the same year. In fact, their representation had varied a great deal amongst various divisions of production work (see Table 3.19). In 1983, in the private sector, the distributional pattern of women employees in various production and other related jobs was different from that of the public sector. In the private sector, women's share was found to be highest in food and beverage spining, weaving, knitting and dying (22.2 per cent), other jobs (12.2 per cent), tabacco preparation (11.9 per cent) and material handling, equipment operation, loading and unloading (4.5 per cent). The point to be noted here is that compared to the public sector, the total number of women employees engaged in production and related occupations was little higher in the private sector.

Table 3.19 : **Distribution of women in production and related occupations in India**

Sl.no.	Occupational category	Public sector, 1982		Private sector, 1983	
		No. of women employees	Percentage to total	No. of women employees	Percentage to total
1.	Blacksmiths, Tool-makers and Machine Tool Workers	519	0.5	2,549	1.2
2.	Bricklayers & other Construction Workers	834	0.9	1,259	0.6
3.	Chemical Processors and Related Workers	220	0.2	3,419	1.6
4.	Electrical Fitters and Related Electrical and Electronic Workers	1,884	2.0	7,234	3.3
5.	Food and Beverage Processor	19,369	20.3	74,980	34.3
6.	Machinery Fitters, Machine Assemblers and Precision Instrument-makers	1,642	1.7	5,487	2.5
7.	Material Handling Related Equipment Operators, Loaders and Unloaders	3,020	3.2	9,753	4.5
8.	Miners, Quarrymen, Well Drillers and Related Workers	3,514	3.7	-	-
9.	Printing and Related Workers	471	0.5	-	-
10.	Spinners, Weavers, Knitters, Dyers and Related Workers	6,119	6.4	48,647	22.2
11.	Tailors, Dress-makers, Sewers, Upholsters and Related Workers	1,593	1.4	7,542	3.3
12.	Transport Equipment Operators	588	0.6	-	-
13.	Labourers	54,342	56.9	-	-
14.	Others	1,620	1.7	26,734	12.2
15.	Glass Farmers, Potters and Related Workers	-	-	3,135	1.4
16.	Tabacco Preparers	-	-	2,61,068	11.9
17.	Wool and Paper Workers	-	-	1,899	0.8
	Total	95,535	100.0	2,18,746	100.0

Sources :(i) Directorate General of Employment and Training (1987) *Occupational Educational Pattern in India (Public Sector-1982)*, Ministry of Labour, Government of India, New Delhi.

(ii) Directorate General of Employment and Training (1987) *Occupational Educational Pattern in India (Private Sector-1983)*, Ministry of Labour, Government of India, New Delhi.

EDUCATIONAL PROFILE OF WOMEN EMPLOYEES

Public Sector : In the public sector, out of a total of 9.75 lakh women employees, 66.1 thousands were graduates, post-graduates in technical and/or professional subjects (see Table 3.20). The distributional pattern of these graduate and post-graduate women amongst various industry divisions shows that the majority of them (93.6 per cent) were in community, social and personal services category, followed by financing, insurance, real estate and business services (2.3 per cent) in 1982. In manufacturing and construction industries, they constituted 1.5 per cent and 1.0 per cent respectively in the same year.

Similarly, it could be found that, out of 9.75 lakh women employed in the public sector, 277.2 thousand were diploma holders in technical and/ or professional subjects in 1982. Of these diploma holders, 96.6 per cent were in community, social and personal services. The percentages of women working in other industries were almost negligible (see Table 3.20).

In 1982, women with general educational qualifications were 631.3 thousands out of which 75.9 per cent were found working in community, social and personal services, followed by financing, insurance, real estate and business services (5.6 per cent), manufacturing (5.5 per cent) and transport, storage and communications (4.6 per cent). Thus, it is now clear that bulk of the educated women employees in the public sector was concentrated in the service sector.

Table 3.20 : Distribution of women employees by industries and broad educational qualification, public sector, India, 1982

Sl. no.	Description of industry division	Percentage of women employees by educational qualifications			
		Graduate, post-graduate in tech./ professional subjects	Diploma holders in tech./ professional subjects	Others those with general educational qualifications	Total
(1)	(2)	(3)	(4)	(5)	(6)
1.	Agriculture, Hunting and Fishing	0.2	0.3	3.2	2.1
2.	Mining and Quarrying	0.3	0.3	2.2	1.5

Contd..

(1)	(2)	(3)	(4)	(5)	(6)
3.	Manufacturing	1.5	1.1	7.9	5.5
4.	Electricity, Gas & Water	0.4	0.2	1.6	1.2
5.	Construction	1.0	0.8	4.5	3.2
6.	Wholesale & Retail Trade and Restaurants and Hotels	0.1	—	0.6	0.4
7.	Transport, Storage and Communications	0.6	0.5	6.8	4.6
8.	Financing, Insurance, Real Estate and Business Services	2.3	0.2	8.2	5.6
9.	Community, Social and Personal Services	93.6	96.6	65.0	75.9
	Total (in '000)	66.1	277.2	631.3	974.6

Source : Directorate General of Employment and Training (1987) *Occupational Educational Pattern in India (Public Sector-1982)*, Ministry of Labour, Government of India, New Delhi

EDUCATIONAL PROFILE OF WOMEN IN MANUFACTURING

Private Sector : In 1983, a total of 23,81,832 employees in various units of the private sector were surveyed out of which 3,00,105 were women. Table 3.21 shows that out of the total women employees, ony 0.2 per cent were graduates and post-graduates in professional and/or technical subjects and 1.1 per cent were diploma holders in professional and/or technical subjects. Women employees with general educational qualifications constituted 9.6 per cent of the total employees. The majority of women employees were below matric and illiterates (89.1 per cent). The point worth noting here is that while in the public sector majority of the highly educated women employees were concentrated in the service sector, nearly 90 per cent of women employees who were below matric or illiterates were clustered in the private manufacturing sector.

Table 3.21 : **Educational composition of female employees in manufacturing industries in private sector, India, 1983**

Sl. no.	Level of educational qualifications	No. of employees			
		All	Percentage	Females	Percnetage
1.	Graduate and or Post-Graduate in Professional and Technical Subjects	47,983	2.0	681	0.2
2.	Diploma in Profesional and of Technical Subjects	2,10,232	8.8	3,267	1.1
3.	Others (with General Educational Qualifications	4,76,273	20.0	28,873	9.6
4.	Below Matric,(including Illiterates)	16,47,344	69.2	2,67,284	89.1
	Total	23,81,832	100.0	3,00,105	100.0

Source : Directorate General of Employment and Training (1987) *Occupational Educational Pattern in India (Private Sector-1983)*, Ministry of Labour, Government of India, New Delhi.

The analysis of the educational status of female employees both in the public and private sectors reveals the important fact that their underrepresentation in education at various levels and branches had been reflected in the pattern of their work participation in different sectors. Since they are disproportionately underrepresented in higher education, their participation in high status jobs which require higher educational qualifications is dismally poor. In fact, employment of women in low status and in certain specific industries and sectors is a global phenomenon :

> Globally, most women are still clustered in low-skill services or clerical jobs with little potential for advancement.... a large percentage of women are in the professional/technical, clerical/service and sales labour force and a small percentage are in manufacturing/ transportation and the administration/management labour force (U.N., 1991:181).

The problem of women's poor participation in high status jobs is predominantly a Third World problem, as could be seen in the case of Kenya :

> The inability of women graduates to reach the policy and decision-making levels of the government infrastructure is quite striking. Only one woman, graduate or otherwise, has held a position of Cabinet rank

or Permanent Secretary since independence. In 1985, of 170 deputy, under-, and senior assistant secretaries in the government ministries, 8(4.7 per cent) were women. Similarly, out of 4356 civil servants classified at 'job group K' or above employed by the government, 313(7.2 per cent) were women. One-third of that number were located in the Ministry of Health. The litany continues in para-statal organisations and private sector. The top two strata of management and governing boards of the organisations in these sectors generally have no female representation. For example, in three private sector firms totalling over 7000 employees, women constituted but 10 per cent of those employees classified as supervisor or above (Ruigu, 1985 : 32-44). It is perhaps in these areas that women have suffered the most egregious exclusion (Hughes and Mwiria, 1989:187).

EDUCATION SPECIFIC WORKER PUPULATION RATI

The education specific usual status worker population ratio for persons of age 15 and above shows that of rural females, per thousand, the ratio was 414 for principal status workers and 526 for all workers not literate. For urban females the corresponding ratios were 230 and 292 per thousand during the same period. The important point which could be noted here is that ratios of female workers 'not literate' are high among rural female workers compared to the ratios of urban female workers 'not literate'.

Similarly, the ratios of rural female principal status workers and all workers with 'literate and upto primary' are less than their male counter-parts and the proportion of such workers is less with regard to urban females as compared to rural females in 1987-88. Similar disparities could also be observed in other education categories also. (see Table 3.22)

Table 3.22 : **Education specific usual status worker population ratio for persons of age 15 and above in India, 1987-88**

Sl. no.	Education category	Rural				Urban			
		Males		Females		Males		Females	
		PS* workers	All workers	PS workers	All workers	PS workers	All workers	PS workers	All workers
(1)	(2)	(3)	(4)	(5)	(6)	(7)	(8)	(9)	(10)
1.	Not Literate	902 (910)	911 (918)	414 (407)	526 (543)	855 (863)	861 (868)	230 (241)	292 (296)

Contd..

(1)	(2)	(3)	(4)	(5)	(6)	(7)	(8)	(9)	(10)
2.	Literate & Upto Primary	870 (885)	890 (901)	274 (277)	391 (418)	827 (841)	839 (852)	132 (134)	175 (181)
3.	Middle	688 (702)	739 (753)	176 (158)	286 (293)	662 (688)	680 (710)	81 (71)	113 (111)
4.	Secondary	664 (665)	729 (733)	175 (158)	262 (269)	645 (652)	664 (676)	125 (134)	151 (156)
5.	Graduate and above	766 (774)	827 (839)	250 (220)	307 (295)	799 (810)	811 (825)	297 (279)	315 (297)
	All Categories	839 (856)	863 (877)	373 (373)	485 (509)	754 (769)	768 (784)	175 (180)	220 (225)

Source : National Sample Survey Organisation (1990) *Sarvekhsan*, Special No. 25, NSS 43rd Round, July 1987-June, 1988, New Delhi.

* : Principal status.

POSITION OF WOMEN IN SELECTED SERVICES

There are some services the selection to which is based on successful performance in the competitive examinations, held at all-India level and in rigorous personal interviews. Most of the services in this category are comparatively 'prestigious' and well paid. An examination of personnel positions of various services, however, reveals that these 'prestigious' and well paid and well provided services are still predominantly male preserves. Entry in these areas by females are very marginal.

It could be seen in Table 3.23 that, in 1987, out of the total of 16,987 personnel in selected services, only 994 were females which accounted for only 5.83 per cent. A service-wise analysis reveals some more interesting aspects of the inter-service distributional patterns of women employees. Out of 553 personnel in the Indian Foreign Services on 1st January, 1987, only 53 were women. Getting into Indian Foreign Services is considered a highly prized achievement. However, the number of female personnel as compared to their male counterparts in these services is marginal : they constituted only 9.58 per cent of the total personnel. Women's representation could be found still very poor in the Indian Customs and Central Excise Services. They constituted only 5.30 per cent of the total personnel in 1987. Similarly, in Income Tax Services the percentage share of female personnel to total is highly disproportionate to their numbers. Only 7.99

per cent were females among a total of 2439 personnel in this service. These figures speak a great deal about women's underrepresentation in various services. In the Indian Audit and Accounts Services also their number was marginal in 1987. They constituted only 10.01 per cent of the total personnel. In Indian Postal Services, the share of female personnel was only 10.27 per cent. Some more important services where women have been dismally underrepresented are Indian Economic Services (1.99 per cent), Indian Statistical Services (4.72 per cent), Indian Forest Service (0.57 per cent), and Central Secretariat Services (3.36 per cent).

Table 3.23 also shows another important dimension, i.e. the representation of the Scheduled Castes and Scheduled Tribes females in various important all-India level services. The figures in Table 3.23 amply demonstrate the fact that women of these deprived sections have been far more underrepresented in various services than their sisters belonging to other social classes. This is despite the fact that these services have been reserved for these sections. Moreover, in some of such services the SC and ST females were totally absent in 1987.

Table 3.23 : **Representation of women in selected services in India, 1987**

Sl. no.	**Services**	**All India**			**Scheduled Castes**			**Scheduled Tribes**		
		M	F	T	M	F	T	M	F	T
(1)	(2)	(3)	(4)	(5)	(6)	(7)	(8)	(9)	(10)	(11)
1.	Indian Foreign Services (IFS)	480 (9.58)	53	553	65	2	67	30	5	35
2.	Indian Customs and Central Excise Services (ICCES)	1,053 (5.30)	59	1,112	187	4	191	64	3	67
3.	Income Tax Services (ITS)	2,244 (7.99)	195	2,439	295	3	298	100	5	105
4.	Indian Audit and Accounts Services (IAAS)	530 (10.01)	59	589	48	1	49	20	1	21
5.	Indian Postal Services (IPS)	454 (10.27)	52	506	34	2	36	16	2	18
6.	Indian Economic Services (IES)	481 (1.99)	71	552	44	3	47	19	0	19

12.86

Contd..

(1)	(2)	(3)	(4)	(5)	(6)	(7)	(8)	(9)	(10)	(11)
7.	Indian Statistical Services (ISS)	645 (4.72)	32	677	56	0	56	4	1	5
8.	Indian Forest Services (IFS)	1,733 (0.57)	10	1,743	133	0	133	80	1	81
9.	Central Information Services (CIS)	770 (8.22)	69	839	69	0	69	30	0	30
10.	Central Secretariat Services (CSS)	976 (3.36)	34	1,010	-	-	-	-	-	-
11.	Indian Administrative Services (IAS)	-	-	-	483	16	499	248	13	261
	Total	15,993 (5.83)	994	16,987	1,1414	31	1,445	611	31	642

Sources :(i) India, Ministry of Human Resource Development (1989) *National Perspective Plan for Women, 1988- 2000 A.D.*, Department of Women and Child Development, Manager, Government of India Press, New Delhi.

(ii) India, Ministry of Human Resource Development(1988) *Women in India - A Statistical Profile, 1988*, Department of Women and Child Development, Raj Prakashan, New Delhi.

(iii) India, Ministry of Home Affairs, Department of Personnel and Administrative Reforms, New Delhi.

(iv) India, Ministry of External Affairs, New Delhi.

(v) India, Ministry of Finance, Department of Revenue, New Delhi.

(vi) Comptroller and Auditor General of India, New Delhi.

(vii) India, Ministry of Communications. Department of Posts and Telegraphs, New Delhi.

(viii) India, Ministry of Planning, Department of Statistics, New Delhi.

(ix) India, Ministry of Environment and Forests, New Delhi.

(x) India, Ministry of Information and Broadcasting, New Delhi.

Note : Figures in parenthesis represent percentages of females with respect to total personnel in the respective services.

WOMEN IN TEACHING PROFESSION

Teaching is the only occupation where women are highly concentrated as compared to their male counterparts. There are several reasons for women's concentration in this occupation. First, the time stringency in this occupation is considerably less, besides flexibility of school hours. These factors seem to help women to cope both with their household chores and professional engagements and in that occupation hours of work and holidays are already almost totally congruent with the care of families (Silverstone and Ward, 1980:15). Second, given the nature of teaching-learning process, the teaching job is not complicated and demanding. Yet, teaching profession is being held as a respectable profession in India. All these factors contribute greatly to the feeling among women to aspire for teaching profession.

Social attitudes also are responsible to a great extent for women's participation in teaching — it is not considered a male profession only. The social attitudes seem to have influenced government's policy decisions too.

Here, an attempt has been made to examine women's employment as teachers at various levels and faculities from school education to collegiate and university level education.

In School Education : It could be seen in Table 3.24 that the proportion of women teachers in higher secondary schools/junior colleges (10+2 new pattern) was 29.47 per cent and in high/post-basic schools, it was 33.14 per cent in 1986-87. In middle/senior basic schools, the percentage of women teachers was 33.25. However, the share of women teachers was relatively less in the case of primary/junior basic schools, it was 27.89 per cent. It has been stated in the Policy document (1986) that each primary school should have one female teacher. This proposition seems to have remained unfulfilled. No wonder, given the overall situation of women's education which is very low as compared to men's, the availability of female teachers in many areas, particularly rural areas, is not adequate. As a result, many schools in this category are without female teachers.

Table 3.24 : **Proportion of women teachers at various stages of school education in India, 1986-87**

Sl. no.	Type of institution	Men	Women	Percentage of women	Total
1.	Higher Secondary Schools/ Junior Colleges (10+2 New Pattern)	3,15,633	1,31,923	29.47	4,47,556
2.	High/Post-Basic Schools	5,2,6813	2,61,161	33.14	7,87,974
3.	Middle/Senior Basic Schools	6,89,179	3,43,355	33.25	10,32,534
4.	Primary/Junior Basic Schools	11,55,843	4,47,215	27.89	16,03,058
	Total	26,87,468	11,83,654	30.58	38,71,122

Source : Ministryof Human Resource Development (1990) *Selected Educational Statistics, 1988-89*, Government of India, New Delhi.

In Higher Education : The disproportionate representation of women in higher education in general and in individual faculties/subjects in particular, is clearly reflected in their employment patterns in different types of institutions of higher learning at different levels. Table 3.25 shows that, during 1986-87, out of the total of 27,461 teachers in the universities only 13.59 per cent were females, that is to say, only 4,322 in number. In other words, in the highest bodies of institutions of higher learning the share of women teachers was highly disproportionate to their numbers. The institutions deemed to be universities constitute an important segment of higher education sector. The percentage of women teachers in these institutions was 15.60 of the total teachers in 1986-87. There are also institutions which are of national importance. The representation of women teachers in these institutions was as low as 7.95 per cent of the total of 2,803 teachers in the same year. There are some institutions established especially for research activities. The proportion of women faculty was not higher in these institutions either. It was only 13.22 per cent in 1986-87 (see Table 3.25).

Degree Standard and Above : Analysis of institution-wise (degree and above) distribution of female teachers in higher education in 1986-87 reveals some interesting aspects relating to the share of women in the adcademic labour market (see Table 3.25). In 1986-87, in arts, science and commerce colleges, the percentage of women teachers was only 25.52. In pedagogical institutions (i.e. education colleges), the women teachers were highly concentrated, their percentage was 29.84 in 1986-87. The relative share of females in the faculties of the colleges offering courses in engineering, technical and architecture was the least (6.68 per cent). In medical colleges, the relative share of women teachers was 23.53 per cent which was certainly high. However, this higher percentage of women teachers in medical colleges can be attributed to high concentration of women in nursing (95.00 per cent).

In the institutions of higher education (below degree), the pattern of distribution of women faculty was the same as could be observed in Table 3.25. The percentage of female teachers in medical colleges was relatively high (49.11 per cent) in 1986-87. Again, this high percentage was due to high concentration of females in nursing (77.60 per cent) in the same year. In 1986-87, the overall share of women teachers in the higher education sector was 21.08 per cent. Thus, despite high rate of participation of women in the academic labour market, they constituted only a little more than one fifth of the total teaching staff in this sector in 1986-87 which was certainly disproportionate to their numbers. (see Figure 3.2.)

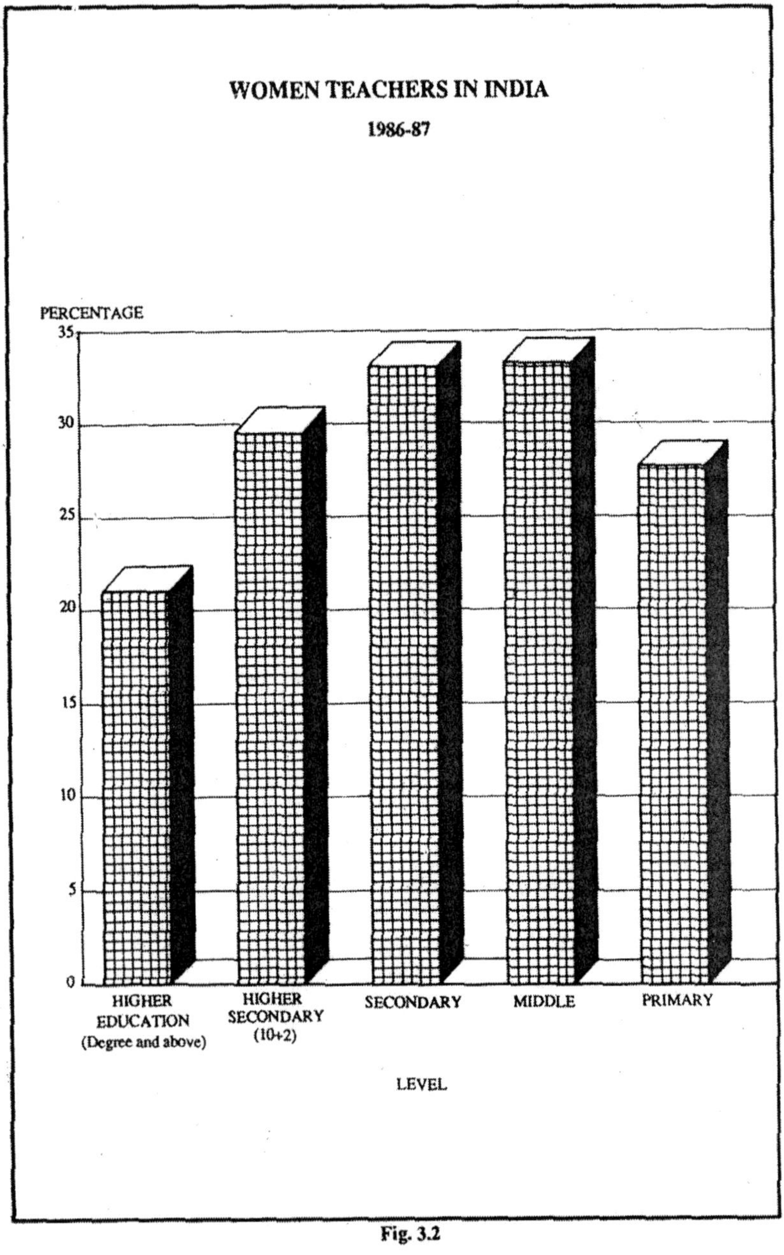
WOMEN TEACHERS IN INDIA
1986-87
PERCENTAGE
35
30
25
20
15
10
5
0
HIGHER EDUCATION (Degree and above)
HIGHER SECONDARY (10+2)
SECONDARY
MIDDLE
PRIMARY
LEVEL

Fig. 3.2

Table 3.25 : **Proportion of women teachers in institutions of higher education in India, 1986-87**

Sl. no.	Type of institution	Men	Women	Percentage of women	Total
(1)	(2)	(3)	(4)	(5)	(6)
A.	Universities	27,461	4,322	13.59	31,783
B.	Institutions Deemed to be Universities	1,876	347	15.60	2,223
C.	Institutions of National Importance	2,580	223	7.95	2,803
D.	Research Institutions	1,047	161	13.32	1,208
E.	(a) Institutions for Higher Education (Degree Standard and above)				
	1. Arts, Science and Commerce	1,31,687	45,129	25.52	1,76,816
	2. Agriculture & Forestry	4,405	404	8.40	4,809
	3. Business Management	299	28	8.56	327
	4. Education	3,717	1,581	29.84	5,298
	5. Engg. Tech. & Archt.	12,001	860	6.68	12,861
	6. Law	2,270	185	7.53	2,455
	7. Medicine: (i) Allopathy	13,720	4,346	24.05	18,066
	(ii) Ayurveda & Unani	2,095	408	16.30	2,503
	(iii) Homeopathy	1,282	127	9.01	1,409
	(iv) Dentistry	432	268	38.28	700
	(v) Nursing	16	304	95.00	320
	(vi) Pharmacy	443	94	17.50	537
	(vii)Public Health	91	17	15.54	108
	Total [7(a)]	18,079	5,564	23.53	23,643
	8. Music & Fine Arts	997	306	23.48	1303
	9. Oriental Studies	2807	314	10.06	3121
	10. Physical Education	527	92	14.86	619
	11. Social Work	138	111	44.57	249
	12. Veterinary Science	1,685	63	3.60	1,748
	13. Other Institutions	420	196	31.81	616
	Total [E (a) (1-13)]	1,79,032	54,833	23.44	2,33,865

Contd..

(1)	(2)	(3)	(4)	(5)	(6)
E.	(b) Institutions of Higher Education (below Degree level)				
1.	Agriculture & Forestry	142	18	11.25	160
2.	Education	5,532	2,952	34.79	8,484
3.	Engg. Tech. & Archt.	31,663	2,591	7.56	3,4254
4.	Medicine:				
	(i) Ayurveda and Unani	31	1	3.12	32
	(ii) Homeopathy	416	56	11.86	472
	(iii) Nursing, Midwifery	204	707	77.60	911
	(iv) Pharmacy	326	22	6.32	348
	(v) Public Health	21	177	89.39	198
	Total [b (4)]	998	983	49.11	1,961
5.	Music & Fine Arts	569	600	51.32	1,169
6.	Oriental Studies	181	4	2.16	185
7.	Physical Education	127	11	7.97	138
8.	Social Work	8	—	---	8
9.	Other Institutions	1,184	404	25.44	1,588
	Total [E (b) (1-9)]	40,404	7,543	15.73	47,947
	Grand Total	2,52,400	67,429	21.08	3,19,829

Source : Ministry of Human Resource Development (1991) *Education in India, 1986-87*, Vol. 1 (c). *Government of India*, New Delhi.

RESEARCH AND DEVELOPMENT

Representation of women in the research and development (R and D) sector is an important indicator of development and the pattern of their participation in the traditionally male dominated areas. Earlier, because of lack of data, it was rather difficult to pin-point exact situation. The Department of Science and Technology of India has, however, collected an impressive amount of data in 1986-87 on women science and technology personnel. The present analysis is based on these data (Rajeswari et al., 1988).

It could be seen in Table 3.26 that most of the women S and T personnel were employed in administration (57.85) followed by R and D and auxiliary service category in 1986. This again clearly shows that women are still underrepresented in the R and D proper. The distribution of

20,221 women personnel in different establishments shows that majority of the women and S and T personnel are in State Government establishments (31.06 per cent) followed by Central Government establishment and in institutional sector. The percentage of the women S and T personnel in industrial sector of both the public and private sectors is very small : 4.75 per cent and 8.90 per cent respectively.

Table 3.26 : **Full-time equivalent of women personnel employed in R and D establishment by nature of work as on April, 1986**

Establishment	R and D	Auxiliary	Administration	Total
A. Institutional Sector				
I. Central Government				
1. Department Atomic Energy	413	452	1301	2166 (10.71)
2. Council of Scientific and Industrial Research	569	565	693	1827 (9.04)
3. Defence Research and Development Organisation	41	254	658	1325 (6.54)
4. Indian Council of Agricultural Research	405	343	938	1686 (8.34)
5. Department of Space	106	75	239	420 (2.08)
6. Indian Council of Medical Research	134	166	117	417 (2.06)
7. Other Central Govt. Ministries/Agencies	587	1202	1552	3341 (16.52)
II. State Governments	541	411	5329	6281 (4.75)
B. Industrial Sector				
1. Public Sector including Joint Sector	554	190	216	960 (4.75)
2. Private Sector	850	295	655	1800 (8.90)
Total	4570 (22.60)	3953 (19.55)	11698 (57.85)	20221 (100.00)

Source: Government of India, DST (1988) *Occasional Paper on Status of Women in R & D*, New Delhi.

Note : Figures in brackets indicate percentages.

FAMILY BACKGROUND OF WOMEN PROFESSIONALS

In the preceding chapter we have already discussed the socio-economic background of females who have access to higher education in India. To be brief, the households, both in rural and urban areas, which have differential access to various types of resources — i.e. material, human, etc. - also have differential access to education and employment. In other words, the absence of females from particular socio-economic groups or communities in the higher education in general and professional education in particular reflects the relative status of these communities in the social as well as economic hierarchy in the country. This pattern of participation of girls and women of various communities or status groups in different levels and types of education is further reflected in the pattern of representation of such educated girls and women across different types of occupations or jobs having differential labour market status and reward structures.

Here, on the basis of the study on 'Women Engineers in India' conducted by the Indian Institute of Technology, Bombay, (Parikh and Sukhatme, 1992), an attempt has been made to show that those girls and women who are getting into engineering jobs have got a family background which is somehow different from that of the girls and women who opt for general education, and hence, are mostly found employed in low status and less rewarding jobs, and which is favourable to persue a career in engineering. In 1990, the total stock of women engineers in India was estimated to be 18,875, out of which the study covered a sample of 2,753 women engineers. According to the study, the analysis of the formal educational levels of parents, brothers and sisters of the sampled women engineers (i.e. mostly employed, some were unemployed and some were in post-graduate courses) reveals that mothers of almost half of the sampled women engineers were matriculates (47.8 per cent), 21.3 per cent mothers were graduates and only around 20 per cent were having lower than high school education (see Table 3.27). So far as formal educational level of fathers of women engineers were concerned, 42.5 per cent were graduates, 24.4 per cent were post-graduates and 25.1 per cent were matriculates. The percentage of fathers of women engineers having lower than high school education was negligible. Thus, between the formal educational achievements of the parents of women engineers, the fathers were relatively better placed, though about 78 per cent of the mothers had education upto matriculation and/or above. It can be seen in Table 3.27 that the brothers and sisters of women engineers were mostly highly educated - i.e. graduates and/or post-graduates. Thus, on the basis of the above evidence, it emerges that ambience of a good educational background of the family, particularly of the parents, supports women to participate in engineering courses and to take up engineering as a career.

Table 3.26 : **Formal educational levels of parents, sisters and brothers of women engineers in India**

Sl. no.	Educational Level	Mother	Father	Sister 1	Sister 2	Brother 1	Brother 2
1.	Post-Graduate	245 (8.9)	672 (24.4)	742 (27.0)	263 (9.6)	536 (19.5)	168 (6.1)
2.	Graduate	587 (21.3)	1171 (42.5)	1018 (37.0)	520 (18.9)	1199 (43.6)	511 (18.6)
3.	High School	1317 (47.8)	690 (25.1)	308 (11.2)	202 (7.34)	345 (12.5)	188 (0.8)
4.	Lower	549 (19.9)	176 (6.4)	26 (0.9)	28 (1.0)	41 (1.5)	21 (0.8)
5.	No Response	55 (2.0)	41 (1.5)	22 (0.8)	36 (1.3)	39 (1.4)	36 (1.3)
6.	Not Applicable	0 (0.0)	3 (0.1)	637 (23.1)	1704 (61.9)	593 (21.5)	1829 (66.4)
	Total	2753	2753	2753	2753	2753	2753

Source : Parikh, P.P., and S.P. Sukhatme (1992) *Women Engineers in India*. Department of Mechanical Engineering, IIT. Bombay, (Sponsored by Department of Science and Technology. Government of India, New Delhi).

Notes : (i) Not Applicable = Do not have sisters/brothers.
(ii) Figures in parenthesis show percentages to total.

Table 3.28 : **Formal educational levels of husbands and parents-in-law of women engineers**

Sl. no.	Educational level	Husband	Mother-in-law	Father-in-law
(1)	(2)	(3)	(4)	(5)
1.	Post-Graduate	577 (47.1)	73 (6.0)	218 (17.8)
2.	Graduate	662 (54.1)	203 (16.6)	505 (41.3)
3.	High School	8 (0.7)	524 (42.8)	372 (30.4)

Contd..

(1)	(2)	(3)	(4)	(5)
4.	Lower	0 (0.0)	407 (33.3)	120 (9.8)
5.	No Response	9 (0.7)	49 (4.0)	41 (3.4)
	Total	1256	1256	1256

Source: Parikh, P.P., and S.P. Sukhatme (1992) *Women Engineers in India*, Department of Mechanical Engineering, IIT, Bombay, (Sponsored by Department of Science and Technology, Government of India, New Delhi).

Note : Figures in parenthesis show percentages to total.

A close look into the formal educational levels of in-laws of the married women engineers shows that most of the women engineers had husbands having equivalent or higher educational achievements (see Table 3.28). The educational achievements of the fathers and fathers-in-law of women engineers were comparable, whereas the educational achievements of the mothers of women engineers was relatively higher than that of the mothers-in-law.

Besides, a large number of husbands of women engineers were also themselves engineers by profession. This was also true in case of the fathers of the women engineers. According to the study, the fathers' occupational background - i.e. engineering - coupled with high educational achievements of the parents of the women engineers had helped women to opt for and persue a career in engineering. Apart from these, encouragement by the parents was one of the important factors determining the rate of participation of women both in engineering courses and in engineering jobs. Thus, it follows that the discouraging attitudes of parents and non-acceptability of women engineers in the society are perceived as the two main reasons of low participation of women in engineering education. Moreover, difficulty in getting suitable jobs is also considered as another important reason of low representation of women in engineering profession. However, it should be noted that, according to the study, the salary levels of women engineers were low and the pace of career advancement was also very slow. Most of the women engineers were crowded into "desk-type" and teaching jobs and, therefore, had less chance of upward occupational mobility.

What follows from this study is that girls and women persuing a career in engineering have the advantage of a sound family background (i.e. in terms of educational level, type of main occupation of parents, particularly fathers and husbands, etc.) and, therefore, untill and unless the disparity with regard to distribution of income and power among communities and/or households are reduced and the attitudes of parents toward the education and participation of girls and women in the labour market in general and in technical and other occupations in particular, are changed, the sex disparity across various types of occupations cannot be bridged, *ceteris paribus*.

CONCLUSION

Subordination of women is a socially, economically and culturally constructed phenomenon. It is clearly proved by the evidence of her preponderance in the peripheral employment market where she is underpaid and where her career prospect, more often than not, is marginal.

She works more hours than a man. Yet her activities go unrecognised as contribution to production. The 'money-god' seems to be unfavourably inclined toward her. And this unfavourable inclination perhaps does not allow her contribution to be given a price tag. It is no wonder that she is still viewed as a dependent of man.

Examination of the Indian labour market scenario shows that women have largely been engaged in jobs which require low levels of skills and lesser education specific qualifications. In organised sectors - both public and private - women are found more or less in teaching, community services, clerical and nursing category of occupations. Their presence in high status jobs is virtually marginal. In research and development sector, their presence is found insignificant.

One more fact of women's underrepresentation is that even women who are in high status professions, for instance, engineering, an examination of their family backgrounds demonstrates that most of them, in fact all of them, come from higher levels of socio-economic hierarchy. What this signifies is that women from lower socio-economic bacgrkounds are totally absent from the vital employment sectors thus indicating that the problems of disproportionate underrepresentation of women in high status jobs is not only between men and women but within women as well. In policy terms, women from lower socio-economic backgrounds have to be provided far more educationally purveyed wherewithals to blunt the undulating edges of intra-gender differentiation. To quote Standing :

> It is crucial that development policy-makers and planners realize that the impact of change and policy varies significantly not only by gender

> but also according to sector, region, class and other factors. To be adequately informed, planners require gender-disaggregated data backed by micro-level studies with a gender perspective. Without such an input, employment policies will continue to be gender blind (1992: 75).

Analysis of data pertaining to various categories of occupations in the Indian employment market also shows that women's presence in higher echelon of job market, for instance in administrative and managerial positions, is negligible because jobs in this category require higher level of educational qualifications and skills, and there are not many women with higher level of educational qualifications. The indepth study of women in various levels of education in chapter two clearly highlights this unpleasant truth. In policy terms, adoption of measures only at employment level will not tilt the balance in favour of women, but it has to be initiated at the level of education more vigorously.

CHAPTER FOUR

THE JAGGED HORIZON

PROLOGUE

Social formations of all kinds by nature and character are oppressive of women everywhere and in every sphere. Her aspirations have been the reflected perceptions of men. In fact, the whole process of being a woman has been designed by men. Men have, in many grabs, prescribed laws to regulate the behaviours of women and ascribed attributes specific to 'women'. These realities are not always captured by mere statistical profiles and their analysis. The objective realities could be more systematically and scientifically examined by observing an on-going scenario where men and women emerge as individuals against the background of different light and shade. Here, an attempt has been made to examine the process of how human beings become women and men and what factors and forces contributed, and at whose advantage and disadvantage, to the emergence of the present unbridgeable gap between the two human beings as woman and man.

Here, we have made an effort to outline the contours of the differentiated status of women in the broad socio-economic and political context in the language and expressions of women whom we had encountered in different situations during a couple of days. We have argued that if perception of the process of differentiation is understood in the context of the person, it would be more systematic and provide a relatively real image of the individual reality and its complex web of interrelationships with other individuals.

HARYANA : HER CURTAINED FACE

Haryana is one of the economically developed states in India. Some parts of the state have experienced remarkable economic progress through the green revolution strategy. During autumn and winter seasons, the vast expanse of emareld green wheat and paddy fields in the north-eastern Haryana adds testimoney to its affluence and development. However, all 'Haryanavis' are not equal beneficiaries of this development - some have done well, whilst some have not, and there are many in the latter category.

The green revolution has not only changed the economic status of the beneficiaries, it has also changed the implements and instruments of economic activities. However, this material prosperity has not changed people's motivation and attitudes toward a better social system. It has remained grossly primordial with respect to men's attitude toward women. In the state, the conditions of women have remained subordinate to men, perhaps in almost all the activities. In the following pages, we have attempted to present the experiences of one of our collegues who happened to be in a village in Haryana in 1991. She had stayed with the family (about which we have discussed here) for a few days and had recorded details of her observations and interactions with the family members. While living with this family, she had tried to closely examine the relative status of females within the family in rural India and the perceptions of the family members, particularly of males, about the need for and opportunities available for educating women in the rural society.

One day, in the late March in 1991, on an early morning, I met Farhana (all the names used in this case study are not the real names) again, clad in a *dupatta*, (a long scurf) trailing behind half a dozen goats and one lone she-buffalo going towards the village wheat fields for grazing purpose. The fields were already ladden with golden wheat. The morning mist was curled up above the wheat fields and over the distant hills.

> "You have, it seems, got up so early in the morning?" I asked Farhana.
>
> "What to do! I am not lucky like men to sleep late and then lazily keep smoking *beedi* and *hukka*!" She said, raising her hand and patting her buffalo.
>
> "Why, your husband too went to bed with you, I suppose". I said, "and he slept late after you?"
>
> "He slept late after me?" Farhana cried and grimaced and added, "men are good for nothing, and still think they are almighty."

Farhana used to get up every morning at around 5 a.m. The first thing she did was to clean her yard which kept collecting dust soon after. However, as usual she would sweep it before everyone got up. She was married four years back and was already a mother of two siblings - one girl and a boy - and the boy was the darling of all including the mother and the little sister. Before leaving her bed she made it sure to feed her baby so that it remained restive for a few more hours before she had completed her early morning chores.

"You should have attended school to become a *memsaheb*," I made a pun at Farhana. Farhana gave me a weary look with a weary smile and said, "*memsaheb*, oh, got a husband after so much of try and by so much of money! That too a lazy guy. And to become like you one requires money. Did my parents have any of these enough? And, the school? Who would allow us to attend? Only educated get educated."

Her already crumpled forehead, mated hair, emaciated body and uncleaned and rough hands and bare feet bore enough testimoney to her hard and rough existence, and also explained the fact, like the inevitable dawn, that it was she who made and maintained the "home". And yet, she was not a worker.

"How many members in your house work, Farhana?" I enquired. "Why, only two - my housband and my brother-in-law," she answered casually, and added, "my mother-in-law, sisters-in-law, and myself do not work, yet though we are poor. Working on others' fields or houses is not our custom."

"But then, what you are doing isn't work?" I asked.

"Yes, it is but it is our own work," Farhana tried to explain.

To her, working for wages should only be considered as work. And, working without wages is not considered work in her sense of the term. How close she is to economists and other experts who have defined what is work and what is not! Or, is it the other way round? Do economists follow her perceptions about work? A woman who gets up two-to-three hours before her husband, "the main worker," leaves her bed and begins work, does not think her work as work nor she considers herself a worker. In fact, the existing social and cultural factors constrain women to reveal their rate of participation in the activities on the family farm.

Farhana left her cattle in the grazing meadows near the ripe wheat fields and came back home within an hour to clean the stable and to dump the earlier day's refuse in the dumping ground. Till then, her husband had not left his bed. However, meanwhile her youngest child was already up and her mother-in-law was trying endlessly to get him to sleep again which the naughty child refused by kicking and crying at the top of his voice. His racket had already awoken all the members of the family - 'the little sister', brother-in-law and two sisters-in-law and a dozen poultry birds hiding in a cage-like structure on the other end of the yard.

Farhana, in between her to and fro to the dumping ground, was chiding her boy and urging her mother-in-law to do some household chores. The mother-in-law got up reluctantly. Accompanied by age and malnourishment she had already acquired a bent back. The wrinkle on her flubby face told the hard life she had had since her birth. The life she led was a grinding experience of hard labour that could be easily seen written on her face, rough palms of her 'once upon a time' tender hands. She knew at once what she had to do — needed to extend her helping hands to prepare the frugal morning breakfast of few *chapatis*(bread) and buttermilk. She went to kitchen gingerly and shouted at her daughters who were still lying in bed idly — perhaps too tired to get up easily as 'yesterday' was a hard day like every other day gone by.

One of the daughters, Sakila, got up, and lazily, without any protest. and before washing her face, began to knead wheat floor for making *chapatis*. Meanwhile, the mother-in-law began to wake up the obstinate *chullah* from its slumber, which used to take considerable time to warm up because the fuel they used was not always properly dry. Immediately the tiny kitchen was filled up with smoke and the mother-in-law seemed to cry — her eyes were filled with tears caused by the irritating kitchen smoke. While waking up the *chullah* (woven) she began to curse her fate. God, and everybody else around.

However, she was cautious, else the guest "me" might hear her. I butted in, and passing by the kitchen door wished her 'salam aunty'. She was sweet and courteous enough and offered me a wooden plank to sit near the door and said, "your breakfast will be ready soon. Then, I will take you to other's house to meet some women with whom you can talk about what you want."

I did not come to see her for my breakfast. I was there just to help her and, in between, to talk about her family. She courteously refused my help saying,

> "You have come for a few days. You should not do any work. You are just like my daughter."
>
> "Are we not your daughters", a little voice crept in from the corner of the yard near the kitchen. Sakila, her daughter, teased her mother. The mother was quick to reply.
>
> "You get married, and then come back, I,'ll not allow you to do any work here."
>
> "Then, soon I want to get married", Sakila said naughtily, "and will sleep here atleast upto 10 O'clock when I come back, well."

For a woman marriage is still a must, a paramount and important event in her life and a milestone too. That married life, a life without rest, that it is full of problems and troubles, the conversation between the mother and the daughter clearly proved that point. Sakila would have to come back to her mother to steal a few days of rest after her marriage which was more poignantly portrayed by Farhana's forage through the whole day from one place to another and from one work to another.

Meanwhile, the *chullah* had now fully warmed up and filled the tiny kitchen with white smoke. The smoke cozily curled up moved towards the sky like a fuzzy fox tail.

Farhana had finished half of her cleaning job and washing her hand with the water from a plastic canister badly frayed at the top, lying across the yard, sat down to roll *chapatis.* The mother-in-law baked them while gossiping with me.

Farhana rolled each *chapati* adeptly and kept talking with me.

"Why don't you send your two daughters to school?" I asked the mother-in-law.

> After a pause, she said, "I wanted but the school is not good. Teachers do not teach regularly. Those girls who had attended the school did not continue for long. Our village people also do not like girls going to school with boys. Besides, what they will do with education? They will do the same thing I am doing, Farhana doing. They will go to somebody's house to *collect garbage and clean yard*" (emphasis added).

"Pheer bhi padhai likhai jaruri hai," (still education is necessary) Farhana said with a serious tone.

"Without education even one will not know how to rear ones children. I wanted to have education. My parents and brothers, though had no objection to my going to school, did not encourage me either."

She continued while kept rolling *chapatis* by her two powerful hands and her fully bloomed bosom heaved with a far away loss which she had unduely suffered. May be my presence had reminded her lost childhood which had graduated her to a womanhood deprived of many fundamentals of life which constitute human dignity.

> "I used to send my daughters to school along with my son. But people began rediculing. 'Tumharee ladki kya Indira Gandhi banegi, oh Maluki'! (Maluki, will your daughter become Indira Gandhi). This is how things are in the village. One does not like others well-being and progress."

The mother-in-law said in detail while baking the *chapatis* and keeping the recalcitrant fire alive. By now the eyes of the three of us had become red and "you are 'crying' without a cause," Sakila joked when she came and saw us crowded in the kitchen. By now she had already made up her hair into a bun and her washed face now glowing with youthful smile spread all over her lovely and innocent face, 'the face that soon would be crumpled like her mother by deprivation, want and hard labour,' I pictured in my mind.

> "Bahenji hamare liye kya alag se school khuloge yehan?" (Sister, will you open a separate school for us) Sakila asked me laughingly.
>
> "Why, will you go to the school if it is opened separately?" I asked. "I think I,ll go there, because, nobody will mind us girls going there and if the teachers are also 'madams'!", she added quite confidently.

The mother-in-law was hearing these conversations without any response. I took this opportunity and said ,

> "Mother will you read if somebody comes and teaches you alphabets?"
>
> She laughed and added, "what is the use of teaching me? I'll do what I am doing — cooking, cleaning, grazing, collecting water and fuel, harvesting, winnowing and what not. I will not become '*memsaheb*' any more."

I paused for a moment and thought how the very concept of education had become synonimous with white collar employment in service sector, factories, etc. May be the illiterate mother was right, "one who is educated do not require to wip, clean and cook food that we keep doing here from our puberty." To her, these were drudgery. And to do any work of drugery one obviously, according to her, might not require any education. In other words, to her perception, if education did not raise quality of human life both in material and spiritual sense then what for education was required. She was logical as far as the existential situation in which she was caught.

By now, breakfast was ready. Farhana packed some *chapatis* and some *achar* (condiments) to be taken to the field for lunch for themselves. She then called one by one and gave them their share. At last she gulped a hot cup of tea and a few *chapatis* while kept feeding her baby son, the apple of every one's eye in the house. During her preparation of breakfast, the child had his best of times. It had gobbled a good deal of mud and muddied himself profusely with mud and dust in the yard. Farhana used her hand vigorously to shed some of it and the baby got filled up with more dust.

Sakila got angry. "Had you been educated, you would have learned some manners and would not have shed dust here like an 'unpadh'," (illiterate) she shouted at her.

"Will you keep quiet? I'll see how you behave when you are educated," Farhana said mockingly.

The mother-in-law kept smiling. Might be she was a little bit embarassed by my presence. However, Sakila did not mind. She knew me for sometime and was already informal with me.

The conversations of Sakila and her sister-in-law Farhana outline a point clearly : education is a must for bringing up children and for "good manners." Then, why have they, especially women, been deprived of ? Who are responsbile? What factors are making whom responsible and why?

During our breakfast in the kitchen Farhana's husband Abdulla coughed noisely outside their bed room. Perhaps, he was trying to make it felt to his wife that he had awaken and required breakfast.

"Rakhu, bring some fire from the kitchen," Farhana's husband asked his daughter mildly.

Rakhu was too busy to hear him. She was playing with her little brother and half a dozen other kids from the neighbourhood.

"What happened?" Abdulla asked with a raised voice. However, Sakila, his sister, fetched him the fire. She brought a paleful of fire for her brother to light his *hukka* for the morning smoke.

Sakila left the pale of fire near her brother who lighted his *hukka* gingerly. It seemed he hadn't yet got rid of his bed time laziness. And March was a marvellous month. Spring had already set in. Wheat fields were golden and swaying rythmically from one side to another creating lyrical pattern on the fields and of course in the minds of the farmers. The weather was langurous. The sun did not rise yet up much ahead of their *neem tree* (azadirachta indica). Its golden rays seemed to create a pattern on their cleaned and well spruced up yard by the deft hand of Farhana, reflecting through the leaves of the neem tree standing elegantly on one side of the yard. Abdulla was smoking with a casual look and sometimes closing his eyes slowly taking a mouthful of steam swathed with water vapour and emitting smoke from the corner of his lips in a curl covering his weather bitten hard face with a weeklong growth of stubs. While he was smoking Farhana brought his breakfast on the *charpoy* (cot).

"Just I'll eat," he said without even looking at Farhana. Farhana did not say anything. She kept the water tumbler near him and disappeared.

I left the kitchen and slowly came to Abdulla and sat near him wishing him a "good morning" loudly. He responded smilingly. I was happy to catch him in a happy and carefree mood. Straight away I asked him, "Abdulla Bhai, tell me why don't the girls in your village study? I could not understand, why? Although there is a school in the village established 30 years ago. How come not a single girl has even passed matriculation?"

Abdulla took a deep breath and thought for a while and then asked his mother to bring some more breakfast for me. "I had already," I told him.

"You see," Abdulla began haltingly, "we are not against sending our children, especially our girl children to school. The problem is that they hardly learn anything in the school. The teachers are mostly absent. When they are there, they do not mind whether children come to school or not."

"I agree with you, but then, why boys do not stop going to school?" I asked.

Abdulla was not prepared for my sudden question. He was a bit confused and there was more to what he said about not sending girls to school. After a pause, he was, however, forthcoming.

"Sometimes we do not also understand the value of education. Some people think that there is hardly any use in educating a girl because, after marriage, they would go to others' households. That is why people mostly take girls' education very casually. "I want that my sisters and daughters should get education, at least upto eighth class. But, unfortunately they are not interested," Abdulla said very nonchalantly.

Our conversations could be heard in other rooms and kitchen. By now, the eldest of the two sisters, Sabina had got up and was doing some work near the kitchen, probaly washing some linen. She overheard our conversations and said straight from there.

"We want to go to school but who will look after our work? Besides, what we learn at school that is to be repeated at home as well. We do not have anybody to help us at home with our problems."

"Why, what do the teachers do?" I asked.

> "They hardly care whether you learn or not. They come, take attendance and repeat something from a book and the class is over in a jiffy. That is what happens in the classroom," Sabina said in a haste and with a little disgust.

"Here lies the problem," Abdulla said, nodding his head, with a gleam in eyes. I understood there is something hidden between the lines of these conversations. Something or certain things which Abdulla, the head of the household and the young patriarch, did not want to talk about, and still there were certain things which his sister did not like or had no audacity to talk to an outsider.

The sun was already up. Farhana who had disappeared meanwhile returned and was preparing to leave for the field with her sisters-in-law, instructing her mother-in-law when to come and with 'what'. The husband was ready to go to his work in the nearby market where he had opened a small '*kokha*' (small roadside shop) to sell some plastic items and assortment of other articles. He took his bicycle and rode off towards the main road leading to the market without exchanging any word.

I requested Farhana and her sisters if I could accompany them to the field. They readily agreed and became pleasantly surprised knowing my intention. The moment Abdulla left, a new atmosphere seemed to have made appearance in the house. Everybody immediately became boisterous and gay. Farhana had her scurf off and the sisters were no more coy and shy. They had instantly given up their '*tehzib*' (culturally induced behaviour).

> "If you work half a day in the field under sun, you will forget your school and a,b,c, altogether. And, if you have goats to look after, then everything is over. Your time will not be yours, I say." Farhana added noisely looking at me.

How rigorous a woman's life was that was what Farhana wanted to depict for me to understand her brutal existence - the existence which brook no sympathy and romantic dream of an urban '*memsaheb*'.

> "Men do not like our going to school, because who will do their work and bake their *chappatis*," Sabina added quietly.

> "I wanted to become a teacher but see what sort of a teacher I am going to become. I have already got my bhabi's two children and our half a dozen goats to teach them not to eat mud, not to stray into others fields!". Sabina recounted laughingly and shouted at one of her companions, "hey! look, your's is coming."

She meant that her companion's husband was coming. In the village it is still a news, especially for a newly married girl, the arrival of her husband, if he happens to belong to other village.

Together we proceeded towards the ripe wheatfield. The day's tasks were to prepare the threshing ground, collect fodder for the cattle, water and irrigate vegetable patches and collect fuel from the field. Trees were all shaved of their branches for fuel. Most of the available land had been brought under cultivation. There was no more any fallow land left. Cultivation of food crops had denunded the land all of its fragile forest cover. Yet, nobody seemed to realise the gravity of the situation. For women, the emergence of this situation had added doubly to their miseries. To collect fuel they had to travel two to three kms. from their homes to the nearby foothills where only acacia bushes thrived. It was also getting depeleted by merciless cutting. Fodder was not easily available either. Foraging from one field to another, one might collect some green fodder for the cattle. Water was also a highly scarce commodity. The village ponds go dry before the summer sets in. The women have to go to distant sites of deep tubewell to fetch water.

We reached soon the site where, within few days, the ripe wheat would be collected and thrashed by machines. Mostly women would do this threshing by indigenous threshers. The machines were not very safe. Some women had lost their hands in those unsafe and hideous looking machines.

After a few minutes rest, Farhana began to make the land plain by her spade. Several others followed, and within three hours the ground was smooth, spick and span.

"Please, come under the shade of the tree and have some rest," I requested Farhana and their collegues.

They all laughed in unison and soon came near the tree and one of them asked me if I could give her a *bidi*? Since I did not smoke, I said, "sorry, I was not knowing it earlier." Farhana took from a tin box several *bidies* and distributed among her collegues.

"Sorry, I hope you do not mind us smoking," she said very apologetically. I nodded and added, "I don't mind."

"Bahenji, now see for yourself, why we do not go to school. Do these works allow us? Are we left with any energy?" Sakila asked me rather sympathetically.

All she wanted to mean was that it was their work which did not allow them enough time to pursue education. Of course, I realised. The much advertised green revolution, introduction of new technology in agriculture and integrated rural development programmes seemed to have done little or nothing to alleviate the deprived conditions of women. In certain cases, it had compounded their problems. The so-called economic development has not emancipated her to any extent. In marginal and small farming households, the women have been doubly burdened, because they are neither well off enough to hire in "other women" as their well off sisters belonging to urban and rural households do.

This is especially true in the marginal and small agricultural households where the husbands happen to work in others' field as wage labourers or work in urban areas as factory workers, as now many do if the industrial areas are near the villages. In such households children are badly neglected. When parents are out for work, the children if not grown-up, either accompany them or remain behind in the care of the grandmothers. The dire economic conditions hardly allow their children to attend school. Girl children remain more neglected than the male children. Both poverty and social traditions and antipathy conspire against girls' development endeavour. The wife also becomes an appendage in the process of existence. Despite her grim struggle she hardly had any individuality of her own. Beauvoir clearly highlights these points in the following terms:

> To 'catch' a husband is an art; to 'hold' is a job and the one which has great competence is called for. A wise sister said to a peevish wife : 'be careful, making scenes with Marcel is going to cost you your job'. What is at stake is extremely serious - material and moral security, a home of one's own, the dignity of wifehood, a more or less satisfactory substitute for love and happiness. A wife soon learns that her erotic attractiveness is weakest of her weapons; it disappears with familiarity; and alas, there are other desirable women all around. Still she endeavours to make herself seductive, to please; she is often torn between the pride that inclines her toward frigidity and the hope that her sensual ardour will flatter her husband and endear her to him. She also counts on force of habit, on the charm of a pleasant abode, his liking for good food, his affection for his children; she makes an effort to 'do him credit' by the way she entertains and dresses, and she tries to influence him by her advice and counsel; in so far as she can, she will make herself indispensable to his social success and to his work (1974: 523).

Farhana may not be articulate enough but she, the wife of a small farmer, nevertheless, remained a shadow of her husband, the master. The master's decisions on every thing only mattered.

Under the spray shadow of the *babul* (acacia arabica) tree I posed again another question to Farhana, "do you think that your husband really is in favour of women's education?" Farhana looked up for a while confused, and rather grimly concluded :

> "No man likes a woman equal to him. It becomes a question of his dignity. And, an educated woman would not accept his right or wrong demand so easily. Man knows for sure that education will open women's eyes. Opening women's eyes is not what he wishes".

Everybody present there echoed the same feeling as Farhana did. Sabina equipped, "educated girl means educated boy for marriage, and an educated boy now costs more. Can we afford it?"

Today, education is not a value free activity and it was never. Education plays a dialectical role in a possessor's life. It may liberate her/him or may enchain her/him and could vitiate social conditions more damagingly.

It was now beyond high noon. The sun had already dimmed. The shadow of the tree was stretching towards east, as if trying to run away from the sun. Farhana and her companions finished their lunch and began to plan about three more tasks that were yet to be completed — irrigating the miniature vegetable patch, collecting fodder and some fuel. Sooner than later they all dispersed in different directions. Sabina left with other girls of her age towards hills to collect thorny fuel in the sparse acacia bush while Sakila with scythe in her hand went to wheat fields to collect some green fodder for the cattle.

Farhana was left to water the miniature vegetable patch where she had planted some tomato and brinjal plants and green paper. Some of them were still bearing fruits. They looked as starved and undernourished as our Farhana and her collegues. Meanwhile, the mother-in-law landed — Farhana's son needed feeding. The child seeing his mother cried more to attract her attention. Farhana left her vegetable patch for a while to feed her baby. The rest of the work was completed by the mother-in-law. She also picked some vegetables and green chillies for preparing dinner.

By now, the sun had disappeared beyond the skyline dotted by the barren Aravalli hills spraying all over the western horizon its departing crimson glow. Some scattered clouds were floating across the already greyish pale blue departing March evening sky. Crows were noisely making felt their return to the village trees from every directions and heralding that dark was falling. Of course, the shadows of the trees had already lengthened enough to remind us to leave for home. Sabina, Sakila and their collegues slowly meandered towards home with their collections of fuel and fodder bundles on their heads. Followed them their cattle blowing clouds of fine dust on their way which curled up against the sky in a myriad pattern.

"Let us go home," Farhana asked her mother-in-law and me and we briskly made a move towards home. Coming back home Farhana splashed a few handful of water on her scorched face and smiled radiantly in the departing evening glow of the spring twilight.

> "Now, you sit for a while on this *charpoy*. I'll make some tea and we all will drink together before getting down to cook the evening meal," Farhana said in a business like manner and pulled a dust-ladden *charpoy* for us to sit. Since 5 O' clock in the morning she had been working and it was now already 7.30 p.m. She worked without rest. "This daily grind has no doubt hardened her physical constitution but what has happened to her spiritual constitution!" I pondered.

Women's liberation, emancipation seemed such a big myth devoid of meaning for Farhana and for her sisters-in-law. Still the basic opportunity like, education and health care are far cry for woman like her. First, there is no time to pursue education. Second, the poverty is of such magnitude that it does not allow them to avail any facility which is ostensibly propagated to be meant exclusively for them. Lewis very scientifically highlights this point :

> The culture of poverty is both an adaptation and a reaction of the poor to their marginal position in a class stratified, high individuated, capitalist society. It represents an effrot to cope with feelings of hopelessness and despair which develop from the realization of the improbability of achieving success in terms of values and goals of the larger society. Indeed, many of the traits of the culture of poverty can be viewed as attempts at local solutions for problems not met by existing institutions and agencies because the people are not eligible for them, cannot afford them, or are ignorant or suspicious of them. For example, unable to obtain credit from banks, they are thrown upon their own resources and organize informal credit devices without interest (1966: 49-50).

Farhana swiftly made tea and giving others first, she then gulped it down quickly and disappeared for a while. Within half an hour she appeared with her cows and the buffalo which she had taken out early in the morning.

Like a wizard Farhana first gave water to her quadrupeds and gave them hay sparsely sprinkled with some green grass which Sabina had brought from the field. On the background some hens clucked to attract her attention for their supper. Farhana attended them too and gave them their due evening supper. By now, it was quite dark. Night was slowly spreading its dark raiment and after sometime enveloped everything. Here and there some electric bulbs on the street poles were dangling, surrounded by hosts of insects and emitting lifeless light. Haryana has provided every village with electricity. That may be true. But what is not true is that many houses have not electric connections. Farhana's house was, of course, one of such houses. She had two kerosene oil lamps which were enough for her to ward off the darkness. One was dimply burning in the kitchen and another was in the veranda of her main room where her daughter was engaged in writing something on a broken slate with a small piece of chalk.

By now, her hens had become quiet, the cows and the buffalo were ruminating. Only occasionaly the bleating of a goat could be heard from the enclosure. Hearing this the mother-in-law reprimanded and the goat stopped bleating and the one who was making trouble probably understood her displeasure.

"Rakhu don't waste your time and read something loudly, and ask your aunty if there is any difficulty."

Farhana mildly shouted at her daughter who was supposed to learn her alphabets in Hindi. Of course, her mother wanted her to learn English alphabets too, and she had brought one two rupee priced English-Hindi book for her from the bus by which she was travelling one day from her mother's house to her husband's. One would not fail to notice that in many buses hawkers would be saying sonorously that they were selling 'such books' for learning English, that, one would be conversant in the language in no time. English is still a craze and necessity. It was reflected in Farhana's effort to teach her daughter the language. Farhana lived in a family characterised by conservative attitudes and outlooks. Still then there was a world where availability of certain things was dependent on certain other complementary achievements and this was not beyond her perceptions.

"Mummy, I don't understand this," a tiny voice floated and once again Farhana asked her daughter, "ask aunty."

Farhana's daughter Rakhu slowly came near eyeing me intently and suspiciously. That was her close encounter with me. In one hand she was holding the kerosene oil lamp and in another one the broken slate and the dilapidated book bought by her mother. She looked beautiful and mysterious in the shadow of light and darkness. Her eyes were her mother's.

Her tiny hands were exact miniature replica of her mother's too. I gently asked her to sit down and slowly taught her how to pronounce English alphabets. Farhana's ears were towards us. Her motherly mind was perhaps ladden with a beautiful dream for her beloved daughter. She probably did not want a life for her daughter like her. Off and on during cooking, she kept repeating to her daughter "Rakhu, ask aunty what you don't know. Don't shy away. Shy children don't learn anything, do you hear?"

It was now 9.30 p.m. when Farhana's husband came back. He left his bicycle and smoking a *bidi* went away to meet somebody in the neighbourhood.

"Come soon," Farhana said to her husband, "food is ready." However, her husband did not reply nor he came back within another half an hour's time. She called me and asked me to take food with her sisters-in-law and daughter. The wife and the mother did not eat and waited for Abdulla to return back from the neighbourhood.

Farhana's life was an unending grind which revolved around 'work'. And still she did not consider herself a worker. She did not get education. She could not afford now the luxury either. Where was the "time and money?" Today, for millions of Farhanas, education is a distant dream and so it is for their children. She is the victim of both her own perception that she is a woman and the purposes and prejudices of man that she is after all a 'woman'. The horizon of her hope and aspiration is jagged and blurred in the mist of doubt and paradoxes.

CHAPTER FIVE

GREY STREAKS IN SYLVAN SURROUNDING

PROLOGUE

In order to outline the gap between the participation of females and males in education and employment a primary survey with a structured household survey schedule was conducted in some villages in three different states of India during 1990-91. We have made an effort to present a picture of representation of women and men at different levels of education and in different occupations according to the age group of the members of the surveyed households. Analyses of data from two villages and a cluster of villages have been presented here separately to show inter-state variations, if any, in the pattern of educational attainment of both females and males and their representation patterns in different occupations in specific age groups.

HARYANA

The Village : The village Harsaru is located at a distance of 30 kms. from Delhi and 7 kms. from the district headquarters, Gurgaon, and it is also the nearest town. An all weather road connects the village with Gurgaon town and the usual modes of conveyances are buses and other automobilies. Not much is known about the begining of the village. However, it is presumed by the villagers that about 250 years ago the village came into being as a sub-village ('dhani' in local parlence). The village is a self-contained entity though it is linked with other villages in the neighbourhood, socio-economically and culturally. Its inhabitants have a strong sense of belonging to this entity and thus it is a distinct though not an isolated village.

This village, like any other village in the state, represents fairly a typical example of the surrounding rural community. The village is inhabited by 223 rural households. The households represent a number of castes - Brahmin, Rajput and Scheduled Castes. The village bears all the characteristics of a heterogeneous society within a homogenous physical framework. According to 1981 census, the total number of population of the village was 1161 which included 398 Scheduled Caste population.

The comparative prosperity of the village could be found largely stamped on the white-washed village walls, T.V. antenae, tractors and electric poles. The village sky-line is criss-crossed by electric wires, and recorded music emanating from many houses could be heard everywhere. The village does not boast much of greenery — blonde eucalyptus trees could be frilling in the air everywhere nonchallantly with a look of disdain on their faces. *Acacia* is growing in gay abandon. It has made its home comfortable in almost every nook and corner of the village.

The agricultural land is cultivated no more with animal labour. Sturdy tractors could be found ploughing and preparing the land. Tubewells dot the fields. Those who now cultivate land are not cultivators like their forefathers. They are 'modern' and 'literate' and all of them invariably wear western-style clothes, and they are all men. They show the sign of apparent change in outlook and attaire.

But the other side of the picture is primordial : women still live and work hiding in veil. Though many things 'modern' perhaps have been creating stir in their hearts, on the surface the signs are remote and oppressed. The technological innovations have also not been directed towards their liberation, for technology is still a male chauvinist creature.

The village has school upto eighth grade. Boys usually dominate. Girls are few. The traditional social attitudes still hold sway. The apparent modernity of material man has not yet become liberated spiritual human. The wizardy of science seems to have failed to loosen the intricate mental complex of human mind. The criss-crossed eletric wires light many dark corners of the village romantically, but it has not enlightened eerie silence of ignorance in men about women.

Our study of the two aspects of the village — education and employment profiles of both males and females in various age groups — is an attempt to highlight the differentiations that exist. Our purpose is to show how the differentiated status in educational scenario is reflected in their employment status.

Educational Profile : The village Harsaru though economically prosperous was educationally backward. Our survey of 111 households of the village in 1991 revealed that out of a total population of 692 in different age groups, there were 157 illiterates which constituted 22.69 per cent. The percentage share of female illiterates was 70.7, more than double the percentage share of their male counterparts (see Table 5.1). The number of persons having education below primary level was 106 which was 15.32

per cent of the total population. The number of females who were literates but below primary level was 55. The percentage of females to the total population in this category was 51.89. In 1991, there were only 36 persons in the surveyed households having education upto the primary level, out of which the number of females was 17 (47.3 per cent).

The number of persons who had education upto primary level but below middle level was 37 only. In this educational status group the number of females was 13 which constituted 35.2 per cent of the total persons having education upto this level. The number of persons who had education upto middle level was 95, out of which the number of females was 33 (34.8 per cent).

Table 5.1 : **Educational profile of males and females of surveyed households in village Harsaru, Haryana, 1991**

Educational level		Males	Females	Total	% of males	% of females
Illiterate		56	111	157	29.3	70.7
Class	I	15	20	35	42.8	57.2
	II	13	15	28	46.4	53.6
	III	09	09	18	50.0	50.0
	IV	14	11	25	56.0	44.0
	V	23	34	57	40.3	58.7
	VI	19	17	36	52.7	47.3
	VII	24	13	37	64.8	35.2
	VIII	62	33	95	65.2	34.8
	IX	27	03	30	90.0	10.0
	X	73	24	97	75.2	24.8
	XI	16	03	19	84.2	15.8
	XII	21	05	26	80.7	19.3
Graduate		23	04	27	85.1	14.9
Post-Graduate		4	01	05	80.0	20.0
Total		389	303	692		

It can be seen in Table 5.1 that the number of persons who had education upto middle level but below matriculation (i.e. upto class X) was only 30 which included only 3 females, their percentage share was only 10.

Similarly, out of the total of 97 persons having education upto high school level, there were only 24 females, less than one-fourth of the total matriculates.

Moreover, the total number of persons who were matriculates but below pre-degree level was 19 which included 3 females (15.8 per cent). In this year, there were only 26 persons having education upto 12th standard. This included 5 females who constituted only 19.3 per cent of the total persons in this category.

Out of the total population of 692 of the surveyed households, the number of graduates was 27 which included 4 females (14.9 per cent). Besides, in this village, there were only 4 males and one female having education upto post-graduation level in 1991. (see Table 5.1)

The analysis of the educational status of population of the surveyed households thus reveals two important aspects of sex disparity in education. First, the number of illiterate women was relatively very high. The relative share of girls who had education upto primary level or below was nearly fifty per cent. Second, beyond the primary level, the rate of participation of girls and women at each higher level of education - i.e. high school, pre-degree, graduation and post-graduation - used to be relatively less and less. Thus, given the improved economic status of the surveyed households in the village, poverty was not the major reason of non-participation of girls and women in education. The main factors explaining the existence of wide disparity between the levels of educational status of males and females could be found embedded within the family. The relative sex roles assigned to girls and women and the social customs and traditions were acting as major impediments constraining girls and women to participate in the school sector. However, the lack of schooling facilities of the type which would suit the requirements of girl students was, to some extent, responsible for their relative low educational status.

Occupational Profile : The level of participation of girls and women in various occupations was not very high in the village Harsaru either in 1991. Out of a total of 260 persons of the surveyed households participating in different occupations, the number of women was only 57 (i.e. 21.92 per cent), slightly more than one-fifth of the total number of males (see Table 5.2). In this village, the number of agricultural labourers in the surveyed households was 51 which included 2 females in 1991. The percentage share of the agricultural labourers in the total working population in the village was 19.62 and within this category of workers the percentage of female agricultural labourers was only 4.0. The number of persons having cultivation as their main occupation was 21 and all of them were males. However, a large number of women were engaged in household activities. In 1991, there were 71 household workers in the village out of which 50 were females who constituted 70.4 per cent of the total workers in this category. A total of 4 males were engaged in trade - i.e. they were village shopkeepers. In the category of skilled workers, there were only 27 males and 2 females in the village in 1991.

However, the number of persons employed in the service sector was the highest compared to the number of persons engaged in any other type of occupation in this village. Out of a total of 74 persons employed in the service sector, 6 (8.11 per cent) and 68 (91.89 per cent) were employed in public sector and private sector jobs. But, there was only one female working in the private sector as an office worker.

Table 5.2 : **Occupational status of males and females of surveyed households in village Harsaru, Haryana, 1991**

Occupational status	Males	Females	Total	% of males	% of females
Agricultural Labourers	49	02	51	96.0	4.0
Skilled Workers	27	02	29	93.2	6.8
Household Workers	21	50	71	29.6	70.4
Shopkeepers	04	-	4	100.0	-
Cultivators	21	-	21	100.00	-
Office Workers (Govt.)	06	-	6	100.00	-
Office Workers (Pvt.)	67	01	68	98.5	1.5
School Teachers	02	02	4	50.0	50.0
College Teachers	01	-	1	100.0	-
Commissioned Officers	03	-	3	100.0	-
Non-Commissioned Officers	01	-	1	100.0	-
Professionals (Doctors, Engineers, Lawyers, etc.)	01	-	1	100.0	-
Total	203	57	260	78.08	21.92

The participation rates of both males and females in the education sector as teachers were too low in 1991. In this village 5 persons were employed as teachers, out of which one male was a college teacher and 4 were school teachers. The number of female school teachers was 2. Similarly, there was only one male who was a professional in this village and the total number of commissioned and non-commissioned officers was 4 which did not include any female. Thus, the largest number of persons were employed in the service sector followed by household workers (who are not paid), agricultural labourers, skilled workers and teachers. The relative numbers of persons engaged in other types of occupations were marginal. Out of the twelve occupational categories, females were participating in only 5 occupations namely agricultural labour activities, skilled work, household work, office work in the private sector and teaching. Except the household sector, the representation of women in any other occupation was almost insignificant. The relative educational status of women in this village was clearly reflected in the distributional pattern of women across various occupations. Women and girls were virtually absent in occupations requiring certified educational achievements. Moreover, it should be noted here that most of the women in this village were engaged in agricultural activities in their own family farms. However, as they were not being paid for their labour input in their own family farms, they did not consider themselves as workers.

UTTAR PRADESH

The Village : The village Khaila is located in the periphery of Delhi - i.e. some 15 kms.away from the boarder of the Union Territory. This is an economically prosperous village in Meerut district in Uttar Pradesh. In 1991, total number of households in this village was 198. According to our census survey in 1991, the total population of the village Khaila was 1,181, out of which 678 were males and 503 were females. Most of the households in the village are engaged in agricultural and other related activities. Some of the households also earn a substantial amount of their total annual income from horticulture. This village is relatively advanced in the sense that it has some of the basic physical and educational facilities. There is a co-educational school having classes upto 8th standard in the village. The high school is situated less than 1 km. away from the village and the nearest college is 7 kms. away from it. Though the village is economically advanced, the socio- cultural forces operating within it are not favourable for the overall development of girls, particularly their relative educational development.

Educational Profile : The village Khaila, though located in the urban periphery and in the 'green revolution belt' which implies a developed agricultural sector, the perceptions and attitudes of the village towards girls' education are still traditional and discriminatory. The statement is well supported by the primary data on educational and occupational status of girls and women in Khaila collected by us in 1991.

Analysis of data on the educational status of males and females in the village Khaila reveals that, in 1991, out of a total population of 1,009 in the age group 6 & above, there were 390 illiterates which included 235 females and 155 males. The percentage of illiterate females to total illiterates in the village was 60.26. In the age group 0-6, there were 141 illiterates out of which 76 were females. However, most of the illiterate females were concentrated in the age group 18 and above (see Table 5.3). In this village, the number of persons in the age group 6 and above who were literates but below primary level was 165, out of which the number of females was 70 (42.42 per cent). It should be noted here that, most of the persons having education below primary level were concentrated in the age group 6 to 11. So far as the primary level of education was concerned, there was not much difference between the educational achievements of males and females in this village. In 1991, there were 46 males and 45 females who had education upto the primary level (see Table 5.3).

The number of persons who had education above the primary level but below the middle level was 23 in the village. The percentage of females having this level of education was only 35.29 in 1991. Moreover, most of such females (66.7 per cent) were found in the younger age group of 11 to 14. Similarly, in the village, there were a total of 37 persons who had education upto the middle level. Out of this total, the number of females was only 7(i.e. 18.92 per cent).

In 1991, out of a total of 173 persons in the village who had education above the middle level but below high school level, the number of females was only 27 (i.e. 15.61 per cent). In the same year, the number of females who were matriculates was only 13 out of a total of 58 such persons in the village. the percentage of female matriculates was 22.41. In this village, there was only one female having education above the high school level but below the higher secondary level. Besides, there were 5 females out of a total of 28 persons in the village who had education upto higher secondary level. In higher education, the participation rate of females was almost marginal. The number of females having education upto graduate and post-graduate levels were only one and two respectively in 1991. Thus, the above analysis clearly reveals the relatively low educational status of girls and women in village Khaila, particularly at higher levels of education.

Occupational Profile : In the village Khaila, the rate of workforce participation of females was very low, especially in the wage employments. In 1991, out of a total of 1,009 persons, including children, participating in various on-farm and off-farm activities, the total number of females was 412 which was 40.83 per cent of the total. However, it should be noted here that more than fifty per cent of working females in this village were engaged in the household chores, though they also worked in their family farms which they did not consider as employment. Moreover, females in this village were not at all participating in occupations such as small trading, .business and government jobs and their representation in the skilled jobs, jobs in the private enterprises and in teaching was almost marginal (see Table 5.4).

The percentage share of females in the on-farm paid activities was only 28.57 as agricultural labourers and 14.76 as cultivators. So far as the off-farm employment was concerned, except the household occupation, the number of females engaged in skilled jobs, private office jobs and teaching were one, three and one respectively. Thus, almost all the females in this village were engaged in both on-and off-farm employments, they were not considering themselves as workers, except the few who had paid jobs.

WEST BENGAL

The Villages : In order to study educational and employment profiles of households belonging to various size-classes of landholding from a cluster of three villages 100 households were identified in 1991 and these 100 households consisted 20 households from each size-class of holding, namely, landless households, households belonging to marginal, small, semi-medium and medium size-classes. Thus, a total of hundred households were surveyed through structured schedules to elicit various informations with particular focus on education and employment.

All the villages are contiguous and geo-physically located in the same setting. The villages are located in Bongaon sub-division of district 24 Parganas (North) in West Bengal and the villages are namely, Bagdaha, Patkelgacha and Mosyampur. The village Bagdaha is connected by an all weather road and the other two villages are connected by unpaved approach roads. During rainy season, communication with these villages become acutely difficult. All the villages are served by a higher secondary school. Besides, each village is provided with a primary school.

People belonging to various social classes inhabit in these villages. Agriculture is the mainstay, though a considerable number of people are engaged in business and trade.

Table 5.3 : Age-wise and sex-wise distribution of educational status in village Khaila, Uttar Pradesh, 1991

Age group	Illiterate		Below primary (Classes I-IV)		Primary (Class-V)		Below middle (Classes VI)		Middle (Class VIII)		Below matric (Classes VIII-IX)	
	M	F	M	F	M	F	M	F	M	F	M	F
(1)	(2)	(3)	(4)	(5)	(6)	(7)	(8)	(9)	(10)	(11)	(12)	(13)
0-6	65 (29.6)	76 (24.4)	16 (14.4)	15 (17.6)	-	-	-	-	-	-	-	-
6-11	16 (7.3)	15 (4.8)	62 (55.9)	42 (49.4)	9 (19.6)	12 (26.7)	-	-	-	-	-	-
11-14	6 (2.7)	9 (2.9)	11 (9.9)	9 (10.6)	10 (21.7)	12 (26.7)	6 (35.3)	4 (66.7)	9 (30.0)	4 (57.1)	17 (11.6)	5 (18.5)
14-18	3 (1.4)	19 (6.1)	4 (3.6)	8 (9.4)	6 (13.0)	3 (6.7)	2 (11.8)	-	11 (36.7)	1 (14.3)	23 (15.8)	9 (33.3)
18-25	19 (8.6)	40 (12.9)	2 (1.8)	6 (7.1)	6 (13.0)	7 (15.6)	2 (11.8)	-	8 (26.7)	2 (28.6)	40 (27.4)	4 (14.8)
25-35	12 (5.5)	53 (17.0)	1 (0.9)	2 (2.4)	-	5 (11.1)	5 (29.4)	-	1 (3.3)	-	35 (4.0)	6 (22.2)
35-55	48 (21.8)	58 (18.6)	10 (9.0)	3 (3.5)	8 (17.4)	5 (11.1)	2 (11.8)	2 (33.3)	1 (3.3)	-	22 (5.1)	3 (11.2)
55 and above	51 (23.2)	41 (13.2)	5 (4.5)	-	7 (15.2)	1 (2.2)	-	-	-	-	9 (6.2)	-
Total	220 (100.0)	311 (100.0)	111 (100.0)	85 (100.0)	46 (100.0)	45 (100.0)	17 (100.0)	6 (100.0)	30 (100.0)	7 (100.0)	146 (100.0)	27 (100.0)

Note : Figures in paranthesis show percentages to total.

Contd..

Matric (Class-X)		Below higher secondary (Class-XI)		Higher secondary (Class XII)		Graduate		Post-graduate		Population		
M	F	M	F	M	F	M	F	M	F	M	F	Total
(14)	(15)	(16)	(17)	(18)	(19)	(20)	(21)	(22)	(23)	(24)	(25)	(26)
-	-	-	-	-	-	-	-	-	-	81	91	172
-	-	-	-	-	-	-	-	-	-	87	69	156
-	-	-	-	-	-	-	-	-	-	59	43	102
14 (31.1)	7 (53.8)	5 (35.7)	1 (100.0)	3 (13.0)	4 (80.0)	-	-	-	-	71	52	123
9 (20.0)	-	7 (50.0)	-	9 (39.1)	-	7 (43.8)	1 (100.0)	2 (50.0)	1	111	61	172
9 (20.0)	6 (38.5)	1 (7.1)	-	11 (47.8)	1 (20.0)	8 (50.0)	-	6 (60.0)	1 (50.0)	89	73	162
8 (17.8)	1 (7.8)	1 (7.1)	-	-	-	-	-	2 (20.0)	-	104	72	176
5 (11.1)	-	-	-	-	-	1 (6.25)	-	-	-	78	42	120
45 (100.0)	13 (100.0)	14 (100.0)	1 (100.0)	23 (100.0)	5 (100.0)	15 (100.0)	1 (100.0)	10 (100.0)	2	678	503	1181

Table 5.4 : Age-wise occupational status of males and females in village Khaila, Uttar Pradesh, 1991

Age group	Agriculture labourers		Skilled workers		Household workers		Shopkeepers		Cultivators	
	M	F	M	F	M	F	M	F	M	F
(1)	(2)	(3)	(4)	(5)	(6)	(7)	(8)	(9)	(10)	(11)
6-11	8 (8.0)	7 (17.5)	-	-	1 (4.5)	4 (1.6)	-	-	2 (1.1)	-
11-14	6 (6.0)	4 (10.0)	-	-	3 (13.6)	7 (2.9)	-	-	5 (2.8)	1 (3.2)
14-18	13 (13.0)	7 (17.5)	2 (9.5)	1 (100.0)	-	23 (9.5)	1 (5.1)	-	11 (6.1)	1 (3.2)
18-25	27 (27.0)	8 (20.0)	4 (19.1)	-	4 (18.0)	58 (23.9)	3 (15.8)	-	21 (11.7)	5 (16.1)
25-35	16 (16.0)	3 (7.5)	8 (38.1)	-	7 (31.8)	52 (21.4)	5 (26.3)	-	32 (17.9)	6 (19.1)
35-55	18 (18.0)	11 (27.5)	6 (28.6)	-	3 (13.6)	68 (28.0)	8 (42.1)	-	62 (34.6)	15 (48.1)
55 and above	12 (12.0)	-	1 (4.8)	-	4 (18.0)	31 (12.8)	2 (10.5)	-	46 (25.7)	3 (9.7)
Total	100 (100.0)	40 (100.0)	21 (100.0)	1 (100.0)	22 (100.0)	243 (100.0)	19 (100.0)	- (0.0)	179 (100.0)	31 (100.0)

Note : Figures in paranthesis show percentages to total.

Contd..

Business men		Govt. office workers		Private office workers		School teachers		Total population		
M	F	M	F	M	F	M	F	M	F	Total
(12)	(13)	(14)	(15)	(16)	(17)	(18)	(19)	(20)	(21)	(22)
1	-	-	-	-	-	-	-	87	69	156
-	-	-	-	-	-	-	-	59	43	102
-	-	4 (12.9)	-	1 (3.2)	-	-	-	71	52	123
11 (55.0)	-	8 (25.8)	-	14 (45.2)	-	2 (50.0)	-	111	61	172
4 (20.0)	-	9 (29.0)	-	9 (29.0)	1 (33.3)	1 (25.0)	-	89	73	162
3 (15.0)	-	9 (29.0)	-	4 (12.9)	2 (66.7)	1 (25.0)	-	102	72	176
1 (5.0)	-	1 (3.2)	-	3 (9.7)	-	-	1 (100.0)	78	42	120
20 (100.0)	- (0.0)	31 (100.0)	- (0.0)	31 (100.0)	3 (100.0)	4 (100.0)	1 (100.0)	597	412	1009

Educational Profile : The villages surveyed were relatively economically developed. In 1991, the total population of surveyed households was 574, out of which 295 were males and 279 were females. Most of the households (i.e. 60 per cent) were either landless or marginal or small land holders. A survey conducted in 1991 revealed some aspects of glaring inequality in educational status of the various groups in these villages.

At the time of the survey, out of a total of 574 persons canvassed, 338 (58.89 per cent) were illiterates which included 156 males (46.15 per cent) and 182 females (53.85 per cent). Analysis of the distributional pattern of the illiterates across different categories of the land holding households revealed that the maximum number of illiterates were concentrated in the marginal land holding households followed by landless households, semi-medium land holding households and medium land holding households (see Table 5.5). Keeping apart the landless households we can infer that the level of illiteracy and the size of land holding of households in this village were inversely related to each other, though we can not say that which was the cause and which was the effect. It could be seen in Table 5.5 that, except in the landless category where the number of illiterate males and females was the same, the relative percentage shares of illiterate females in all other land holding categories was higher than that of their male counterparts. In the medium class land holding households there was not a single illiterate male whereas the number of illiterate females in this category was 4.

Table 5.5 : **Educational pattern of males and females in various size class of households, 24 Parganas, West Bengal, 1991**

	No. of house-hold	Total	M	F	Illiterate		Primary		Secondary		Above matric		Graduation & above	
					M	F	M	F	M	F	M	F	M	F
Landless	20	93	50	43	43 (50.0)	43 (50.0)	7	-	-	-	-	-	-	-
Marginal (0.2-1.0 ha.)	20	122	65	57	49 (48.0)	53 (52.0)	6 (60.0)	4 (40.0)	-	-	-	-	-	-
Small (1.0-2.0 ha.)	20	118	60	58	38 (42.7)	51 (57.3)	8	5	5	2	5	-	-	-
Semi-Medium (2.0-4.0 ha.)	20	127	67	60	26 (45.6)	31 (54.4)	20	-	13	-	7	-	-	-
Medium (4.0-10.0 ha.)	20	114	53	61	-	4 (100.0)	4	25	25	30	17	6	7	-
Total	100	574	295	279	156	182	45	34	43	32	29	6	7	-

In 1991, the number of persons who had education upto the primary level was 79. Out of which 56.96 per cent and 43.04 per cent were males and females respectively. In the landless and semi-medium land holding households there was not a single female having education upto primary level. The maximum number of females who had education upto primary level were found in the medium size land holding households, followed by small and marginal land holding households (see Table 5.5). In this case, it can also be observed that the level of educational achievements of the members of households and the relative land holding size was directly related to each other.

So far as secondary education was concerned, the number of persons in the surveyed households having education upto matriculation was only 77 which included 55.84 per cent males and 44.16 per cent females. It should be noted here that in the landless and marginal and semi-medium size land holding categories, there was not a single matriculate. Most of the female matriculates were concentrated in the medium size land holding households. Moreover, all the 35 persons who had education above matriculation but below graduate level were from the medium size land holding households. The percentage of female matriculates was only 2.69, nearly one-fifth of the total persons having education above matriculation. Similarly, a total of 7 males from medium size land holding households were having education upto graduation and/or above.

Thus, analysis of the educational profile of the members of households in different land holding categories revealed that, in 1991, irrespective of the size of land holding, the educational status of girls and women was low and their representation in the higher levels of education was almost marginal. Moreover, there existed a direct relationship between the levels of educational achievements of individuals and the relative land holding size of the households to which they belonged. Here, however, poverty was the main reason of low educational status of girls and women and the consequent wide disparity between the educational status of males and females. Apart from this, the prevailing culture, social customs and traditions, the sex stereotyping of roles of boys and girls within the family and the lack of desired level of schooling facilities were also equally important in explaining the low participation rates of girls and women in various stages of education.

Occupational Profile : It has already been mentioned earlier that most of the households had agriculture as the main occupation. The adult members, males and females, of these households irrespective of the size class of land holding, participate in agriculture either as the supplier or employer of labour. However, the number of persons who were hiring out labour on the farm was relatively higher than that of persons engaged in any other type of employment. In 1991, in these surveyed households, there were 122 agricultural labourers which included 27 females. Out of the total number of agricultural labourers, the highest number of persons were from the landless households. Their percentage share in the total agricultural labour force was 36.89 (see Table 5.6). Other types of households the members of which were hiring out labour were the marginal size land holders, small size land holders and medium size land holders. It should be noted here that not a single member from the semi-medium size land holding households was hiring out labour. Besides, women only from the landless and the marginal size land holding households were working as agricultural labourers. Similarly, the highest number of cultivators was found from the semi-medium size land holding households in these villages. Except from the landless households, members from all other types of households were engaged in cultivation (see Table 5.6). However, the number of female cultivators was only 2 who belonged to marginal size class of land holding households and their percentage share in the total number of persons engaged in agriculture was only 2.6.

Table 5.6 : **Occupational pattern of members of different size class of households, 24 Parganas, West Bengal, 1991**

	No. of house-hold	Agricul-tural		Cultivator		Trade & Buss.		Service		Total		Total popul.
		M	F	M	F	M	F	M	F	M	F	
Landless	20	28	17	-	-	-	-	-	-	28	17	93
Marginal (0.2-1.0 ha.)	20	23	10	10	2	-	-	-	-	313	12	122
Small (1.0-2.0 ha.)	20	24	-	20	-	-	-	-	-	44	-	118
Semi-Medium (2.0-4.0 ha.)	20	-	-	25	-	4	-	2	-	31	-	127
Medium (4.0-10.0 ha.)	20	20	-	20	-	2	-	10	7	70	7	114
Total	100	95	27	75	2	24	-	12	7	206	36	574

In these villages, the total number of traders found in the surveyed households was 24 in 1991, out of which nearly 83 per cent belonged to the medium size land holding households and the rest 17 per cent from the semi- medium size land holding households. In the service sector, only 19 persons were participating and they were mostly from the medium size land holding families. The percentage share of females in this sector was 36.84. Thus, the occupational status of the members of various size class of households had close correspondence to the relative educational status of the members of these households. Moreover, the comparative low educational status of females in this surveyed households was reflected in their marginal rates of participation in various off-farm occupations, particularly in the service sector in 1991.

CONCLUSION

Analysis of education and employment profiles of both males and females in the villages in the three states of India show that despite the availability of schools and other educational facilities, women are disproportionally underrepresented in education as compared to men in various age groups and in various size classes of land holding. Poverty is no doubt an important obstacle to girls' education. But, it is more often than not, men's negative attitude which contributes a great deal towards perpetuating discrimination against girls.

The edu-employment profiles of both males and females not only highlight the gap, they also, though indirectly, underline the relative position of women both in terms of their intellectual capability and material capacity. Education is intrinsic to development, and development of women in particular. It also empowers a person to understand and analyse his/her existential situation. Apart from this, it plays the role of a catalyst which helps the person in possession of it to apply it for her/his betterment. Today, as we see here at a mico level, she is deprived of this life-preparing and life-sustaining process. The natural consequence of this deprivation is contributing to her inability to get recognition as worker and entry into paid labour market. The micro level study attempted here does not hower show any noticeable and significant difference in the relative positition of women as compared to their male counterparts in any of the three states. However, the intersting point which emerges is that women in the households belonging to medium-size class are better educated than their counterparts in other lower size-classes (see West

CHAPTER SIX

POSTSCRIPT

PROLOGUE

Development of women has to be addressed keeping gender question in view, for gender epitomizes relationships between man and woman and determines its socio-economic, political and cultural ramifications, and any effort to bring about equality between man and woman has to be in terms of narrowing down gender gaps in the availament of opportunities in education, employment, health, finance and other assorted areas in equal measures. The patriarchally attributed woman's 'womanliness' has to be replaced by contexts in which both man and woman could interact without bringing in sex status as the symbol of differentiation.

The data and informations marshalled in the preceding chapters and its analysis very clearly demonstrate that women as a group have been discriminated against in every field of activity, especially in education and employment which, to our view, constitute the major plank for development of human society in general and women as a gender group in particular.

Development cannot be seen purely as an economic affair. Development rather is an "overall social process" which is dependent upon the outcomes of the human being's efforts to manipulate and control his natural environment. In our society, however, underdevelopment is the reality. This implies that development exists for a select group of people who have access to resources and power. In this context, underdevelopment of our society can be viewed as the product of the historical (i.e. colonial) and contemporary exploitative relationship between classes, castes, religious and gender groups within the nation. In fact, the present paradox of development is that increase in the production of goods and services would improve the satisfaction levels of the basic needs of people belonging to various sections of our society. In reality, this is not a fact. Because, evidences show that economic development does not automatically eradicate poverty through "trickle-down" effects. Nor does it improve the position of disadvantaged groups, particularly women. The contemporary development process does not provide women and other sections of our society equal access to existing opportunities, and it has also failed to distribute the benefits, be it economic or social, or educational, equally among the various segments of population. As a result, this has become a major concern in the present day development theory.

Even though economic development, in many cases, has met the "practical needs" (i.e. food, clothing, shelter, health care, etc.), it has failed to meet the "strategic needs" of women, for example, educational, political, occupational and the like which would empower them in real life as equal to men. This calls for adopting entirely a different type of development strategy in our society. In the changed form, development should entail improvement in the quality and quantity of life of various sections of population in the country. Here, for example, "quality" can refer to social, health, and educational concerns, while "quantity" may involve the amount of economic and political involvement of women and other disadvantaged groups. To achieve this, the development planners have to take into consideration women's needs, especially their strategic needs and view points. It other words, now the development theory in our society should be development with women.

It is apparent in our discussions in this volume that in societies and cultures where there is still resistance to changing the status of women, the renewed development efforts have failed to change the status of women in the form of raising the quality and quantity of their lives. Women enjoy differential status, be it economic, social, political and the like, within the same social strata. In other words, they are unequals among the equals. Because, the real dimensions of equality are missing in our society. On equality Mullings notes:

> Equality refers to a situation wherein all members of a society have the same relationship to the society's resources. Such a situation would exist in a truly communal society. Symmetry refers to a situation in which males and females have access to similar roles and statuses. Inequality occurs when society's resources are appropriated by a certain social strata as private property, which limits access to resources for other strata. This increased throughout the Third World during the colonial period. In asymmetrical relationships, access to the same means of production may be equal, but males and females may not have access to the same roles and statuses (1976 : 240).

In other words, in our society, women are left with limited means to new avenues of production. This exclusion of women from relatively viable modes of production has made women unequal to men. Moreover, we can identify four major social fields - i.e.status hierarchies - comprising economic setting, political organisation, legal system and ideology, and religion. A number of socio-cultural factors such as education, division of labour, and mass media, intervene between each social field and intrafamilial arrangements in which women are cocooned much more so than men (Epstein, 1989 : 42). Besides, the oppressive effects of religion, or class, or sex, or a combination of the three have adversely affected the status of women. The institutional factors have and continue to play an important role in stagnating (in many cases, lowering down) the status of women. Particularly in our society, the institutionalised male dominance has not changed. Women are highly dependent on men, even for their own social identify. They are the members of the social class of their husbands, fathers, or other significant males in their lives. Helen Safa states this point very clearly in the following terms :

> Women themselves are not a class, but members of another class, depending on their socio-economic position in society...... This class position of women is defined not by women themselves, even when they are working, but by their husbands or fathers, whose status they assume. While this is another clear reflection of women's dependency on men, it does not mean that women cannot acquire class consciousness independently. It does suggest that the process by which women acquire class consciousness will be different and more difficult than it is for men (quoted in Lindsay, 1980 : 305-6).

In fact, dependency of women on men and the consequent subjugation of women have become a part of the culture in our society. Because, subjugation of women (i.e. the process of snatching away the opportunities available to women to meet their strategic needs) as a complex phenomenon has never been confined to particular class, or caste, or race or religion. Rather it has been and continue to be reflected in the ideologies, cultures and practices of all types of groups though in different forms and degrees. Even in the socio-economically, culturally and politically conscious communities, the process of subordination of women has always been designed and maintained in such a manner that it has kept their status both within and outside the family institution unaltered, irrespective of the levels of economic and educational development (which is perhaps not visible in many cases). And this is a fact (see Box 6.1).

Women's participation in various activities — activities which are formative and summative — has remained marginal as compared to their male counterparts. In other words, with the development of our economy, women's status in the labour market has become marginalised. This has already been mentioned while discussing the participation rates of women across different occupations in our economy. However, female

Box 6.1 : **On her palm leaves**

Now approaching 65, Rama Kumari, schooled upto 8th standard and mother of five children, two daughters and three sons, lives in a city which is also the headquarters of one of the districts in Bihar. She was born in a Brahmin family in 1928 in a *kashba*, a small urban outback, in the same district. Her father was a reputed *pundit* (Brahmin priest), and therefore was enjoying relatively a higher social status. He was rich. He, however, sent Rama Kumari to the missionary school, largely controlled by the Christian Chruch. She was a brilliant student, according to her teachers, she claims. At home, she was the most loving daughter of her parents. At the age of 5 or so she started helping her mother in household chores, and that did not stop her being regular at school. Unlike today, the lessons they were being taught at that time were written on the palm leaves. She simillingly recalled and showed us the palm leaves she had preserved for nearly 52 years. She had taken a lot of pain to maintain her palm leaves.

Everything was going on fine. One day, when she was entering into her thirteenth spring, she heard about her father's plan to marry her off to a boy of 18 years old of another kashba who was working in a small private manufacturing unit. She ran to her school and told everything to her favourite teacher, and till then she had not forgotten the hide and seek game she loved to play under her mother's *anchal*. Her teacher suggested her to become a nun which she conveyed to her mother. However, her mother did not have a say at home and she was married off at the age of 13 in 1941 and she had to leave the school. She came as a daughter-in-law to a large joint family of pattidaris(persons having share in the property). Her husband was too busy in seeking a suitable employment and he used to stay away from home for months together leaving his bride to become the victim of *pattidari* system. However, in due course of time, she became the mother of five children. From the very corner of her heart, she had always wanted to educate her children, particularly her daughters. This was perhaps because of the fact that she had failed (rather circumstances both within and outside her family

Contd..

had compelled her to leave the school) to realise her own desire to be highly educated. With this desire, she sent her children to school.

Unfortunately, when her eldest daughter was 14 years old and in the school, her own story was again repeated. She was married off and though she did not like this, she could not oppose her husband's decision on whom she was totally depending for her economic and social existence. A few years after this event, her youngest daughter was also married off at the age of 15 and this time too she could not do anything either. In due course of time, her highly educated sons brought home three loving daughters-in-law. She could not find any difference between the unfortunate educational and occupational careers of her own daughters and that of her own daughters-in-law. The case of her youngest daughter-in-law was somehow different from other two daughters-in-law in the sense that when she was studying in pre-degree level she was married off, nobody tried to peep into her heart where her emotions were dashing against the existing insensitive social culture and traditions, Rama Kumari thought. However, she allowed her youngest daughter-in-law to continue her study and, for this, she used to send her off to her parents.

Time passed away. All the three sons became employed and now living away at distant places. She was not sad. At least her youngest daughter-in-law was with her. And she used to experience a sense of belonging to her. But, one day, in the afternoon, she had to see her youngest daughter-in-law off along with her husband, her son, whom she used to love a lot. Leaning against the bannana tree under its thin consoling shadow she was gazing blankly at the ever distancing tiny feet of her daughter-in-law. Tears silently rolled off her trembling cheeks. She was perhaps strolling down her memory lane trying to make vein efforts to find out any change that might differentiate her own status and the present status of her youngest daughter-in-law. Probably, she could not find any silverlining.

Source : Our personal interview and observations in 1992.

marginalisation in the labour market can be ascertained at least on the basis of either of the four dimensions (Scott, 1986) : (i) exclusion of women from productive employment which can be manifested either in the form of a decline in their overall work participation rates or a decline in their share in wage and salaried employment; (ii) concentration of working women in the margins or periphery of the labour market thereby over-crowding the marginal occupations, industries and sectors of employment; (iii) segregation of women in certain types of jobs which are low in the occupational hierarchy and are low paying and low status, comonly referred to as 'feminisation' of 'segregation' in employment; and (iv) economic inequality reflected through wage differentials and casualisation of female labour force. If not all, more than one dimension of female marginalisation in the labour market are found in the data furnished in this volume. The questions which normally arise are :

Why have women occupied subordinate position in almost all the societies ?

What are the factors responsible for the emergence of women's subordinate status ?

Are the factors exogeneous or endogenous to the process of sex differentition ?

How gender relations exist in various socio-cultural, economic, political and ideological institutions ?

And how are gender relations reinforced and reshaped in the historical processes ?

Answers to these questions may not be easy. Notwithstanding, here, we have made an attempt to outline the contours of the situation which are both the cause and effect of gender relations between man and woman. To us, the material basis of the gender relations is enveloped in myth, mystry and reality. The myth and mystry have been invented, perpetuated, and practised to disguise the 'disadvantages' that would have robbed of the 'advantages' obtained by subjugating half of the human race. The family institution is the birth place of gendered differentiation - it is first here that relation of subordination germinates between a male and a female. It is also the home where sex status and biologically reproductive function 'disfigure' an equal human manifestation into an unequal 'woman'.

It is again within the family institution where biological reproductive necessity carried out by woman becomes a factor of her subjugation by man. It may possibily be hypothesied that in the far away past when human species were not very good in number, and when human beings needed more to add to their numbers to survive over the massive depeletion by ravages of diseases and internecine conflicts, that subjugation of woman became paramount, for it is through her that reproductive function was possible. This assumption further leads to an answer as to why she has accepted her subordination ? Since she was subordinated to perform reproductive function in the family institution, and the family institution was one of the many constituents of any organised group. The group's male, to perpetuate their authority over other groups, clans and races, needed human labour power. And what was the source? Only female. To maintain any domain of authority and exploitation, man needed to control his woman who reproduced and replenished human beings. The evidence of the historical past indicates this very fact - the fact which is enshrined in 'religions' because 'religions' are the first organised socio-politico and economic ideology clothed in a myriad of myths and mystry. Since human being is an intelligent and cunning animal, he/she is also a myopic animal in the sense that in order to exploit other they forget to see the consequences of their actions in the long run.

To continue his own convenient perpetuation he has subjugated his source by myth and rhetorics at superstructural level by eulogiging her as 'mother'. *In a family institution the* 'father' as a male 'progenitor' and the 'mother' as a female 'receiptor' have mutually agreed to a disagreement of domination and subordination. For the father it was a triumph over his victim and for the mother if became a triumph being victimised. In due course, she has become a reflected reality of the male orchestrated reality. Historical evidence amply suggests that many myths and tricks have been generated to subordinate women. It is no wonder that today she is discriminated not only within her natal institution, the family, but also in other life preparatory and sustaining institutions — social, educational, political and economic. In other words, her subordination begins at womb and ends in tomb.

We have seen how reproductive function of the women has been a cause of her subjugation. Besides reproduction, she is also a productive human being. She not only produces human labour as individuals, but herself contributes a great deal to the production process that sustain material existence of the family and the society. Subordination of woman has one more dimension - she is not only a reproducer of human beings and labour but is also a source of great physical pleasure in terms of sexual interplay and interaction. She is subjugated for rendering her sexual services from a disadvnataged position. Since this labour is the result of intensely intra physical manipulation, the female mostly does it out of material compul sion of her being in subordination. Upto this, her subordination can be conceived within a '*sexual paradigm*'. Of course, reinforced by external forces. The biological reproductive activities of procreation and recreation (pleasure) are endogenous factors which men have exploited at their advantage. The exogenous factors are woman's role in material production both in the 'domestic' domain and at the 'outside' domain.

The process of subordination is further institutionalised by allowing women in activities which are supplementary or complementary (though essential) to total activity. This a gain is strengthened by unequal distribution of wealth and other means of producation — land, capital, etc. Evidence indicates that women have been systematically deprived from owning resources as that of men. Pearson describes this situation very clearly :

> Systems of land tenure and inheritance vary widely. In most cases women have used rights other than outright ownership rights to land. Where full rights to ownership exist in traditional legal codes, a woman's share is not usually equal to a man's. And even where traditional women are entitled to inherit land, new laws often reduce women's rights to succession. For example, the Colombian land reform law confined land redistribution to married males over 18, and deprived women of rights they had in the pre-reform system (Whitehead, 1985 : 53).
>
> Even where women have customary use rights to land, these are rarely exercised in their own right, but only through kin relationships with individual men - brothers, fathers, other male relatives or, most commonly, husbands (1990 : 291).

This unfavourably skewed rights of women to land and other properties reinforce her subordination and makes her as dependant of man. We have presented the 'vicious circle' of subordination of women in Figure 6.1.

It emerges from Figure 6.1 that subordination is the end result of a number of interrelated factors which act simultaneously to widen the gender gaps between men and women. The gender gaps eventually determine the position of women in the society's various interrelated areas of activities. The wider the gender gap greater will be the differentiated socio-cultural, economic and political status of women in terms of their participation in education, employment and politics. Gender gap will lead to woman's dependence on man and their dependence will eventually lead to their deprivation. The policy measures to be designed in such a manner that it first preempt the process of dependence and slowly but steadily brings about socio-economic autonomy for women.

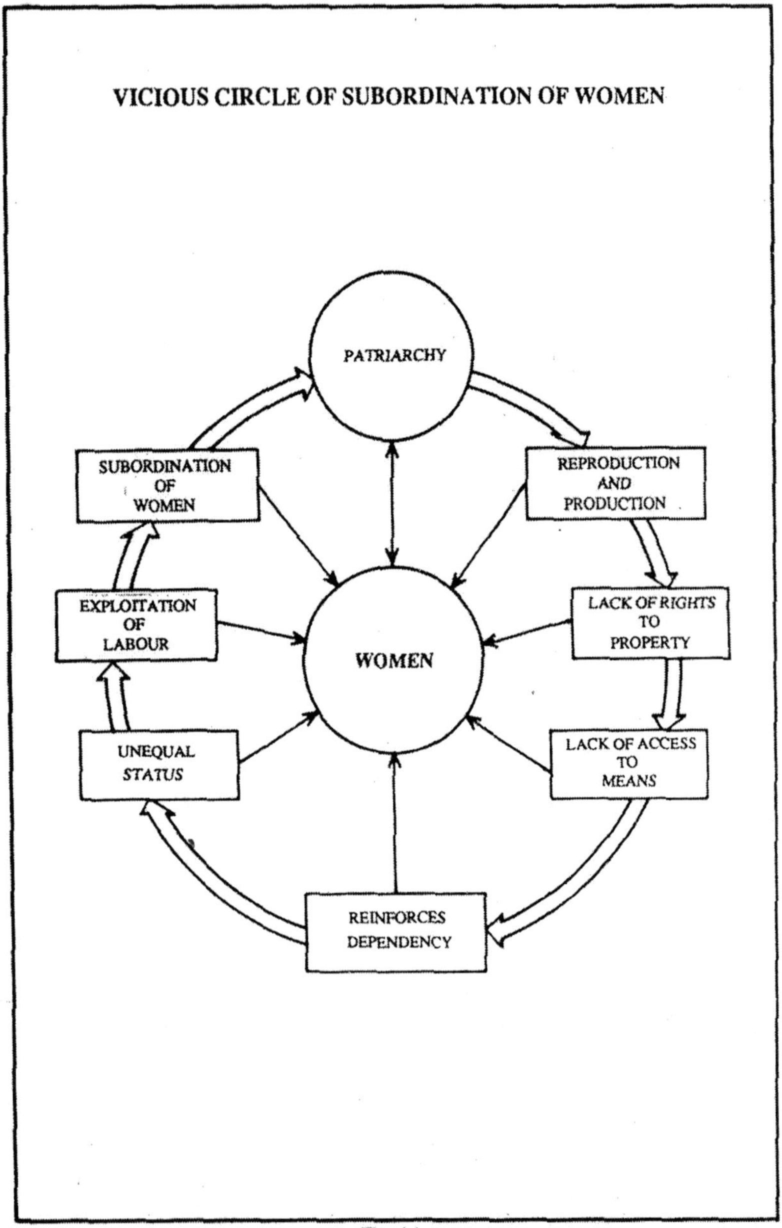
VICIOUS CIRCLE OF SUBORDINATION OF WOMEN
PATRIARCHY
REPRODUCTION AND PRODUCTION
LACK OF RIGHTS TO PROPERTY
LACK OF ACCESS TO MEANS
REINFORCES DEPENDENCY
UNEQUAL STATUS
EXPLOITATION OF LABOUR
SUBORDINATION OF WOMEN
WOMEN

Fig. 6.1

ROLE OF THE STATE

In the preceding chapters, we have examined in detail the pattern of representation of women in education and employment at global, national, village and at individual levels and indicated that women's representation is highly disproportionate to their numbers. We have also hinted the role of the state policy in perpetuating gendered differentiation in socio-economic spheres. Here, we shall examine briefly the role of the state and representation of women in state organisations. Also briefly, we would discuss the negative impact of some of the state polices on women's access to existing opportunities and their overall status.

The state and its organization — i.e. the government — is a male dominated framework, which could be clearly seen by looking at the level of representation of women in parliaments. The figures in Table 6.1 indicate the level of participation of women in parliaments across different regions of the world under different political systems. The data suggest that in the highest political and policy making body — the parliament — the representation of women in highly disproportionate to their numbers. Except in the former USSR, the percentage of women representatives in parliament ranges between a minimum of 4.9 in Africa to a maximum of 22.4 Oceania. This clearly shows the state's partial role in bringing about equality in women's participation in highest decision-making body. Stromquist clearly delineates the role of the state in perpetuating gendered institution:

> The state is a key actor in the management of gender relations. As Connell observes (1987; 1990), the state is a gendered and gendering institution. It is *gendered in the composition of its authorities and it is gendering through its management of ideology and economic relations* (emphasis added). All contemporary states are predominantly male : male in terms of their top and mid-level leadership and in terms of the interests they seek to serve (see also Chafez, 1990). This condition does not forecast that the state will always be oppressive of women. It simply acknowledges that the parameteres for state support give priority to heterosexual males, who carry the highest prestige in any modern society.
>
> The state creates a 'hegemonic gender consciousness', or a form of society based on the assumption that one's own gender interest can be generalised for all (Livingston and Luxton, 1989). At the same time, the state sharpens and froms masculinity and feminity through institutions such as prisons, the military, and the police apparatus, and by the creation of powerful categories of social relations and as homosexu-

ality, prostitution, marriage and family (Connell, 1989). This double play of hiding the gendered-based nature of prevailing interests and, at the same, time defining masculinity as superior creates the basis for the difficult to contest subordination of women (1991 : 112).

Table 6.1 : **Percentage of women in parliaments**

Region	Labour chamber of bicameral assembly		Upper chamber of bicameral assembly	
	1975	Latest year	1975	Latest year
Africa	4.1	6.3	-	4.9
Asia	13.2	12.8	6.9	6.9
Latin America and Caribbean	3.4	10.6	4.2	6.5
North America	3.6	7.0	2.9	7.4
Oceania	1.9	4.9	9.4	22.4
Europe	13.2	17.6	6.4	8.2
Soviet Union	32.1	34.5	30.5	31.1

Source : U.N. (1989) *Report of the World Social Situation*, Geneva, (as quoted in Pearson, 1990 : 295).

A state, whether it is patriarchal, transitional or androgynous, is a key organisation, and as a key and most powerful organisation, has a strong command over the process of generation of knowledge, its dissemination and distribution to various sections of the society. It also directly and indirectly determines the curricula of education system; and through it, the state engenders gender differentiated socio-economic and political relations and thereby creating institutions and structures to sustain it.

The institutions and structures thus created and maintained by the state feed the process of growth of a parallel society the members of which are the disadvantaged groups, including women. Similarly, policies and strategies framed and implemented by the state, in many cases, also negatively affect particular sections of the population. The policy of economic restructuring, for example, usually affects women adversely in many ways. Because, generally, the structural adjustment (the type of adjustment mostly done in the Third World countries) involves an increase in production for export coupled with demand-reducing policies such as removal of subsides on basic necessities, reduction in welfare services, price rises, wage cuts and job loses. The restructuring process also helps in expanding a peripheral industrial sector within the economy

Box 6.2 : **Employment seen as aberration?**

Prejudices of the employers or beliefs about the natural distribution of talents between sexes often lead to discrimination against women workers. ... even in a situation where there is little scope for such forces to operate systematically, women may still receive unequal treatment because of their particular vulnerability. Employers are quick to recognise the profitability of exploiting this vulnerability and naturally take full advantage of it. This vulnerability of women in the labour market has been imposed on them by society which has conditioned them to accept certain norms. These norms teach a woman to believe that she should fuction only as a wife and mother, that having to work is an aberration in the same sense that unemployment is an aberration of a working male. At the same time she bears the ultimate responsibility for the cohesion of the family. The upshot of all this is that she is altogether unprepared for the labour market and totally desperate when the time comes for her to join it. She has no training in the skills required in the labour market and, at work, feels little affinity with other similarly placed workers. Also, her loyalty remains within her family and she makes frantic efforts to adjust to her working life without disturbing too many of the family mores.

Investment in the further expansion of women's education or employment opportunities in the "women prone" industries as the draft Indian Sixth Plan envisages will not improve this situation single handedly. What is needed is a change in the attitudes of women towards economic activities. Expansion of women's jobs can bring about this change in the long run provided it is on a large enough scale. Further spread of education is also a vital *al beit* limited force, especially since the current education pattern itself embodies and reinforces these social values. To alter this, the educators themselves have to be reeducated and this promises to be a long drawn out process.

Source : Benerjee, Nirmala (1984) "Why They Get a Worse Deal: Report on Unorganised Women Eorkers in Calcutta", *Manushi*, No. 20 (Vol. 4, No.2), pp.22-23.

thereby even reducing the labour market status of the available jobs. Structural adjustment of the economy thus shifts the burden of welfare from the state to individual families, particularly to women. Given the price rise and shifting of the burden of welfare to individual families, more and more women go out for seeking employment in the peripheral economy. This ultimately increases the level of competition in this sector and women in turn are discriminated against both at the entry into and within the labour market (see Box 6.2).

Besides, the overall workload of women also increases because of addition of the out-of-home work to the existing household chores, particularly in nuclear families. However, in response to such policies women have always tried to develop new survival strategies. This behaviour has been termed as "the invisible adjustment". This implies that women make adjustment policies socially possible by increasing their own economic activities by working harder and 'self-abnegation' (Momsen, 1991).

Moreover, the state has designed and maintained its machineries in such a manner that opportunities—educational, occupational and the like—are not really available to a large section of disadvantaged population. And this is more so in the case of women if they happen to belong to socio-economically disadvantaged groups. The dual educational system, the rigid procedures and the ever increasing importance of family background and parental educational and occupational achievements make it very difficult for girl children to get access into the school sector thereby keeping them away from fulfilling their strategic needs (see Box 6.3).

What we emphasize here is that, to bring about equality between sexes and again between sexes belonging to different groups having differential access to resources and power, the state should ensure access to opportunities that would avail women the things that meet their strategic needs. To have a balanced development of our society empowerment of women is a prerequisite and to empower women, a strong political will of the state is a must.

AREAS OF INTERVENTION AND FUTURE RESEARCH

Before identifying some of the important areas of future research that would help the development planner to frame policies and programmes to improve the overall status of women in our society, it is pertinent here to throw some light on some of the areas of intervention to bridge the gender related dispariaties. So far, the state has intervened to improve sex

Box 6.3 : Give me my a.b.c.

I, Rani, wife of Shri Dori Lal, resident of Jhuggi No. 503, Raghubir Nagar (Near bus stop No. 857), New Delhi-27, earn my living by cleaning utensils and floors at residences of some people living in Tagore Garden, New Delhi. My husband is not living with me. I have got three dependents - my elder daughter aged 14 years, who also cleans utensils and floors; my younger daughter aged 5 years and a son aged 4 years.

I, want my daughter to be literate and wanted her to be admitted to some school. I took her to an MCD Primary School at Tagore Garden, New Delhi, for admission to class I. They required her birth certificate, which I did not have because she was born in my village and we did not prepare one. My advocate babu helped me and got an affidavit about my daughter's birth. When I approahced the school with the affidavit, I was told that my daughter could not be admitted because the last date was over.

I wonder whether the people who talk so much about literacy of the poor, particularly the 'girl child', realise how difficult it is for the poor to get an affidavit. They cannot by themselves get one. Moreover, it means a lot of money and time. To admit our children to school and make them literate, the authorities should realise the realities and should come to our help, instead of creating hurdles.

Now that I have got an affidavit, my daughter is not being admitted to class I. It is not a higher class. Moreover, they don't admit her to the Nuresery class, because she is five years old. That means she should join my work and remain illiterate like me.

Literacy campaigns and celeberations of the 'years or decades of the child' and several campaigns and serials on radio and TV are not going to help. What will help is understanding of our problems and finding their solutions the moment we send our children to schools.

Is there anyone in authority, in voluntary organisations or any of your readers who can help my daughter's admission to class I so that she does not have to waste full one year? I am asking for a chance for my child. Is it too much to ask?

Rani

Source : Hindustan Times, November 9, 1992

equality by designing and implementing many actions and programmes. Some of these efforts have involved policies and practices to counter discriminatory behaviour of organisations as well as individuals to improve the status of women in general; and some others involved interventions mostly targeted specifically at the areas such as education, employment, health care and the like. However, all these efforts of the state have failed to bring about any visible change in the status of women. This is perhaps due to the very general nature of the state policies and programmes which have not differentiated between the degree of intra-gender disparities.

Even today, some of the important areas of intervention to improve the general and specific status of women are : (i) political recognition; (ii) legal recognition; (iii) access to education; (iv) access to employment; (v) access to health care; and (vi) empowerment.

The first move to improve the status of women is to ensure equal political rights to them, for example, in the from of more representation of women in the parliament and in other political bodies and giving political power to women's organisations to fight for their rights. Similarly, legal recognition can be accorded to women by enacting laws and other legislations which would ensure them economic, social and political rights. To be specific, laws should be enacted to : counter discrimination based on sex; allow women to own property; grant equal rights in matters relating to inheritance and succession; allow women to institute legal action in courts of law in their own name; remove restrictions which prohibit women from entering into commercial transactions in their own capacity; and the like. No doubt, a number of laws relating to the above mentioned rights of women have been enacted, but the enforcement of these laws has always remained weak due to many reasons. Therefore, what is required is to ensure a strong and viable enforcement machinery in our society. Apart from this, a large section of women are unaware of their legal rights. Strategies should be evolved to disseminate informations with regard to legal rights to such disadvantaged women.

Education is the most important strategic variable affecting the status of women. Apart from its positive impact on fertility, productivity, child care and creation of future human capital, education facilitates the process of conscientisation of women. Education is also the prerequisite for women to become economically self-sufficient, which is a must to get themselves out of the vicious circle of dependency on men. Thus, ensuring access to education, particularly quality education, is important to improve the status of women. As we have already discussed earlier, women are discriminated, both at the entry into and within the labour market.

They have no access to certain kinds of jobs : partly, because of lack of required human capital; and partly because of discrimination based on sex. Even if they have access to these jobs, they are paid less wages compared to their male counterparts. Jobs in the urban labour market have been segregated and termed as 'masculine' and 'feminine' occupations. Women are found concentrated in low paying lower status unstable jobs in the periphery of the urban industrial sector. Interventions, therefore, are required to eliminate sex disparities in employment and wages in the urban labour markets.

Women's access to health care facilities is also very low compared to their male counterparts. This differential access to health care facilities has not only affected the development process of our society, it has also affected the future generation. However, the major factors affecting women's health are : health-oriented discriminatory practices against women and girls; lack of education; and lack of employment opportunities. All these factors have together affected the efficiency of women. Increasing investment on health care facilities and access of the women belonging to disadvantaged groups to existing health care facilities would go a long way in bringing about critical changes in the gender relationships. Finally, the most important areas of intervention is empowerment of women. Because, empowerment of women would help them asserting their due place, rights and priviledges in our society. This can also help women to maintain their immediate environment and break the vicious circle of social traditions. Besides, women need to be empowered to organise themselves to fight for their due rights. Actions and programmes therefore should be evolved to empower women, especially rural women and women from disadvnataged groups.

Given the above areas of intervention, the strong and complex institutional factors and a persistent resitance to changing the status of women in our society, the following areas of future research on women's development can be identified :

(i) What conceptual views most adequately provide explanations of the relative status of women in different fields such as education, employment, politics, etc. and between women belonging to different socio-economic groups ?

(ii) What are the indicators of low status of women vis-a-vis men in these fields ?

(iii) How are sex stereotyping of roles of boys and girls created and maintained within the family and how does this role affect the level of achievement of girls and women ?

(iv) Why are girls and women caught in the "vicious circle of dependency" and what are the interactive effects of institutional patterns on the status of women ?

(v) What are the "process variables" responsible for creation of institutions — social,economic, cultural and political— which exert a negative effect on the development of women ?

(vi) What are women's home background or in the wider social setting in where they are found, from the schooling point of view, be regarded as the relevant factor ?

(vii) How is the family institution important in explaining the status of women in the education sector? What are the cultural and attitudinal factors which have a strong relationship with the level of educational achievement of women ?

(viii) Given the existing level of economic development and the availability of employment opportunities, what efforts should be made to improve the quality of female education so as to make them more employable ?

(ix) What should be the proper definition of work force participation of women? How do the concepts relating to the work force participation of women be clarified to take into account their actual contribution to the development of our society ?

(x) What are the factors explaining employment and wage discriminations against women in different sectors in the labour market?

(xi) Given the supply side deficiencies, what are the demand side factors responsible for marginalisation of females in the labour market ?

(xii) What policies and strategies should be evolved to counter the discriminatory practices against women in the labour market ?

(xiii) What are the 'process variables' in the segregation of occupations in our economy ?

(xiv) What models of 'self-empowerment' of women having differential social, educational,occupational and political status would help them assert their rights ?

(xv) What should be the models of participation which would increase the share of women in various activities ?

(xvi) How to develop data banks on various aspects of women's development at the national as well as sub-national levels ?

EMANCIPATION OF WOMEN

Emancipation of women from subordination has to be achieved at two stages :

(i) Preparatory stage; and

(ii) *Contributory stage.*

The emancipation at preparatory stage implies imparting cognitive, communicative and work skills through institutional framework at par with males without resorting to sex bias.

The emancipation at contributory stage implies access of females to all sectors of occupations at par with men. Besides, women must be given status of heads of households as that of men when it comes to owning property, access to credit facilities and any other economic activities.

We feel if equalising measures are adopted at preparatory stage, it will cumulatively contribute to the equalising process at contributory stage leading to gradual emancipation from subordination.

We are also of the view that the problem of emancipation has to be conceptualised both at the class and gender levels. This, we argue, will perhaps help correct the situation arising out of gendered differentiations within home and outside. The elimination of differentiations for achieving emancipation of women demands dramatic restructuring of structural parameters - social, economic, educational, political and cultural - and redistribution of resources - land, labour, capital, and reshaping of human attitudes towards a humane equality. This can be achieved by giving women a *carte blanche* in both preparatory and contributory stages.

APPENDIX

Table 1 : **Faculty-wise percentage distribution of girls' enrolment in post-matric-below degree level**

Sl. no.	States/ union territory	General education			Professional education						Other edn.		Total
		Arts	Science	Commerce	Agricultural	Education	Eng./ Tech.	Law	Medicine	Veter. science	Others	Oriental studies	
(1)		(2)	(3)	(4)	(5)	(6)	(7)	(8)	(9)	(10)	(11)	(12)	(13)
1.	Andhra Pradesh	0.00	0.00	0.00	0.00	24.16	58.40	0.00	0.42	0.00	8.85	8.18	100.00
2.	Assam	0.00	0.00	0.00	0.00	68.12	20.72	0.00	2.36	0.00	8.81	0.00	100.00
3.	Bihar	0.00	0.00	0.00	0.00	56.55	0.78	0.00	9.94	0.00	3.83	28.93	100.00
4.	Gujarat	0.00	1.08	0.00	0.00	0.00	57.04	0.00	38.13	0.00	3.76	0.00	100.00
5.	Haryana	1.14	0.00	0.00	0.00	0.00	3.57	0.00	70.95	0.00	17.36	7.01	100.00
6.	Himachal Pradesh	0.00	0.00	0.00	0.00	35.53	35.16	0.00	14.33	0.00	0.00	15.00	100.00
7.	Jammu & Kashmir	0.00	0.00	0.00	0.00	13.79	70.68	0.00	0.00	0.00	0.92	14.62	100.00
8.	Karnataka	0.11	0.08	0.00	0.00	53.15	8.95	0.00	0.15	0.00	35.73	1.85	100.00
9.	Kerala	0.00	0.00	1.02	0.00	66.15	22.63	0.00	3.30	0.00	6.93	0.00	100.00
10.	Madhya Pradesh	0.00	0.00	0.00	0.00	37.00	28.02	0.00	3.46	0.00	31.53	0.00	100.00
11.	Maharashtra	0.00	0.39	5.33	0.00	57.87	10.70	0.00	22.50	0.00	3.38	0.07	100.00
12.	Manipur	0.00	0.00	0.00	0.00	0.00	55.08	0.00	22.47	0.00	22.47	0.00	100.00
13.	Meghalaya	0.00	0.00	0.00	0.00	100.00	0.00	0.00	0.00	0.00	0.00	0.00	100.00
14.	Nagaland	0.00	0.00	0.00	8.60	3.91	7.82	0.00	0.00	0.00	79.69	0.00	100.00
15.	Orissa	0.00	0.00	0.00	0.00	81.47	3.21	0.00	0.00	0.00	12.95	2.39	100.00
16.	Punjab	1.16	0.71	0.00	0.00	13.37	38.59	0.00	39.83	0.00	6.07	0.31	100.00
17.	Rajasthan	2.16	0.00	0.00	1.25	29.17	51.85	0.00	12.88	0.00	2.70	0.00	100.00
18.	Sikkim	.	.	.	.	.	.	.	.	.	.	.	.

Contd..

(1)		(2)	(3)	(4)	(5)	(6)	(7)	(8)	(9)	(10)	(11)	(12)	(13)
19.	Tamil Nadu	0.00	0.00	0.00	0.08	25.00	53.19	0.00	16.90	0.00	3.55	1.30	100.00
20.	Tripura	0.00	0.00	0.00	0.00	0.00	0.00	0.00	35.31	0.00	27.45	37.25	100.00
21.	Uttar Pradesh	2.49	0.00	0.00	0.00	0.00	85.00	0.00	0.00	0.00	12.02	0.52	100.0
22.	West Bengal	0.00	0.00	0.00	0.04	2.90	1.04	0.00	10.04	0.00	86.01	0.00	100.00
23.	A & N Islands	0.00	0.00	0.00	0.00	75.65	24.36	0.00	0.00	0.00	0.00	0.00	100.00
24.	Arunachal Pradesh	.	.	.	.	.	.	.	.	.	.	.	.
25.	Chandigarh	0.00	0.00	0.00	0.00	0.00	91.71	0.00	0.00	0.00	8.30	0.00	100.00
26.	D & N Haveli	.	.	.	.	.	.						
27.	Delhi	18.95	0.00	0.00	0.00	17.05	44.75	0.00	9.24	0.00	9.74	0.31	100.00
28.	Goa, D. & Diu	0.00	0.00	0.00	0.00	52.85	34.74	0.00	11.27	0.00	1.16	0.00	100.00
29.	Lakshadweep	.	.	.	.	.	.	.	.	.	.	.	.
30.	Mizoram	0.00	0.00	0.00	0.00	56.85	10.79	0.00	26.56	0.00	5.81	0.00	100.00
31.	Pondicherry	0.00	0.00	0.00	0.00	0.00	44.19	0.00	55.82	0.00	0.00	0.00	100.00
	Total	0.83	0.13	1.05	0.06	34.02	22. 26	0.00	12.45	0.00	26.65	2.59	100.00

Source : Ministry of Human Resource Development (1991) *Education in India, 1986-87*, Vol. 1 (c), New Delhi.

Note : Others include Business Management, Library Science, Music & Dance, Physical Education, Social Work and other professional subjects.

Table 2 : **Faculty-wise percentage distribution of girls' enrolment in degree level**

Sl. no.	States/ union territory	General education			Professional education						Other edn.		Total
		Arts	Science	Commerce	Agricultural	Education	Eng./ Tech.	Law	Medicine	Veter. science	Others	Oriental studies	
(1)		(2)	(3)	(4)	(5)	(6)	(7)	(8)	(9)	(10)	(11)	(12)	(13)
1.	Andhra Pradesh	35.73	26.27	25.70	0.66	3.29	1.20	1.10	4.58	0.11	0.11	1.29	100.00
2.	Assam	80.62	10.08	1.48	0.16	1.60	0.45	2.73	2.47	0.29	0.11	0.06	100.00
3.	Bihar	71.62	14.72	3.38	0.02	1.78	0.53	1.71	2.46	0.05	0.16	3.84	100.00
4.	Gujarat	44.70	9.81	34.52	0.04	2.33	1.06	4.73	2.39	0.01	0.47	0.01	100.00
5.	Haryana	62.76	11.81	7.78	0.12	10.80	0.28	0.26	4.00	0.12	0.09	2.03	100.00
6.	Himachal Pradesh	76.18	12.60	2.34	0.80	0.19	0.15	0.00	2.59	0.04	2.43	2.75	100.00
7.	Jammu & Kashmir	56.40	24.47	6.16	0.61	5.88	0.76	1.75	2.63	0.00	0.92	0.48	100.00
8.	Karnataka	41.11	20.67	28.75	0.09	2.33	2.03	1.58	3.02	0.03	0.42	0.03	100.00
9.	Kerala	35.88	42.38	7.81	0.49	3.26	2.69	1.19	4.40	0.18	0.33	1.44	100.00
10.	Madhya Pradesh	56.72	27.14	5.38	0.04	3.87	0.70	3.24	2.07	0.05	0.79	0.07	100.00
11.	Maharashtra	33.44	14.76	38.84	0.14	2.48	1.22	2.94	5.63	0.04	0.55	0.01	100.00
12.	Manipur	67.80	22.51	1.90	0.47	0.00	0.00	4.38	2.07	0.00	0.00	0.00	100.00
13.	Meghalaya	70.74	13.20	1.76	0.00	7.01	0.00	7.31	0.00	0.00	0.00	0.00	100.00
14.	Nagaland	75.64	7.45	1.70	2.88	4.40	0.00	0.00	0.00	0.00	7.96	0.00	100.00
15.	Orissa	69.34	13.07	2.19	0.31	7.60	0.31	1.81	3.37	0.06	1.77	0.23	100.00
16.	Punjab	76.89	11.22	3.33	0.08	4.88	0.19	0.27	2.58	0.08	0.41	0.13	100.00
17.	Rajasthan	53.49	19.29	13.95	0.01	6.75	0.46	1.35	4.08	0.08	0.53	0.06	100.00
18.	Sikkim	55.71	13.43	4.03	0.00	0.00	0.00	26.85	0.00	0.00	0.00	0.00	100.00

Contd..

(1)	(2)	(3)	(4)	(5)	(6)	(7)	(8)	(9)	(10)	(11)	(12)	(13)
19. Tamil Nadu	32.31	39.56	13.34	0.77	1.91	5.26	0.88	5.35	0.13	0.18	0.35	100.00
20. Tripura	77.99	13.29	1.81	0.00	0.00	1.41	0.37	0.00	0.00	4.34	0.84	100.00
21. Uttar Pradesh	77.34	11.32	0.86	0.12	5.97	0.34	2.22	1.59	0.02	0.25	0.04	100.00
22. West Bengal	70.87	17.28	5.46	0.02	3.12	0.32	0.95	0.68	0.02	0.78	0.02	100.00
23. A & N Islands	79.96	11.54	1.83	0.00	6.69	0.00	0.00	0.00	0.00	0.00	0.00	100.00
24. Arunachal Pradesh	92.45	7.56	0.00	0.00	0.00	0.00	0.00	0.00	0.00	0.00	0.00	100.00
25. Chandigarh	62.99	19.84	7.92	0.00	5.13	2.14	1.14	0.52	0.00	0.36	0.00	100.00
26. D & N Haveli	.	.	.	.	.	.	.	.	.	.	.	.
27. Delhi	63.46	11.26	16.28	0.00	1.07	0.60	0.90	3.78	0.00	2.36	0.34	100.00
28. Goa, D. & Diu	30.00	16.53	39.16	0.00	1.76	1.64	3.09	6.50	0.00	1.36	0.00	100.00
29. Lakshadweep	.	.	.	.	.	.	.	.	.	.	.	.
30. Mizoram	86.59	5.63	5.14	0.00	2.65	0.00	0.00	0.00	0.00	0.00	0.00	100.00
31. Pondicherry	38.02	35.44	14.20	0.00	0.00	3.23	2.75	4.79	0.00	1.62	0.00	100.00
Total	52.87	19.88	16.21	0.20	3.34	1.27	1.89	3.26	0.06	0.56	0.46	100.00

Source : Ministry of Human Resource Development (1991) *Education in India, 1986-87*, Vol. 1 (c), New Delhi.

Note : Others include Business Management, Library Science, Music & Dance, Physical Education, Social Work and other professional subjects.

Table 3 : **Faculty-wise percentage distribution of girls' enrolment in post-graduate level**

Sl. no.	States/ union territory	General education			Professional education						Other edn.		Total
		Arts	Science	Com-merce	Agri-cultural	Edu-cation	Eng./ Tech.	Law	Medicine	Veter. science	Others	Oriental studies	
(1)		(2)	(3)	(4)	(5)	(6)	(7)	(8)	(9)	(10)	(11)	(12)	(13)
1.	Andhra Pradesh	46.64	31.26	7.80	2.13	1.24	1.46	0.27	5.72	0.18	1.53	1.76	100.00
2.	Assam	68.47	27.77	0.55	0.62	0.00	0.00	0.43	0.62	0.18	1.35	0.00	100.00
3.	Bihar	76.23	15.60	0.94	1.43	2.01	0.30	0.17	1.29	0.08	0.83	1.13	100.00
4.	Gujarat	50.68	13.46	24.36	0.01	2.27	0.95	1.75	4.58	0.01	1.92	0.00	100.00
5.	Haryana	72.79	11.85	4.81	2.58	3.46	0.22	0.18	1.62	0.22	2.27	0.00	100.00
6.	Himachal Pradesh	55.92	11.29	4.55	2.37	1.28	0.73	8.74	0.00	0.00	6.38	8.74	100.00
7.	Jammu & Kashmir	65.70	16.56	4.71	0.00	8.40	0.00	0.31	3.14	0.00	1.18	0.00	100.00
8.	Karnataka	65.49	13.51	2.38	0.46	1.66	0.77	0.12	8.77	0.33	6.34	0.19	100.00
9.	Kerala	42.23	38.86	6.97	2.16	1.22	2.34	0.59	3.25	0.18	2.21	0.00	100.00
10.	Madhya Pradesh	56.72	27.14	5.38	0.04	3.87	0.70	3.24	2.07	0.05	0.79	0.07	100.00
11.	Maharashtra	45.20	21.98	19.09	0.09	2.88	1.64	0.28	3.60	0.08	5.07	0.09	100.00
12.	Manipur	65.15	33.20	1.66	0.00	0.00	0.00	0.00	0.00	0.00	0.00	0.00	100.00
13.	Meghalaya	78.82	21.18	0.00	0.00	0.00	0.00	0.00	0.00	0.00	0.00	0.00	100.00
14.	Nagaland	100.00	0.00	0.00	0.00	0.00	0.00	0.00	0.00	0.00	0.00	0.00	100.00
15.	Orissa	69.20	18.41	2.63	0.00	3.46	0.94	0.83	2.56	0.00	0.11	1.87	100.00
16.	Punjab	78.29	11.09	0.92	2.68	2.34	0.29	0.00	1.43	0.04	2.75	0.18	100.00
17.	Rajasthan	66.48	12.64	18.15	0.05	0.76	0.23	0.16	1.20	0.13	0.19	0.03	100.00
18.	Sikkim	.	.	.	.	.	.	.	.	.	.	.	.

Contd...

(1)		(2)	(3)	(4)	(5)	(6)	(7)	(8)	(9)	(10)	(11)	(12)	(13)
19.	Tamil Nadu	39.64	40.29	8.75	0.62	0.60	4.38	0.18	3.09	0.08	1.41	0.95	100.00
20.	Tripura	63.33	36.67	0.00	0.00	0.00	0.00	0.00	0.00	0.00	0.00	0.00	100.00
21.	Uttar Pradesh	83.80	11.88	1.30	0.13	1.30	0.29	0.15	0.58	0.01	0.46	0.10	100.00
22.	West Bengal	71.48	18.38	1.58	0.17	2.75	1.81	0.06	0.87	0.00	2.91	0.00	100.00
23.	A & N Islands	100.00	0.00	0.00	0.00	0.00	0.00	0.00	0.00	0.00	0.00	0.00	100.00
24.	Arunachal Pradesh	100.00	0.00	0.00	0.00	0.00	0.00	0.00	0.00	0.00	0.00	0.00	100.00
25.	Chandigarh	73.17	12.92	2.25	0.00	0.00	0.00	1.17	7.33	0.00	3.17	0.00	100.00
26.	D & N Haveli	.	.	.	.	.	.	.	.	.	.	.	.
27.	Delhi	58.63	15.66	13.03	0.77	0.59	1.65	0.51	4.45	0.00	2.55	2.16	100.00
28.	Goa, D. & Diu	45.21	32.42	19.63	0.00	2.74	0.00	0.00	0.00	0.00	0.00	0.00	100.00
29.	Lakshadweep	.	.	.	.	.	.	.	.	.	.	.	.
30.	Mizoram	100.00	0.00	0.00	0.00	0.00	0.00	0.00	0.00	0.00	0.00	0.00	100.00
31.	Pondicherry	26.35	27.70	9.46	0.00	0.00	0.00	0.68	35.81	0.00	0.00	0.00	100.00
	Total	62.61	20.85	7.73	0.73	1.57	1.06	0.38	2.53	0.07	2.06	0.41	100.00

Source : Ministry of Human Resource Development (1991) *Education in India, 1986-87*, Vol. I (c), New Delhi.

Note : Others include Business Management, Library Science, Music & Dance, Physical Education, Social Work and other professional subjects.

Table 4 : **Education specific 'worker population ratio' for persons of age 15 years and above according to usual principal status, rural males**

Sl. no.	State / union territory	Not literate	Literate and upto primary	Middle	Secondary	Graduate & above	All
1.	Andhra Pradesh	904	916	717	662	753	870
2.	Assam	882	882	615	519	722	793
3.	Bihar	909	857	696	645	674	839
4.	Gujarat	868	871	714	729	758	833
5.	Haryana	816	783	578	733	674	761
6.	Himachal Pradesh	895	824	602	724	706	809
7.	Jammu & Kashmir	913	791	651	714	772	825
8.	Karnataka	902	918	718	692	859	861
9.	Kerala	726	809	680	502	701	717
10	Madhya Pradesh	925	884	663	800	878	883
11.	Maharashtra	903	890	685	646	860	833
12.	Manipur	868	777	538	536	779	695
13.	Meghalaya	920	843	717	694	876	848
14.	Nagaland		—	No Survey	—		
15.	Orissa	904	901	691	550	604	848
16.	Punjab	878	844	683	728	873	821
17.	Rajasthan	895	806	656	689	808	836
18.	Sikkim	883	794	476	626	1000	772
19.	Tamil Nadu	886	902	749	673	699	851
20.	Tripura	884	831	589	629	739	781
21.	Uttar Pradesh	914	866	700	688	790	848
22.	West Bengal	922	852	685	669	768	842
23.	A & N Islands	884	899	599	805	990	831
24.	Arunachal Pradesh	886	696	603	725	977	802
25.	Chandigarh	948	870	911	783	849	886
26.	D & N Haveli	924	921	595	682	1000	894
27.	Delhi	750	830	617	678	821	733
28.	Goa, D. & Diu	886	897	570	325	842	712
29.	Lakshadweep	830	852	547	544	1000	730
30.	Mizoram	851	870	806	624	912	828
31.	Pondicherry	875	852	673	653	905	805
	All-India	902	870	688	664	766	839

Source : National Sample Survey Organisation (1990) *Sarvekhana*,(Special Number), July, 1987 - June, 1988, 43rd Round, New Delhi.

Table 5 : **Education specific 'worker population ratio' for persons of age 15 years and above according to usual principal status, rural females**

Sl. no.	State / union territory	Not literate	Literate and upto primary	Middle	Secondary	Graduate & above	All
1.	Andhra Pradesh	635	379	242	165	362	584
2.	Assam	126	61	39	85	144	101
3.	Bihar	218	83	80	89	171	202
4.	Gujarat	485	350	188	213	217	432
5.	Haryana	197	117	88	186	-	181
6.	Himachal Pradesh	584	477	331	321	257	533
7.	Jammu & Kashmir	154	107	66	216	381	149
8.	Karnataka	515	329	276	161	246	459
9.	Kerala	316	292	162	175	381	254
10	Madhya Pradesh	572	387	196	241	124	544
11.	Maharashtra	668	550	369	257	225	611
12.	Manipur	294	272	95	126	401	259
13.	Meghalaya	682	627	291	404	621	617
14.	Nagaland	---- No Survey -----					
15.	Orissa	369	128	93	136	159	309
16.	Punjab	119	111	35	96	182	110
17.	Rajasthan	608	419	288	368	435	592
18.	Sikkim	407	407	262	543	501	401
19.	Tamil Nadu	607	490	329	305	292	553
20.	Tripura	170	84	53	196	134	130
21.	Uttar Pradesh	289	129	93	133	107	264
22.	West Bengal	189	83	75	113	375	158
23.	A & N Islands	201	164	73	314	465	183
24.	Arunachal Pradesh	576	87	71	-	-	432
25.	Chandigarh	249	245	31	61	-	205
26.	D & N Haveli	775	538	334	483	158	732
27.	Delhi	66	-	-	21	778	63
28.	Goa, D. & Diu	191	153	49	327	283	175
29.	Lakshadweep	79	86	-	188	-	79
30.	Mizoram	311	533	466	310	356	466
31.	Pondicherry	578	257	69	150	271	417
	All-India	414	274	176	175	250	373

Source : National Sample Survey Organisation (1990) *Sarvekhana*, (Special Number), July, 1987 - June, 1988, 43rd Round, New Delhi.

Table 6 : **Education specific 'worker population ratio' for persons of age 15 years and above according to usual principal status, urban males**

Sl. no.	State / union territory	Not literate	Literate and upto primary	Middle	Secondary	Graduate & above	All
1.	Andhra Pradesh	883	846	659	601	798	758
2.	Assam	866	863	691	625	818	744
3.	Bihar	842	846	689	538	673	722
4.	Gujarat	819	793	681	732	866	774
5.	Haryana	877	825	732	773	875	811
6.	Himachal Pradesh	883	778	534	569	825	684
7.	Jammu & Kashmir	896	841	623	660	761	771
8.	Karnataka	866	878	651	594	806	749
9.	Kerala	673	783	674	519	825	688
10	Madhya Pradesh	868	801	607	639	798	741
11.	Maharashtra	809	775	622	664	776	720
12.	Manipur	718	714	453	522	754	595
13.	Meghalaya	763	874	574	575	765	669
14.	Nagaland	858	926	737	800	932	838
15.	Orissa	849	860	726	604	768	764
16.	Punjab	876	836	725	747	848	799
17.	Rajasthan	861	813	661	614	786	748
18.	Sikkim	839	764	805	749	990	791
19.	Tamil Nadu	821	856	733	701	844	788
20.	Tripura	780	771	512	659	767	684
21.	Uttar Pradesh	885	862	633	641	780	777
22.	West Bengal	836	830	644	596	781	740
23.	A & N Islands	970	848	721	744	889	810
24.	Arunachal Pradesh	857	800	847	696	970	808
25.	Chandigarh	969	815	591	632	809	737
26.	D & N Haveli			No Urban Areas			
27.	Delhi	869	807	639	707	874	774
28.	Goa, D. & Diu	941	728	497	610	763	680
29.	Lakshadweep	352	647	418	800	1000	618
30.	Mizoram	109	861	732	735	992	782
31.	Pondicherry	722	824	822	564	711	750
	All-India	855	827	662	645	799	754

Source : National Sample Survey Organisation (1990) *Sarvekhana*, (Special Number), July, 1987 - June, 1988, 43rd Round, New Delhi.

Table 7 : **Education specific 'worker population ratio' for persons of age 15 years and above according to usual principal status, urban females**

Sl. no.	State / union territory	Not literate	Literate and upto primary	Middle	Secondary	Graduate & above	All
1.	Andhra Pradesh	349	150	94	113	346	248
2.	Assam	81	31	42	48	350	65
3.	Bihar	133	45	21	43	186	98
4.	Gujarat	166	106	58	97	270	131
5.	Haryana	92	24	47	141	256	97
6.	Himachal Pradesh	241	114	131	156	368	192
7.	Jammu & Kashmir	61	81	45	154	346	98
8.	Karnataka	332	216	126	129	297	240
9.	Kerala	210	153	139	176	493	185
10	Madhya Pradesh	259	116	26	103	282	180
11.	Maharashtra	275	150	113	146	359	201
12.	Manipur	195	144	83	153	437	174
13.	Meghalaya	204	330	205	326	629	305
14.	Nagaland	539	18	53	172	835	79
15.	Orissa	176	68	16	85	312	117
16.	Punjab	101	41	38	101	189	89
17.	Rajâsthan	280	141	54	107	257	215
18.	Sikkim	152	97	93	320	860	191
19.	Tamil Nadu	351	241	133	186	362	261
20,	Tripura	103	82	43	106	250	92
21.	Uttar Pradesh	133	48	24	90	218	110
22.	West Bengal	167	78	60	109	245	123
23.	A & N Islands	101	21	85	273	508	138
24.	Arunachal Pradesh	140	128	212	274	11	179
25.	Chandigarh	170	280	-	209	542	236
26.	D & N Haveli			No Urban Areas			
27.	Delhi	94	40	20	84	361	117
28.	Goa, D. & Diu	232	94	53	195	460	173
29.	Lakshadweep	38	84	41	433	542	83
30.	Mizoram	20	469	396	584	595	439
31.	Pondicherry	403	186	233	236	464	289
	All-India	230	132	81	125	297	175

Source : National Sample Survey Organisation (1990) *Sarvekhana*,(Special Number), July, 1987 - June, 1988, 43rd Round, New Delhi.

Table 8 : **Education specific 'worker population ratio' for persons of age 15 years and above according to usual principal status and subsidiary status (all workers), rural females**

Sl. no.	State / union territory	Not literate	Literate and upto primary	Middle	Secondary	Graduate & above	All
1.	Andhra Pradesh	916	929	758	734	806	890
2.	Assam	893	898	670	599	777	821
3.	Bihar	917	881	749	716	787	864
4.	Gujarat	881	893	765	801	850	862
5.	Haryana	826	818	656	798	770	796
6.	Himachal Pradesh	907	869	734	835	815	862
7.	Jammu & Kashmir	923	834	731	803	839	862
8.	Karnataka	909	922	740	738	875	873
9.	Kerala	769	851	723	572	753	764
10	Madhya Pradesh	932	902	706	836	898	898
11.	Maharashtra	911	903	732	704	882	855
12.	Manipur	870	782	552	568	791	707
13.	Meghalaya	941	890	784	779	876	888
14.	Nagaland			No Survey			
15.	Orissa	916	915	730	589	618	866
16.	Punjab	884	864	749	786	928	847
17	Rajasthan	905	837	724	752	863	861
18.	Sikkim	895	824	518	707	1000	800
19.	Tamil Nadu	901	920	781	706	741	872
20,	Tripura	893	840	628	656	788	799
21.	Uttar Pradesh	918	883	759	762	859	871
22.	West Bengal	931	875	755	764	850	872
23.	A & N Islands	887	905	659	835	1000	849
24.	Arunachal Pradesh	887	697	657	725	977	808
25.	Chandigarh	959	870	911	826	849	984
26.	D & N Haveli	925	961	718	811	1000	918
27.	Delhi	750	830	617	678	821	733
28.	Goa, D. & Diu	898	907	629	399	842	746
29.	Lakshadweep	893	889	596	698	1000	791
30.	Mizoram	887	900	842	766	927	870
31.	Pondicherry	890	852	687	679	905	815
	All-India	911	890	739	729	827	863

Source : National Sample Survey Organisation (1990) *Sarvekhana*,(Special Number), July, 1987 - June, 1988, 43rd Round, New Delhi.

Table 9 : **Per 1000 distribution of persons usually employed in the principal & subsidiary status (all) by industry section in different states and union territories, rural females**

Sl.no.	State / union territory	Industry section							
		Agriculture	Mining and quarrying	Manufacturing	Elect., Gas and water	Construction	Trade	Transport	Services
(1)	(2)	(3)	(4)	(5)	(6)	(7)	(8)	(9)	(10)
1.	Andhra Pradesh	821	5	77	-	12	39	1	45
2.	Assam	823	-	98	-	3	17	1	56
3.	Bihar	902	9	41	-	8	18	-	21
4.	Gujarat	758	2	36	-	169	8	1	26
5.	Haryana	925	2	28	-	4	4	1	36
6.	Himachal Pradesh	964	-	18	-	3	3	1	11
7.	Jammu & Kashmir	939	1	87	-	1	2	-	19
8.	Karnataka	855	4	88	-	10	28	-	13
9.	Kerala	657	5	190	1	8	37	7	94
10	Madhya Pradesh	911	8	50	-	17	10	-	9
11.	Maharashtra	914	1	27	-	29	12	-	16
12.	Manipur	799	-	101	3	-	35	1	60
13.	Meghalaya	926	5	6	1	2	31	-	23
14.	Nagaland					No Survey			
15.	Orissa	780	11	114	-	25	34	-	35
16.	Punjab	915	1	28	-	-	11	1	42
17.	Rajasthan	888	5	41	-	102	6	-	10
18.	Sikkim	888	-	3	-	31	3	-	79

Contd..

(1)	(2)	(3)	(4)	(5)	(6)	(7)	(8)	(9)	(10)
19.	Tamil Nadu	771	3	129	-	12	41	2	41
20.	Tripura	661	3	75	-	6	27	4	224
21.	Uttar Pradesh	913	1	88	-	4	15	-	26
22.	West Bengal	708	2	196	-	6	26	1	61
23.	A & N Islands	669	4	25	5	102	47	-	146
24.	Arunachal Pradesh	897	-	1	-	16	11	1	74
25.	Chandigarh	727	-	135	-	-	24	-	114
26.	*D & N Haveli*	906	3	33	-	17	8	3	30
27.	Delhi	360	-	117	-	-	-	-	523
28.	Goa, D. & Diu	696	-	57	-	10	98	-	139
29.	Lakshadweep	695	-	133	-	-	42	-	130
30.	Mizoram	946	-	2	-	1	25	-	19
31.	Pondicherry	773	16	32	-	37	74	-	68
	All-India	847	4	69	-	27	21	1	30

Source : National Sample Survey Organisation (1990) *Sarvekhana*,(Special Number), July, 1987 - June, 1988, 43rd Round, New Delhi.

Table 10 : **Per 1000 distribution of persons usually employed in the principal & subsidiary status (all) by industry section in different states and union territories, urban males, Urban males**

Sl.no.	State / union territory	Industry section							
		Agriculture	Mining and quarrying	Manufacturing	Elect., Gas and water	Construction	Trade	Transport	Services
(1)	(2)	(3)	(4)	(5)	(6)	(7)	(8)	(9)	(10)
1.	Andhra Pradesh	107	17	203	12	77	220	121	234
2.	Assam	68	6	91	15	37	288	89	400
3.	Bihar	140	74	209	8	42	213	84	226
4.	Gujarat	63	5	333	8	42	228	97	207
5.	Haryana	55	48	304	5	45	258	69	210
6.	Himachal Pradesh	63	3	115	98	59	212	50	400
7.	Jammu & Kashmir	91	5	237	21	82	204	53	306
8.	Karnataka	147	4	247	14	50	218	94	218
9.	Kerala	191	5	200	7	69	202	115	205
10	Madhya Pradesh	115	25	216	8	48	188	102	294
11.	Maharashtra	70	4	290	10	52	184	115	268
12.	Manipur	323	1	77	-	29	151	21	391
13.	Meghalaya	170	5	59	5	44	158	23	508
14.	Nagaland	21	-	58	3	55	208	148	479
15.	Orissa	103	34	157	19	45	228	97	316
16.	Punjab	73	-	296	15	45	248	87	229

Contd..

(1)	(2)	(3)	(4)	(5)	(6)	(7)	(8)	(9)	(10)
17.	Rajasthan	91	11	195	19	118	224	87	249
18.	Sikkim	13	-	44	9	207	190	78	459
19.	Tamil Nadu	75	3	310	8	73	212	85	233
20.	Tripura	62	3	60	2	32	193	88	553
21.	Uttar Pradesh	115	-	229	9	51	237	89	270
22.	West Bengal	47	24	321	10	50	202	108	236
23.	A & N Islands	89	-	73	27	169	125	150	359
24.	Arunachal Pradesh	112	-	15	-	172	181	2	513
25.	Chandigarh	31	-	115	63	38	171	41	518
26.	D & N Haveli				No Urban Area				
27.	Delhi	9	-	279	35	61	232	84	287
28.	Goa, D. & Diu	77	40	166	3	96	213	129	271
29.	Lakshadweep	293	-	53	24	90	37	68	435
30.	Mizoram	328	46	65	1	64	97	24	357
31.	Pondicherry	119	-	345	3	91	123	68	251
All-India		91	13	257	12	58	215	97	252

Source :National Sample Survey Organisation (1990) *Sarvekhana*,(Special Number), July, 1987 - June, 1988, 43rd Round, New Delhi.

Table 11 : **Per 1000 distribution of persons usually employed in the principal & subsidiary status (all) by industry section in different states and union territories, urban females**

Sl.no.	State / union territory	Industry section							
		Agriculture	Mining and quarrying	Manufacturing	Elect., Gas and water	Construction	Trade	Transport	Services
(1)	(2)	(3)	(4)	(5)	(6)	(7)	(8)	(9)	(10)
1.	Andhra Pradesh	316	9	278	1	36	152	5	200
2.	Assam	222	-	129	1	4	47	6	569
3.	Bihar	349	73	204	9	27	109	6	207
4.	Gujarat	226	-	238	3	62	120	12	324
5.	Haryana	315	65	174	-	29	31	-	386
6.	Himachal Pradesh	435	-	92	-	5	40	1	427
7.	Jammu & Kashmir	377	1	329	-	1	21	6	265
8.	Karnataka	392	-	323	-	38	101	2	143
9.	Kerala	402	-	176	10	18	64	19	307
10	Madhya Pradesh	265	3	287	2	61	78	5	296
11.	Maharashtra	268	8	233	1	41	98	24	326
12.	Manipur	289	11	196	-	-	203	-	296
13.	Meghalaya	477	-	4	3	1	130	4	377
14.	Nagaland	149	-	30	-	-	309	58	423
15.	Orissa	262	22	230	2	89	74	13	303
16.	Punjab	435	2	166	7	4	51	12	323
17.	Rajasthan	542	8	177	-	49	51	8	164

Contd..

(1)	(2)	(3)	(4)	(5)	(6)	(7)	(8)	(9)	(10)
18.	Sikkim	33	-	43	16	191	146	-	571
19.	Tamil Nadu	207	3	404	1	42	113	3	225
20.	Tripura	293	-	13	-	-	21	51	621
21.	Uttar Pradesh	310	-	242	3	24	89	3	329
22.	West Bengal	154	20	269	5	13	75	16	446
23.	A & N Islands	56	23	20	27	12	130	101	631
24.	Arunachal Pradesh	295	-	-	-	53	102	-	541
25.	Chandigarh	96	-	152	18	-	36	-	698
26.	D & N Haveli				no urban areas				
27.	Delhi	24	-	162	2	29	116	26	621
28.	Goa, D. & Diu	330	-	44	10	118	146	-	321
29.	Lakshadweep	467	-	352	-	19	34	-	128
30.	Mizoram	650	31	19	1	7	141	-	135
31.	Pondicherry	350	-	188	-	39	90	-	403
All-India		294	8	270	2	37	98	9	278

Source : National Sample Survey Organisation (1990) *Sarvekhana*,(Special Number). July, 1987 - June, 1988, 43rd Round, New Delhi.

REFERENCES AND SELECT BIBLIOGRAPHY

Afshar, H. 1991. *Women , development and survivals in the Third World.* London : Longman.

Agarwal, Bina. 1986. Women, poverty and agricultural growth in India. *Journal of Peasant Studies* 13.

Agarwal, B. 1981. "Agricultural modernization and Third World women : Pointers for the literature and an empirical analysis". World Employment Programme Research Paper No. WEP 10/WP 21, Geneva, ILO.

Agarwal, A., and A. Anand. 1982. Ask the women who do the work? *New Scientist*, 4 November.

Ahmed, Mirza R. 1983. "Law and child labour - Problems and prospects". Paper read at Seminar on Child Labour, 30 June - 2 July, at the Regional Office of National Institute of Public Cooperation and Child Development, Lucknow, U.P.

Anker, Richard. 1983. Female labour force activity in developing countries : A critique of current data collection techniques. *International Labour Review*, 122(6).

Ahooja-Patel, Krishna. 1979. Women, technology and development. *Economic and Political Weekly* 14(36).

Apter, David. 1987. *Rethinking development.* Beverly Hills, Calif : Sage.

Ballara, M. 1992. *Women and literacy.* London : Zed.

Banerjee, Nirmala. 1979. Women in the urban labour market. *Labour, Capital and Society* 12.

Banerjee, Nirmala. 1985a. "Women's work and discrimination". In *Tyranny of the household : Investigative essays on women 's work,* eds. Devika Jain, and Nirmala Banerjee. New Delhi : Vikas.

Banerjee, Nirmala. 1985b. *Women workers in the unorganized sector.* Hyderabad : Sangam.

Banerjee, Nirmala, ed. 1991. *Indian women in changing industrial scenario.* New Delhi : Sage.

Baster, N. 1981. "The measurement of women's participation in development : The use of census data". Discussion Paper No. 159, Institute of Development Studies, Brighton, England.

Beauvoir, Simone. 1974. *The second sex.* New York : Vintage.

Becker, Gary S. 1971. *The economics of discrimination.* Chicago: The University of Chicago Press.

Becker, Gary S. 1981. *A treatise on the family.* Cambridge, Mass : Harvard University Press.

Backer, Gary S. 1985. Human capital effort, and the social division of labour. *Journal of Labour Economics* 3(1), Part 2.

Bhatty, Zarina. 1980. "Economic role and status of women : A case study of women in the beedi industry in Allahabad". ILO Working Paper. Geneva.

Bodrovia, V., and R. Anker, eds. 1985. *Working women in socialist countries. The fertility connection.* Geneva : ILO.

Boserup, Ester. 1970. *Women's role in economic development.* New York : St. Martin's Press.

Boserup, Ester, and Christian Liljenerants. 1975. *Integration of women in development : Why, when and why.* New York : UN Development Programme.

Briggs, S. 1987. "Women and religion". In *Analyzing gender : A handbook of social science research,* eds. B.B. Hess, and M.M. Ferec. Newburg Park : Sage.

Brown, H.P. 1977. *The inequality of pay.* London : Oxford.

Buvinic, M. 1984. "Projects for women in the Third World : Explaining their misbehaviour". Office of Women in Development, USAID, Mimeo.

Carnoy, Martin, ed. 1974. *Education as cultural imperialism.* New York : David Mackay.

Carnoy, Martin. 1975. *Can educational policy equalise income distribution in Latin America?.* Geneva : ILO, Mimeo.

Carter, R., and G. Kirkap. 1990. *Women in engineering.* London : MacMillan.

Chafez, J. 1990. *Gender equity : An integrated theory of stability and change.* Newburg Park : Sage.

Chen, Lincoln C. 1982. Where have the women gone? *Economic and Political Weekly* 17.

Clark, Kenneth. 1965. *Dark ghetto.* New York : Harper & Row.

Connel, R. 1987. *Gender and power : Society the person and sexual politics.* Stanford : Stanford University Press.

Connel, R. 1990. The state, gender and sexual politics. *Theory and Society* 19.

Davies, M. 1979. "Women's place is at the typewriter : The feminisation of the clerical labour force". In *The case for socialist feminism,* ed. S.R. Eisensteir. New York : Monthly Review Press.

Deaux, K., and Mary E.Kite. 1987. "Thinking about gender". In *Analyzing Gender,* eds. B.B. Hess, and M.M. Ferree. Newburg Park : Sage.

Desai, N., and V. Patel. 1985. *Indian women : Change and challenges in the International Decade, 1975-85.* New Delhi : Sangam.

Desai, N., and M. Krishnaraj. 1987. *Women and society in India.* Delhi: Ajanta.

Dixon-Mueller, R. 1985. "Women's work in Third World agriculture : Women, work and development". Geneva : ILO.

Dixon, R.B. 1982. Women in agriculture : Counting the labour force in developing countries. *Population and Development Review* 8(3).

Doeringer, Peter B., and Michael J. Piore. 1971. *Internal labour markets and manpower analysis.* Lexington, Mass : D.C. Heath.

Engels, F. 1977. *The origin of the family, private property and the state.* Moscow : Progress.

Epstein, T.S. 1989. "Socio-cultural and attitudinal factors affecting the status of women in South Asia". ESCAP, Status of Women in Asia and the Pacific. Bangkok.

Farley, Lin. 1978. *Sexual shakedown.* New York : Warner.

Fawcett, Millicent. 1917. "The position of women in economic life". In *After war problems,* ed. W.H. Dawson.

Filer, R.K. 1983. Sexual differences in earnings : The role of individual personalities and tastes. *Journal of Human Resource* 18.

Food and Agriculture Organization. 1986. "Programme for the 1990 world census of agriculture". Statistical Development Series. No. 2, Rome, United Nations.

Finn, Jeremy, Janet Reis, and Loretta Dulberg. 1982. "Sex differences in educational attainment : The process". In *Women's education in the Third World,* eds. Gail P. Kelly and Carolyn Elliott. Albuny : Suny.

Friedan, Betty. 1986. *The second sex.* New York : Summit.

Gailey, C.W. 1987. "Evolutionary perspectives on gender hierarchy". In *Analyzing gender,* eds. B.B. Hess, and M.M. Ferree. Newburg Park : Sage.

Gardner, Katy. 1992. Songs at the river's edge : Stories from a Bangladeshi village. Calcutta/Delhi/Allahabad/Bombay : Rupa.

Githens, Marianne, and Jewell Prestage. 1977. *A portrait of marginality.* New York: Longman.

Gordon, David M. 1972. *Theories of poverty and underdevelopment : Orthodox, radical and dual labour market perspectives.* Lexington, Mass: D.C. Heath.

Government of India. 1974. "Towards equality". Report of the Committee on the Status of Women in India, Department of Social Welfare, New Delhi.

Government of India. 1977. *The Constitution of India.* New Delhi.

Groot, J. 1991. "Conceptions and misconceptions : The historical and cultural context of discussion on women and development". In *Women, development and survival in the Third World,* ed. H. Afshar. London : Longman.

Hate, Chandrakala A. 1969. *Changing status of women in post-independent India.* Bombay : Allied.

Hensmen, Rohini. 1988. "The gender division of labour in manufacturing industry : A case study of India". Discussion Paper No. 253, Institute of Development Studies, Sussex.

Hess, B.B., and M.M. Ferree. 1989. *Analyzing gender : a handbook of social science research.* Newbury Park: Sage.

Hughes, R., and K. Mwiria. 1989. Kenyan women, higher education and the labour market. *Comparative Education* 25 (2).

Humm, M., ed. 1992. *Feminism - a reader.* New York : Harvester.

Hunter College Women's Studies Collectives. 1983. *Women's realities, women's choices.* New York : Oxford University Press.

ICSSR. 1975. "Status of women in India : A synopsis of the report of the national commission on the status of women, 1971-74". New Delhi.

ICRW. 1980. *The productivity of women in developing countries : Measurement issues and recommendations.* Washington, D.C. : ICRW.

Jain, Devika. 1980. *Women's quest for power.* New Delhi : Vikas.

Jain, D., N. Singh, and M. Chand. 1980. "India : Status and role of women". In *Women in Asia,* ed. R. Johan. London : Minority Rights Group.

Jenness, Linda. 1977. *Feminism and socialism.* New York : Pathfinder.

Koedt, Anne, et al. 1973. *Radical feminism.* New York : Quadrangle.

Lane, Ann J. 1976. "Women in society : A critique of Frederick Engels". In *Liberating women's history : Theoretical and critical essays,* ed. Bernice A. Carroll. Urbana : University of Illinois Press.

Larguia, Isabel. 1975. "The economic basis of the status of women". In *Women cross - culturally : Change and challenge,* ed. Ruby Rohrlich-Leavitt. The Hague : Mouton.

Lewis, O. 1966. *La vida.* London : Panther

Lindsay, Beverly. 1975. Socio-cultural factors influencing career choices of Kenyan women. *The Kenya Education Review* 2.

Lindsay, Beverly, ed. 1980. *Comparative perspectives of Third World women : The impact of race, sex and class.* New York : Praeger.

Livingstone, D.W., and M. Luxton. 1989. Gender consciousness at work : Modification of the male breadwinner norm among steel workers and their spouses. *Canadian Review of Sociology and Anthropology* 25.

Madden, J.F. 1975. "Discrimination - A manifestation of male market power"? In *Sex discrimination and dualism of labour,* ed. C.B. LLoyed. New York : Colombia University Press.

Mazumdar, Vina. 1985. *Emergence of women's questions in India and the role of women's studies.* New Delhi : Centre for Women's Development Studies.

Mencher, J., and K. Sardamoni. 1982. Muddy jeet and dirty hands : Rice production and female labour. *Economic and Political Weekly* 17 (52).

Mies, M. 1986. *Patriarchy and accumulation on a world scale.* London : Led Books.

Mill, John Stuart. 1948. *Principles of political economy.* London : Parker and Co.

Ministry of Education and Social Welfare. 1977. "National policy on education, 1968". Government of India, New Delhi.

Mitra, A., L.P. Pathak, and S. Mukerji. 1980. *The status of women : Shifts in occupational participation, 1961-1971.* New Delhi : Abhinav.

Ministry of Human Resource Development. 1990. "Report of the committee for reivew of national policy on education, 1986". Government of India, New Delhi.

Ministry of Human Resource Development. 1992. "National policy on education, 1986". Government of India, New Delhi.

Molyneux, M. 1991. "The 'women question' in the age of perestroika". In *After the fall,* ed. Robin Blackburn. London : Verso.

Momsen, Janet Henshall. 1991. *Women and development in the Third World.* London : Routledge.

Moran, R., and J. Tansey. 1986. "Distance working : Women and environments". Occasional Paper, No. 78, Commission of the European Communities.

Mullings, Leith. 1976. "Women and economic change in Africa". In *Women in Africa : Studies in social and economic change,* ed. by Nancy J. Hafkin and Edn G. Bay. Stanford, Calif : Stanford University Press.

N.C.E.R.T. 1971. "Education and national development : Report of the education commission, 1964-66". New Delhi.

National Commission on Self-Employed Women and Women in the Informal Sector, 1988. *Report.* New Delhi.

Nayar, Usha. 1991. *Measures to increase participation of girls and women in vocational, technical and professional education in India.* New Delhi : NCERT.

Nuss, S. 1989. *Women in the world of work : Statistical analysis and projections to the year 2000.* Geneva : ILO.

Omvedt, G. 1986. *Women in popular movements: India and Thailand during the Decade of Women.* Geneva : U.N.R.I.S.I.D.

Ostergaard, L. 1992. *Gender and development : A practical guide.* London : Routledge.

Osterman, P. 1975. An empirical study of labour market segmentation. *Industrial and Labour Relations Review* 28(4).

Palmer, I. 1985. "The impact of agrarian reform on women". In *Women's role and gender differences in development : Case studies for planners,* prepared by the Population Council. West Hartford, Conn. : Kumarian.

Parikh, P.P., and S.P. Sukhatme. 1992. *Women engineers in India.* Bombay : Indian Institute of Technology.

Pastizzi-Ferencic, D. 1986. *Redesigning women's work - New approaches and concepts in statistics on women.* Santo Domingo : INSTRAW.

Pearson, R. 1990. "Gender matters in development". In *Poverty and Development in the 1990,* ed. T. Allen, and A. Thomson. Oxford : Oxford University Press.

Phelps, E.S. 1972. The statistical theory of racism and sexism. *American Economic Review* 62.

Planning Commission. 1951. *First five-year plan*, New Delhi.

Rajeswari, et al. 1988. "Status of women science and technology personnel in research and development". Occasional Paper, Department of Science and Technology, Government of India.

Ram, Rati. 1980. Sex differences in the labour market outcomes of education. *Comparative Education Review* 24 (Part 2).

Ramu, G.N. 1987. *Women, work and marriage in urban India*. New Delhi: Sage.

Rathbone, Eleanor. 1917. The remuneration of women's services. *Economic Journal* 27.

Rehman, M.M. 1992. *Society, economy and education of the deprived.* Delhi : Anupama.

Reich, Michael. 1981. *Racial inequality*. Princeton, N.J. : Princeton University Press.

Rodgers, Gerry. 1986. Labour markets, labour processes and economic development. *Labour and Society* 11(2).

Rodney, Walter. 1972. *How Europe underdeveloped Africa*. Dar es Salaam, Tanzania : Tanzania Publishing.

Rogers, Barbara. 1980. *The domestication of women : Discrimination in developing societies*. London : St. Martin's Press.

Roos, P.A. 1985. *Gender and work : A comparative analysis of industrial societies*. New York : State University of New York Press.

Rosenberg, Sam. 1980. Male occupational standing and the dual labour market. *Industrial Relations* 19(1).

Rubin, Gayle. 1975. "The traffic in women : Notes on the political economy of sex". In *Towards an anthropology of women*, ed. Rayna Reiter. New York : Monthly Review Press.

Rumberger, R.W., and M. Carnoy. 1980. Segmentation in the US labour market : Its effects on the mobility of whites and blacks. *Cambridge Journal of Economic 4(2).*

Safa, Helen Icken. 1976. "Class consciousness among working class women in Latin America : Puerto Rico". In *Sex and class in Latin America*, eds. Jane Nash, and Helen Icken Safa. New York : Praeger.

Saffioti, H. 1986. *Women in class society*. New York : Monthly Review Press.

Scott, A.M. 1986. Women and industrilisation : Examining the female marginalisation thesis. *Journal of Development Studies* 22(4).

Sen, A., and S. Sengupta. 1983. Malnutrition of rural Indian children the sex bias. *Economic and Political Weekly* 18.

Sen, G. 1982. "Women workers and the green revolution". In *Women and development : The sexual division of labour in rural socieities,* ed. L. Beneria. New York : Praeger.

Sen, G., and C. Sen. 1985. Women's domestic work and economic activity : Results from national sample survey. *Economic and Political Weekly* 20.

Sharma, U. 1980. *Women work and property in north-west India.* London: Tavistock.

Silverstone, R., and A. Ward, eds. 1980. *Careers of professional women.* London : Croom Helm.

Smock. A.C. 1981. *Women's education in developing countires.* New York : Praeger.

Standing, H. 1992. "Employment". In *Gender and development,* ed. L. Ostergaard. London : Routledge.

Staudit, K.A. 1980. *Women in development : Women's organizations in rural development.* Washington, D.C. : USAID.

Stromquist, N.P. 1991. Educating women : The political economy of patriarchal states. *International Studies in Sociology of Education* 1.

Tinker, Irene. 1990. *Persistent inequality.* New York : Oxford University Press.

Tinker, Irene, and Bo Bromsen. 1978. *Women and world development.* Washington, D.C. : Overseas Development Council.

Tomsic, V. 1982. "Policy of Non-Alignment struggle for the NIEO and the role of women in development." Paper presented at Golden Jubilee Symposium on Women, Work and Society, ISI, New Delhi, mimeo.

UNESCO. 1981. Women and development : Indicators of their changing role. *Socio-economic Studies* (3).

United Nations. 1989. *World survey on the role of women in development. 1989.* New York : UN

United Nations. 1991. World economic survey. *New York : UN.*

Vanek, J. 1974. "Time spent in housework". In *The economics of women and work, ed. A.H. Amsden. Harmondsworth : Penguin.*

Varghese, N.V. 1989. *Education and labour market in India.* Paris : International Institute of Educational Planning.

Varghese, N.V. 1991. Women and work : An examination of the female marginalisation thesis in the Indian context. *The Indian Journal of Labour Economics* 34 (3).

Webb, Sidney. 1891. The alleged differencies in the wages paid to men and women for similar work. *Economic Journal* 1.

Walker, S., and Len Barton, eds. 1983. *Gender, class and education.* Sussex : The Falmer.

Witting, M. 1992. *The straight mind.* New York: Harvester

Wolpe, A.M. 1977. *Some process in sexist education.* London : Women's Research and Resource Centre.

World Health Organization, Division of Family Health (WHO). 1980. "Health and the status of women". FHE/80.1.

INDEX